BLACK WOMEN AND WHITE
WOMEN IN THE PROFESSIONS

PERSPECTIVES ON GENDER

Pleasure, Power, and Technology: Some Tales of Gender, Engineering, and the Cooperative Workplace

Sally Hacker

Black Feminist Thought: Knowledge, Consciousness, and the Politics of Empowerment

Patricia Hill Collins

Understanding Sexual Violence: A Study of Convicted Rapists

Diana Scully

Feminism and the Women's Movement: Dynamics of Change in Social Movement Ideology and Activism

Barbara Ryan

Maid in the U.S.A.

Mary Romero

BLACK WOMEN AND WHITE WOMEN IN THE PROFESSIONS

OCCUPATIONAL SEGREGATION BY RACE AND GENDER, 1960–1980

Natalie J. Sokoloff

Routledge
New York • London

Published 1992 by
Routledge, an imprint of
Routledge, Chapman and Hall, Inc.
29 West 35 Street
New York, NY 10001

Published in Great Britain by
Routledge
11 New Fetter Lane
London EC4P 4EE

Library of Congress Cataloging-in-Publication Data

Sokoloff, Natalie J.
  Black women and white women in the professions: occupational
segregation by race and gender, 1960–1980. / Natalie J.
Sokoloff.
    p. cm.—(Perspectives on gender)
  Includes bibliographical references and index.
  ISBN 0-415-90608-3. — ISBN 0-415-90609-1 (pbk.)
  1. Women in the professions—United States. 2. Minority women in the
professions—United States. 3. Afro-Americans in the
professions. 4. Professional employees—United States.
  5. Discrimination in employment—United States.   I. Title.
  II. Series: Perspectives on gender (New York, N.Y.)
HD6054.2.U6S65 1992
331.4'133'0973—dc20   92-3988
                                                                         CIP

British Library Cataloguing in Publication Data Available on Request
ISBN 0-415-90608-3 hb
ISBN 0-415-90609-1 pb

For my son,
Joshua Mark Pincus-Sokoloff,
and his generation:
through struggle,
change is always possible

CONTENTS

Foreword by Julianne Malveaux   ix

Preface   xiii

Acknowledgments   xvii

Chapter 1
THE HALF-FULL GLASS: PARTIAL INTEGRATION IN THE
PROFESSIONS   1

Chapter 2
THE PROFESSIONS: STRUCTURAL CHANGE AND GROUP
ACCESS   33

Chapter 3
"GAINS" AND "LOSSES" FOR BLACK AND WHITE MEN
AND WOMEN IN THE PROFESSIONS   43

Chapter 4
WHITE MEN: THE MORE THINGS CHANGE, THE MORE
THEY STAY THE SAME   55

Chapter 5
BLACK MEN: AFFIRMATIVE ACTION OR REACTION?   65

Chapter 6
WHITE WOMEN: MOVEMENT AND CHANGE   75

Chapter 7
BLACK WOMEN: BEYOND THE MYTH OF DOUBLE
ADVANTAGE   93

Chapter 8
THE HALF-EMPTY GLASS: CAN IT EVER BE FILLED?   113

Appendix 1
METHODOLOGY   135

Appendix 2
DETAILED OCCUPATIONAL CENSUS CATEGORIES FOR
PROFESSIONS AND TECHNICAL FIELDS   147

Notes   151
References   159
Index   171

FOREWORD

I was recently talking to a white male student about his prospects for employment in the future. "I think affirmative action is okay," he told me, "but is there any room in the labor market for me?" From this student's perspective, white men were being forced to take a back seat to minorities and women in the labor market. Occupational data are at odds with his perspective, but the numbers on the spreadsheets seemed distant from his plight. I asked the young man to clear his calendar and spend some time with me, stopping at a university print shop, a television station, a newspaper, a library, a bank. The ethnic composition varied from place to place, but the faces of those in authority were almost uniformly white. At the end of our three-hour jaunt, my student seemed somewhat reassured that people of color were not going to dominate the labor market any time soon.

It is easy to rail against the myth that white men are being elbowed out of the best jobs in the labor market, or to bristle when President Bush calls a tepid civil rights measure a "quota bill." It takes a bit more work to decompose the myths and explain how the labor market is changing. Natalie Sokoloff has done the work of decomposition in her book, *Black Women and White Women in the Professions*.

Most of those who write about race and gender in the labor market compare black and white women to each other. Sokoloff undertakes the painstaking task of comparing these women to each other, but also to black men and white men, by both general and detailed occupational categories. By undertaking this detail of analysis, Sokoloff brings forth the facts behind the headlines. Writing that "black women in no way reached parity with black men in either group of the professions," she debunks the myth of the "twofer" (the notion that black women are double-counted in affirmative action statistics, as black and as female, providing measurement conscious affirmative action officers with two for the price of one) that has divisively defined much of the discourse on race and progress in the African American community.

The "twofer" myth is not the only one that gets an argument from Sokoloff. In her chapter on white men in the professions (aptly titled, "The More Things Change, The More They Stay the Same"), she responds directly to the notion of white male displacement by noting that "white men continued to be the overwhelming majority in the most desirable and visible of the professions." White men lost some ground, says Sokoloff, but only in moderate status professions. Meanwhile, white male overrepresentation in the elite male professions "increased from moderate to severe."

Sokoloff produces similar, myth-shattering findings about the status of white women in the labor market, showing that white women remain more concentrated in the female professions, with "fewer than one percent of all employed white women . . . represented in the elite male professions." Sokoloff's findings might seem incredible, given all the hype that we've heard about white women taking over the typically male professions. But after having been bombarded with the 1991 picture of an all-white-male Senate Judiciary Committee, this work becomes all the more compelling.

Although Sokoloff's analysis stops in 1980, it is interesting to think about her findings in the context of the 1980–1990 decade. Socioeconomic data suggest that the status of working people, especially African Americans, has deteriorated in the 1980–1990 period. Wages bifurcated in the 1980s and the amount of black poverty grew to the point where one in three African Americans (and the majority of black children) live in poverty. Even among the professionals that Sokoloff discusses, there was significant job insecurity. This insecurity combined with the concept of "glass ceilings," perhaps explains the dramatic increase in the number of self-employed workers in the late 1980s.

How do we measure the status of these "new independent" professionals, and how do we quantify the fact that many will operate at the periphery of the economic mainstream, with influence diminished by their distance from corporate employment? Does it matter if African American and women professionals are more likely to be self-employed? How are social policy issues affected by this distribution? Sokoloff does not answer those questions, but her framework provides a useful basis for analysis.

Similarly, and in the context of comparison, it is interesting to note that the foreign-born population increased by more than 8 million in the last decade. One in twelve of those counted in the 1990 Census were foreign born. Some have called the 1980s "the decade of the immigrant" and lauded our country's ability to absorb new people. In the same sense that Sokoloff asks if white men have been displaced by women and minorities, one might ask if American workers have been displaced by immigrants, and if so in which occupations.

In her closing chapter, "The Half-Empty Glass," Natalie Sokoloff explores some of the current implications of her research, and the impact that the economic and political climate has on the status of minorities and women in the professions. In speaking to the gossamer threads that bind women, minorities, and those that are "other," Sokoloff gets to the meat of the matter in much the way Rodney King did when he asked if we can all get along.

Who has gained and who has lost in the labor market and in society in the decades that can be described as "social change" decades? Who will gain and who will lose as our country enters a world market more competitive than any we have ever faced? Should we be more concerned with gains and losses in the professions than in the changing ways that the professions are organized, and how this differs by occupation, race, and gender? And must we move past a dialogue of gainers and losers as we deal with more diverse populations in the labor market?

Although it was not the case in 1960, by 1980 job announcements routinely carried the phrase "equal opportunity employer." There is a large gap between opportunity and outcome, between good intentions and measurable results. What I find so very valuable about Natalie Sokoloff's work is her ability to combine measurement with socioeconomic commentary as she makes the case that no matter how diverse the labor force, there has been woefully little change in the ways power and influence are distributed in the labor market. The white male student who worried about his job prospects has, on the basis of race and gender, little to worry about if the trends from 1960 to 1980 continue. On the other hand, if 1960–1980 trends hold true, much more has to be done before women and minorities are better represented in top professional jobs.

Because Sokoloff has measured occupational change so precisely, she has provided important information for theorists and practitioners about the trends that have affected women, black and white, in the professions. This is an important contribution to research on the labor market, and on the oscillating status of women.

Julianne Malveaux
San Francisco
June, 1992

PREFACE

Headlines in the 1990s express a far different reality than a decade ago when I began this research. Today we are regularly told about the severe and debilitating downturn of the U.S. economy, the continual crises caused by scandals in the savings and loans and banking industries, and the difficulties of holding onto a middle class way of life. Wall Street and the financial industry were heavily hit with the "stock market crash of 1987;" and service industries as well as factory employment are suffering greatly in the 1980s and early 1990s. The loss of federal monies to cities and states led to sharp cutbacks in government employment and services at all levels. Much of this employment provided a step on the ladder to a middle class way of life for the first time to many women and minorities.

These economic setbacks were coupled with the heated attacks on affirmative action, continual erosion of women's rights to control their own destinies (e.g., threats to women's rights to control their own bodies, set-backs in their ability to challenge discrimination in employment), and cutbacks for welfare recipients. Blatant "Racial Politics: Back with a Vengeance" (Toner, 1991) was headlined as David Duke, the former Ku Klux Klan leader, ran for governor of Louisiana, and then later for the Republican presidential nomination. The racist Willie Horton campaign created by the Republicans in the 1988 elections and the anti-affirmative action campaign that led to the defeat of Harvey Gantt, who would have been the first black senator from South Carolina since Reconstruction, were precursors of the 1992 presidential campaign. And the appointment of Clarence of Clarence Thomas in late 1991, one of the few black conservative judges, made prospects even dimmer for women, minorities and the poor with the shift of the Supreme Court to a conservative majority.

When I began this research in the early 1980s, despite early rumblings to the contrary, the situation was indeed much more hopeful. The country had just experienced a period of economic expansion and liberal politics that heated up in the 1960s. Thus, the period under study in this book, from 1960 to 1980, represents some of the best possible results for the advancement of women and racial/ethnic minorities in the U.S.: a "best case" scenario, if you will.

Being skeptical of the sweeping claims about women's advancement in the labor force, I tried to locate those studies that would document, at a national level, the progress that women from various racial/ethnic backgrounds had made in a more "generous" post World War II era. Much to my surprise, there simply were no such in-depth studies. Moreover, since affirmative action was said to be beneficial to relatively more advantaged women, I wanted to see what happened to women in the professions. I became increasingly convinced that it was not possible to evaluate women's progress in the professions without likewise comparing them to men's fortunes in these fields. Again, nothing existed that provided a detailed analysis of race *and* gender in the most desired jobs in U.S. society. And yet, as we will see (Chapter 1), claims were being made that women had not only done better, but had "surpassed" men in the professions, and that black women had made the greatest advances of all.

Having just completed *Between Money and Love: The Dialectics of Women's Home and Market Work* (Sokoloff, 1980), a book that looked at the long-term transformation of the 20th century economy and women's position in the U.S. labor force, I was curious whether some of the same phenomena that explained women's overall increase in the labor force were likewise applicable to their increase in the professions. For example, was there an expanding number of jobs lower down the professional hierarchy—as there had been in lower-level service-sector jobs—that provided a larger number of professional jobs to women, but not of the same high status and rewards as had traditionally been available to men? Were women being allowed to enter newly created lower-level positions within high status professions or were they, perhaps, being shunted into already existing "female" identified subsectors or specialties? Thus, while women gained the necessary education and training for "men's" jobs in the professions, were they being allowed to enter primarily those places that were in some way devalued by the labor process or by the men themselves? Moreover, I was particularly interested in learning what differences existed between majority and minority women, since it was abundantly clear that not only class, but race, too, was *necessary* for understanding gender differences in the job market. At the time I began this research, this was simply an under-researched area (Sokoloff, 1986, 1987b).

The current study reflects basic (or "bare bones") research that looks at the "overall" picture. It requires a good deal of follow-up and asking of questions that need to be funded for research: not only how has the picture changed since 1980, but how does the picture differ for younger professionals compared to older ones; how did changes in educational opportunity and specialization affect the placement of black women and white women in the professions; to the degree that employment in the professions increased for black women and white women in comparison to black men and white men, how are these changes related to increased hours of work for certain groups of women or deteriorated work conditions and wages for these very groups. Although mention is made of some of these issues in this book, they are clearly the subject of further in-depth study. When the census data from 1990 and 2000 are accessible to the public,[1] we will be able to see if and how the downturn in the economy and a more conservative environment affected women and minorities as they entered the 21st century. Until then, the current study tells a story of how several disadvantaged groups in American society—black women, white women, and black men—progressed during more hopeful times in the 1960s and 1970s in comparison to each other as well as to the more advantaged group of white men. As I indicate in Chapter 1, this book, should be seen as a base-line or taking-off point to such later studies. Most important, I hope it is used for greater action to improve the conditions of each of the disadvantaged groups studied in this research.

ACKNOWLEDGMENTS

This book is a tribute to all women who have combined motherhood along with their many other activities and responsibilities. The research for this book was the first work I did after the birth of my son, Joshua, in 1982. It has taken almost a decade to complete this work, as I have parented and worked full-time. This book is dedicated to Josh, just for being the wonderful, incredible person that he is, and for giving me perspective not only on my own life, but making even more meaningful the work that I do as teacher, scholar, feminist, and activist.

Along the way there are many points at which I have been delayed: the numerous bouts of a child's ear infection; parent involvement in a public school in New York City; the failure of all major funding agencies to support this project despite their overwhelming praise for my work; my own illness (nonlife-threatening, but debilitating) that laid me low for two different stretches of time; the sale of the publishing company not just once but twice within two years thereby necessitating my working with four different editors over the life of my contract.

Because it has taken so long to complete, I have become indebted to many people who have helped me with this project. While I take full responsibility, it is with great joy that I am able to acknowledge these wonderful people. I begin by thanking first those who have been the most supportive and helpful over the years. Key in this process is Myra Marx Ferre, who has struggled through the long years with me and helped to shape the early form of the manuscript. Hours-long long-distance phone calls provided both hard-hitting criticism and abundant nurturance. Danny Choriki, who spent the better part of four years helping me with the data analysis, was an invaluable computer assistant. He taught me much. His willingness to work for such low wages on such complicated data earned my deepest gratitude. And Carol Ehrlich, who painstakingly edited the entire manuscript with care, diligence, and creativity, was supportive through the most traumatic changes caused by the various buyouts of my contract. To the degree the book is more readable and accessible, she deserves much of the credit. Finally, while many funding agencies praised my work, it was the Professional Staff Congress–City University of New York (PSC-CUNY) Faculty Research Award Program that provided me with the resources to pay for the computer work in this book. I am deeply grateful to them and hereby acknowledge the grants I received from that program, and in particular its Women's Studies Panel: grant numbers 665399, 666245, and 669257.

I first presented some of the ideas found in this book to a graduate class in women's studies organized by Sarah Begus and Emily Martin at the Johns Hopkins University. I was then invited to present a paper on the contradictory ways in which black women and white women had increased in the professions at a conference on Ingredients for Women's Employment Policy at the State University of New York, Albany, organized by Chris Bose and Glenna Spitze. Since then, I have presented different aspects of the findings from this research to many different groups of women and men, black and white, professional and community groups. All of these audiences provided valuable feedback, which I hope is well reflected in the book.

In the early stages of the research the following people were very important in helping me figure out how to develop the methodology and make the data comparable from one census year to the next: Suzanne Bianchi, John Priebe, and Nancy Naples were key in this process; likewise Pam Stone and Jack Hammond were important sounding boards in this early stage. Later, Danny Choriki, Myra Marx Ferree, Chris Bose, and Greg Robinson helped me deal with "trouble spots" in the data, how to understand, best use, and analyze them. Without their help, the data would never have been as meaningfully analyzed and presented as they are.

Along the way many people and groups were of tremendous help. In fact, at each stage that I might have given up struggling with either the data or the analysis, people kept "coming through" for me. In addition to Myra Marx Ferree, Danny Choriki, and Carol Ehrlich, Leslie Morgan provided a much needed "push" to help me reorganize how I would present the findings at one of the many points at which I got "stuck." And Elizabeth Almquist gave a 15-page, single-spaced critique of the manuscript that was both remarkably supportive and wonderfully critical and helpful in pointing out weaknesses that needed to be addressed. To each person, I am most appreciative.

I would also like to thank several people who provided helpful comments on individual papers or chapters over the course of my work: Regina Arnold, George Fischer, Patricia Gwartney-Gibbs, Elizabeth Higginbotham, Barbara Re-

George Fischer, Patricia Gwartney-Gibbs, Elizabeth Higginbotham, Barbara Reskin, Patricia Bell-Scott, and Joan Smith. Members of the Women and Work Research Group have probably had the longest and most continual relationship to this work. They have put up with re-reading countless versions of various chapters, papers, and presentations based on this work. I am most grateful to all of them: Chris Bose, Nancy Breen, Carol Brown, Peggy Crull, Roslyn Feldberg, Nadine Felton, Myra Marx Ferre, Amy Gilman, Evelyn Nakano Glenn, Amy Kesselman, Susan Lehrer, Fran Rothstein, Joan Smith, and Carole Turbin.

I have also benefited greatly from receiving pre-publication work especially from Barbara Reskin and Patricia Roos and their colleagues. In addition, they graciously shared income and education data made comparable for 1970 and 1980 for each of the detailed professions (see Chapter 6). I hereby acknowledge the use of their materials: Roos, Reskin, Donato, and Hein (1990). Two other people who shared pre-publication materials with me over the years, and from which I have greatly benefited, are Elizabeth Higginbotham and Gwyned Simpson.

I also wish to acknowledge the four editors with whom I have worked over the life of this book. Despite the sometimes rocky experiences of continually changing editors due to company buy-outs, a sign of the times in the late 1980s-early 1990s, my thanks to the following people for their efforts and support: Lisa Freeman and Lauren Osborne (at the time at Unwin-Hyman), Sarah Dann (at the time at Harper-Collins), and Max Zutty (now at Routledge, Chapman and Hall).

Finally, I want to acknowledge and thank my husband and son. To Josh, who has had to share me with interruptions too numerous to elaborate, I simply want to say thank you. His pride in my accomplishments is both rewarding and humbling. And even though he claims that I work too hard, near the completion of this project, Josh said to me: "You work too hard; but you always find time for me."

To Fred Pincus, my partner for 20 years, it is hard to put into words the love, support, and help he has given me over the years. Not only has he done more than his share of the domestic and child-care support in our family, but he has spent many late-night hours listening to me struggle with the problems associated with the elaborate data sets with which I chose to work for this project. Although not always "smooth sailing," without his support I would never have been able to accomplish this project.

Chapter 1

THE HALF-FULL GLASS: PARTIAL INTEGRATION IN THE PROFESSIONS

INTRODUCTION

The 1960s and early 1970s were a time of expanding political, social, and economic opportunities in the United States. Since the end of World War II, the economy had continued to grow, particularly in the service area. This growth, combined with an ever-expanding government, created correspondingly more white-collar and public-sector jobs. In this same period, the civil-rights and women's movements pushed for and won legislation that prohibited discrimination in areas such as employment, housing, and voting rights. The combined expansion of the economy and of civil rights was hailed as benefiting women from all backgrounds, including racial/ethnic[1] minority groups, and minority-group men as well. Increased employment opportunities were now supposed to exist in all occupations—including the highest levels of the professions.

For women, these changes led to far greater numbers than ever before entering professional schools: from single-digit percentages in the early 1960s to one-third of the students entering medical and law schools by the 1980s (Epstein, 1983; Bowman and Gross, 1986). In addition, women doubled and in some cases tripled their representation in elite professions such as law, medicine, science, and college teaching, traditionally the domain of white men of higher socioeconomic origins (USDL, Bureau of Labor Statistics, 1980; USDC, Bureau of Census, 1983). In fact, Samuel Ehrenhalt, a regional commissioner of the Bureau of Labor Statistics, reported that by the mid-1980s, the barriers to women's equality had clearly fallen as women "edged out" men who "are no longer the majority among the professional workers in this country" (quoted in Greer, 1986:C1).

For racial/ethnic minorities, especially blacks,[2] the legislation of the mid-1960s did more than put an end to segregated lunch counters, restaurants, and hotels. For the very first time, racially based discrimination in employment was illegal (Landry, 1987). The most important civil-rights laws dealing with employment were the Equal Pay Act of 1963; Title VII of the Civil Rights Act of 1964 and amendments to it expanding coverage to federal employees in 1972; and several Executive Orders issued in the 1960s and early 1970s by President Lyndon Johnson (11246, which applied to race, religion, color, and national origin; and 11375, which applied to gender). This legislation required that businesses as well as governmental bodies not discriminate against minorities and women, particularly regarding access to education and employment. (For a brief review of affirmative action and equal employment opportunity legislation, see Burstein, 1985, DiTomaso and Thompson, 1988.)

In the context of a period of U.S. economic expansion and the growth of government, these laws contributed to the creation of a new black middle class and a new group of black professionals within it (Higginbotham, 1987; Landry, 1987). This middle class tripled in the quarter century between 1950 and 1976, with the proportion of black professionals increasing from 3.4 to 10.1 percent of all employed blacks. In contrast, the corresponding figure for white professionals did not even double, rising from 8.6 to 16.2 percent (Landry, 1987). The 1970s was a particularly remarkable period for black women, who, it was frequently noted, experienced a tenfold increased presence in law, medicine, and other prestigious professions (Herbers, 1983).

Despite the many advances made by women and blacks in the wake of economic expansion and changing antidiscrimination legislation, many contradictions have lingered. On the one hand, despite certain changes in the 1970s, occupational gender segregation has persisted throughout the 20th century (Gross, 1968; England, 1981; Jacobs, 1984, 1986). Yet, as we have seen, the increased numbers of women in traditionally high-status professions such as law and medicine between 1960 and 1980 is nothing short of remarkable. On the other hand, when one looks at those jobs with the largest expected numerical growth between 1978 and the year 2000, not a single one is in the high-status, male-dominated professions (Carey, 1981; Leon, 1982; Silvestri, Lukasiewicz and Einstein, 1983). Consider registered nursing, which is the largest profession in the list of the 20 occupations that are expected to grow the most by the year 2000.[3] In 1988, 97 percent of nurses were women. And, as we will see, nursing has never ranked near the top in any of the studies of occupational status or prestige.[4]

In contrast, occupational segregation by race has decreased substantially since the early part of the century (Treiman and Terrell, 1975; Farley, 1984). Yet minorities, particularly blacks, have made very little progress, especially within the more prestigious professions. Despite the economic and legislative changes that began in the 1960s, very few blacks have managed to obtain professional educations and to enter doctoral programs: by the early 1980s, blacks earned only 4 percent of all doctorates and first professional degrees (Carter and Wilson, 1989) while only 2 percent of all physicians, lawyers, and dentists throughout the United States were black (Blackwell, 1981). This underrepresentation is especially striking, given that blacks are at least 12 percent of the U.S. population (U.S. Bureau of Census, 1984).[5]

As the 1980s census data were analyzed and the results were displayed in newspaper headlines, these contradictory findings demanded an explanation. Moreover, as a more conservative mood hit the country during the 1980s and the economy became substantially less expansive than in the previous two decades, the political terrain shifted once again. Claims of "reverse discrimination" from white men became legitimized by the Reagan administration. Yet many women and minorities felt that the changing economic and labor-market landscape was particularly detrimental to them.

THE PARAMETERS OF THE STUDY

In 1960, the opening year of the period under study, there had been virtually no contemporary studies of women in the occupational structure. In the more than 30 years since then, there has been an outpouring of books and articles on the subject. In far too many, however, gender has been treated as the primary factor, with race (and class) as distinctly secondary, if indeed considered at all.[6]

Although discrimination on the basis of gender has been (and continues to be) directed against women of all races, racial discrimination is at least as important a factor in the work lives of racial/ethnic minority women. In short, the experiences of minority women and white women are not the same.[7] For this reason, I focus not simply on women in the professions between 1960 and 1980, but on black women and white women. And because both race and gender are bases of discrimination, in the professions as well as throughout the occupational structure, I also examine the position of white men and black men in the professions during the same period, in order to show how both factors work together and separately.

Why Focus on Blacks and Not Other Minorities?

I have chosen to focus on blacks, and not women and men of all minority groups, for four reasons: First, the attention of the civil-rights movement of the 1960s and 1970s (and of the anti–affirmative action backlash of the 1980s and

1990s) was on blacks. Second, blacks constitute the largest proportion of the combined racial/ethnic minority populations in the United States (92 percent in 1960, 89 percent in 1970, and 85 percent in 1980). As the largest minority group, they are often targets of the most vicious and systematic discrimination and hostility. Third, although women in general are believed to have made great inroads into the professions, one piece of conventional wisdom has it that black women in particular have done well. In Chapter 7, "Black Women: Beyond the Myth of the Double Advantage," one of my major purposes is to examine the merit of the claim that black women are "doubly advantaged," and that because of this they were said to be the primary beneficiaries of the expanded economy and the social-change legislation of the 1960s and 1970s. Fourth, Census Bureau materials, which provide the data on which this book is based, are more adequate for blacks than for other racial/ethnic minority groups during the 1960–1980 period.[8]

It is, of course, equally important to attempt to document the occupational experiences of all racial/ethnic groups during this same period. However, each group needs to be analyzed within the context of its unique historical experience and not to be subsumed under the black experience. This is a massive undertaking, one made more so by the sketchiness of Census Bureau data on groups other than blacks and whites over time. For this reason, such a broad-ranging analysis is not within the parameters of my book.

Why Study the Professions?

Even though the professions represent less than one-fifth of all workers in the United States, they are seen as some of the most desirable occupations in our society. The ability to enter and rise in a profession has always been regarded as assuring middle-class status in American society. Despite the many changes affecting the professions and their relation to the social-stratification system, they have always offered relatively greater control, autonomy, power, and rewards than have the "nonprofessional" occupations. To a very large extent, this is where people want to be. In fact, when we look at the possibilities for progress, the professions provide a "best case" scenario; nevertheless, the vast majority of women and black men do not acquire professional status.[9] Those who do are the most privileged among the disadvantaged groups and have the best chances to achieve occupational mobility and economic security.[10] For this reason we need to remember that they are in a better position than most of the other members of their racial/ethnic or gender groups, often serving as role models and/or mentors for others who are talented but more disadvantaged.

Not only are the professions desirable, but they have also expanded at an incredibly high rate in the post–World War II era. In the 1960s and 1970s, job opportunities grew faster in the professions than in any other occupational group

(Leon, 1982; Levin and Rumberger, 1983; Rumberger, 1983). Some professions expanded and new ones emerged. For example, in 1960, computer programmers did not even exist as an occupational category recognized by the Census Bureau; but by 1980, they numbered over 300,000 and were categorized in three distinct professional classifications. Likewise, the number of lawyers increased dramatically. In the 1970s alone, the number of lawyers grew by approximately 200,000. By 1986 there were more than 800,000 lawyers. The expansion was so great that more women entered the legal profession during the 1970s than during the rest of the 20th century up to that point (Epstein, 1983).

A Brief History of Women and Minority Men in the Professions until 1960

It was evident to the American public that expansion was occurring for women and minorities during the 1960–1980 period. Up until the 1960s, however, it was very clear that women and minority men were excluded from most of the professions.[11] Between 1870 and 1930, the percentage of women in the professions increased steadily from less than 5 percent of all employed women to just over 14 percent. For the next 20 years, largely as a direct result of the Great Depression, there was a steady decline in the number of women professionals; in 1950 they were only 10.8 percent of all women workers. By 1960 the percentage of women in the professions had started to climb once again, but women had a long way to go before they would recoup their losses. It was not until 1970 that among all women who worked, women once again could claim approximately the same share of the professions (14.3 percent) that they had had in 1930 (14.2 percent) (Bernard, 1971).

Despite these changes, women were largely confined to those professions that were overwhelmingly "female": that is, elementary education, nursing, and librarianship, which were at least 85 percent female in 1960. Even at that time women represented a very small percentage of the classical elite professions. For example, although women constituted a full one-third of the labor force, they made up only 3.5 percent of all lawyers, 5.8 percent of clergy, 6.8 percent of doctors, and 4.2 percent of physicists (Oppenheimer, 1970; Bernard, 1971).

Women could not enter training or practice in the classical professions in the same way that men could. Formal barriers to women's participation existed throughout the first half of the 20th century, including, for example, legal restrictions, quotas, administrative regulations, and antinepotism rules (Scharf, 1980; Cott, 1987).

Until the 1960s, the received wisdom that women did not belong in the classical professions, save for women's enclaves, was seldom questioned. In each of the male-dominated professions, women were recruited into sectors of the legal, medical, scientific, and professiorial structures that were said to be "women's domain." Women lawyers were able to find work in such "female" sectors as family law or trusts and estates. In the latter case, firms could put women in back offices where they would not have contact with the most important clients. In medicine, women physicians worked in pediatrics and psychiatry. And at the university, women predominated in the "soft," or female, areas of concentration: for example, foreign languages, literature, and home economics (Theodore, 1971; Kaufman, 1984). In each case, these were lower-prestige specialties, lower-paid areas, and/or at the lowest and least-permanent ranks of the profession.

A look at the history of women in the professions is primarily a look at the history of white women, since blacks (both men and women) have almost entirely been denied entry. The small number of blacks in the professions is related to the history of both legal and extralegal restrictions against blacks in this country. Thus by 1960 only 4.7 percent of all black workers were able to find employment in the professions (Landry, 1987).

Prior to the civil-rights era, racial segregation limited the demand and opportunity for most black professionals to the provision of services where white professionals refused to go (Higginbotham, 1987; Landry, 1987). Thus black professionals were allowed to work in the small and often poor private sector in the black community or in a segregated public sector. This resulted in the limited employment of black professionals as teachers, ministers, social workers, and occasionally doctors and lawyers (Woodson, 1934; Frazier, 1957; Dubois, 1967; Landry, 1987). Thus the nature of professional employment for black women was shaped by both racism and sexism. While black men were confined to a somewhat greater variety of professional jobs, the primary profession for black women was teaching; social work and nursing ran far behind in second and third place (Kilson, 1977). Within these professions, black women did not work with white women. In the South, Jim Crow legislation ensured that black women taught in segregated schools and practiced nursing in offices of black male doctors. In the North, rigid racial barriers and de facto segregation restricted the employment of black professional women to segregated schools, hospitals, churches, and welfare agencies (Higginbotham, 1987). The numbers of black women educated to be physicians, lawyers, or college teachers were outrageously small. In 1960, in the entire country, there were only 176 black women lawyers and judges and 490 physicians and surgeons documented by the census (USDC, Bureau of Census, 1963, Table 205).

Clearly the degree of exclusion and segregation has lessened. By 1980 black men and black women in the professions were more likely to enter institutions in the mainstream and work alongside whites. White women were no longer confined to female-dominated professions as they had been in the past. But important questions remain: do the 1980 data show women and blacks entering the core professions so highly prized and protected by the interests of white men?

Do they indicate that white women have been restricted in new ways to women's enclaves, not only in such professions as nursing and teaching, but also in medicine and law? Which professions have expanded the most? Have they become accessible to black women and white women alike? Have black men and black women been able to increase their numbers in the coveted white male professions as much as white women have? Or have totally new places emerged for men and women from different racial/ethnic groups as the professional job market has expanded? Have any professions declined in status over the years? If so, is the decline correlated with increased access for members of disadvantaged race/gender groups?

JUST WHAT ARE THE PROFESSIONS?

In many ways the professions are *the* elite occupations. Since professions are accorded a high degree of honor and status in our society, their members can expect greater rewards for their services. The autonomy of professionals and the respect they elicit can be largely attributed to their very high levels of education: their specialized training is said to allow them to draw on a body of knowledge inaccessible to the general public. The exclusivity of the professions is in large part a result of their right to exercise a virtual monopoly over who can legitimately do the work, how that work should be done, and who can judge their performance. Professionals are thought to derive a great deal of fulfillment from their work and to enjoy a high degree of respect, autonomy, control, and status.[12]

There are two major schools of thought about the place of the professions in society: they have been labeled the *American approach* and the *British approach* by Macdonald and Ritzer (1988). The American perspective has been dominated by the structural-functional approach, which attempts to define the distinctive characteristics of the professions. This includes listing attributes that help to define the degree of professionalization of an occupation along several key dimensions (see, for example, Montagna, 1977:196,197): autonomy, control, monopoly, and so forth. In the 1970s, structural-functionalism was challenged by theorists such as Eliot Freidson (1973).

The British perspective involves a more theoretical approach that tries to understand the place of the professions (and, more generally, of the middle class) in the stratification system. It calls upon both Marxian and Weberian theory in doing so (see, for example, Macdonald and Ritzer, 1988). Those who adhere to the British perspective look at theoretically informed work around the issues of inter- and intraprofessional conflict, the relationship between the professions and the state, and the place of the professions in the stratification system.

Within this perspective are those who see professionals as part of a new middle class: the professional managerial class.[13] In contrast to manual laborers, the professional managerial class is defined as those who plan, manage, and monitor the labor of the working class. They are the thinkers, the creators, the controllers; the workers are the doers. What is important is the social relations of subordination and dominance—subordination of the professional managerial class to capital and their control over workers—which creates a separate and distinct "middle" class in modern industrial capitalism (Ehrenreich and Ehrenreich, 1979; Vanneman and Cannon, 1987).

The Core Professions

The classic case of the core professions traditionally has been exemplified by law and medicine (Rueschemeyer, 1964, 1973; Freidson, 1973; Laumann and Heinz, 1977; Heinz and Laumann, 1982; Starr, 1982). Other established professions include architecture, the ministry, dentistry, the judicial profession, science, and university teaching. These are the highest-paid professions with the greatest autonomy and control where white men from more privileged backgrounds have traditionally predominated.[14]

The Semiprofessions

The core professions are theoretically and empirically distinct from those occupations more recently defined as the *semiprofessions*. The semiprofessions have been characterized as the "handmaidens" to the professions. They include occupations such as nursing, teaching (elementary, kindergarten, and nursery school), librarianship, and social work. According to Theodore (1971), it is no accident that the semiprofessions and the professions are correlated with the extremes of gender segregation. Thus the semiprofessions are heavily female dominated, and the professions (in which she includes medicine, dentistry, law, science, engineering, and the ministry) are largely reserved for men. As we will see, the core professions tend to include what I later define as the *elite male professions,* while the semiprofessions correlate most closely with what I define as the *female professions.*

The semiprofessions have shorter training periods than the established professions and, according to Etzioni (1969:v) "their status is less established, there is less of a specialized body of knowledge, and they have less autonomy from supervision or societal control than 'the' professions." The semiprofessions are more entrenched in bureaucracies and are often controlled by the more traditional professions. Nursing work, predominantly hospital based, flows directly from the doctor's orders and is thereby defined as a subordinate part of the technical division of labor surrounding medicine (Freidson, 1973). Moreover, rules and regulations guiding the performance of medical workers who are not physicians are in large part determined by physicians (Brown, 1974). Simpson and Simpson (1969) argue that the semiprofessions lack autonomy and are subject to numerous rules governing both central work tasks and extraneous details, precisely because of the prevalence of women in them.

The Technical Fields

Not only does the popular meaning of the term *professions* tend to be restricted to the most visible and highly paid male-dominated fields (law, medicine, etc.), thereby overlooking the even larger grouping of the semiprofessions, but it also excludes another group of occupations: the *technical fields*. Until 1950 the Census Bureau used only the category "professions and semiprofessions," and included within it an array of technical fields (laboratory and X-ray work, electrical engineering, and agricultural work, for example). In 1950, owing to the expansion of these far lower-status, lesser-paid occupations requiring less education and training, the Census Bureau created a new category, "professional, technical, and kindred workers" and classified the technicians there.

In 1980, in recognition of the further expansion of this lower-status group, the Census Bureau separated technicians from professionals. However, there is still much overlap between them. Certain occupations moved from profession to technical field over time: computer programming and airline piloting, to mention two. In contrast, licensed practical nursing moved from a lower-status service occupation to a technical field over time. For the most part, these changes reflected the upgrading or downgrading of an occupation from one census decade to another. Like the semiprofessions, the technical fields contain large numbers of women. In addition, they are highly segregated by race/gender, as we shall see.

Since technical fields have experienced considerable growth (in fact, their overall growth between 1970 and 1980 was greater than for the professions), and since they have historically been included conceptually and empirically in the census definition of professions, I have included them in this study. However, my focus is on the professions, with more limited analysis of the much smaller group of technical occupations.

THE CHANGING OCCUPATIONAL LANDSCAPE

There are continual shifts in occupations and the people who enter them. New professions emerge; old ones change their organization and control; some totally drop from view; and new groups of men and women vie for positions in this changing economy. None of these distinctions are taken into account when news-paper headlines, such as "Women Now the Majority in Professions" (Greer, 1986), lead the reader to believe that the movement of women and minorities into elite male professions continues to increase (see also Prial, 1982; Herbers, 1983; Hacker, 1984; Castro, 1985). In fact, the possibility clearly exists that these gains have been in professions outside the highly desirable core.

Race/Gender Segregation in the Professions

The importance of the professions as an avenue of advancement for disadvan-taged groups in our society cannot be underestimated. In order to answer the question, To what degree were black women and white women as well as black men able to gain greater *access* to the professions during a period of massive social change?, we need to understand the nature of race/gender segregation.[15] Not only do women (both black and white) and blacks (both women and men) tend to be highly concentrated in certain occupations, which are usually less desirable and/or lower paid, but black women stand in a quite different relation to both white women and men (both white and black), in a labor market simul-taneously structured on the basis of race and gender.

What this typically means is that most of the earlier studies of gender segre-gation either assumed that all women are alike or considered only the experi-ences of the dominant group, white women. Likewise, studies of racial segre-gation have either subsumed the experiences of black women under those of black men or simply ignored black women's unique experiences (Hull, Scott, and Smith, 1982).[16] My goal is to develop an understanding of the actual gains of black women and white women, compared both with each other and with black men and white men, in the context of the changing nature of the economy and specifically the professions within it. This research strategy allows us to look at the larger picture while considering diverse categories of men and women in several sectors of the highly desired professions, rather than lumping all women or all blacks into a single group.

In short, I focus on the changes in *access* and *equity* of diverse race/gender groups in the professions at the same time that I examine the diverse nature of the professions themselves. What this analysis means is that though my focus is on the changing occupational experiences of black women and white women, this occurs in the context of what happens for black men and white men in a changing economic and political landscape. Moreover, while the professions are the major occupational group I study, it is important to keep in mind that the professions are a diverse group of occupations within the larger stratification system. Thus I explore how the different race/gender groups do or do not gain access to the various levels of the professional job structure in a period of mas-sive social, political, and economic change. Most important, I operate under the guiding principle that the structures of race, gender, and class continuously work in historically specific ways to affect the occupational opportunities that are available to women and men, black and white.

THE NEED FOR A STRUCTURAL APPROACH

The focus on individual mobility is often more appealing than a broader analysis because individuals who have risen despite being black, female, or working class seem to validate the American dream. However, a structural approach provides a *context* for individual success stories; it is not an alternative to them. Moreover, the need to explore the more structural levels of analysis is a major part of feminist and antiracist approaches, as well as the sociological enterprise.

One way of considering this distinction between individual mobility and structural forces is to compare our own knowledge of individual women who have moved into the professions with the broader changes occurring within the occupations themselves. For example, we all can cite impressive examples of contemporary women whose mothers and grandmothers were domestics and typists and homemakers, but who, themselves, have "made it" as lawyers, doctors, schoolteachers, accountants, affirmative-action officers, and so on. These individual accomplishments are mirrored in the experiences of hundreds of thousands of women who have gained access to occupational positions typically reserved for white men and, therefore, often not available to preceding generations of women.

For individual women in the professions, or male-dominated professions in particular, this movement may represent genuine improvement over other less powerful, less remunerative work they would otherwise have had to do. This is true despite the fact that black women and white women (and black men) are more likely to enter at lower levels even within the elite male-dominated professions. For example, in medicine women are more likely to be recruited into family practice than surgery; in law women tend to go into domestic relations rather than corporate practice (Epstein, 1983; Bowman and Gross, 1986). Black women, in contrast, are more likely than white women to be found in public hospitals and municipal clinics as physicians. As lawyers, they tend to end up in government-funded legal aid and attorney general's offices (Higginbotham, 1987).

Moreover, it should be clear that many women prefer these specialties to the more male-dominated ones. This is likewise the case for female professions: many black women and white women want to work as nurses, schoolteachers, and social workers. The problem is that many women working in these jobs might want to enter higher-paying and more male-dominated professions but are *prevented* from doing so. Thus the fact that a female profession or a female enclave in a male profession is lower status or is lower paid may well be due to the social devaluation of a job where women are concentrated, not because of characteristics intrinsic to the job itself (see Phillips and Taylor, 1980).

Much about these individual gains in social mobility is problematic, however, when looked at from a broader perspective. First, at the same time that individual black women or white women are experiencing upward mobility, the occupation itself may be in the process of being downgraded or rationalized, with less autonomy and control and fewer rewards for those individuals. The downgrading of an occupation correlates with the proportion of women entering it—that is, if it is "women's work," it is less highly valued by our society; and both prestige and earnings decline. Reskin and Roos (1990) call the point at which the proportion of women reaches a certain number in an occupation's transition from male to female the "tipping effect." This effect has certainly occurred in the past as clerical work (Davies, 1974) and teaching (Tyack and Strober, 1981; Strober, 1984) shifted from male to female domination. It currently appears to be occurring with pharmacists, who are becoming less autonomous businesspeople (Phipps, 1990a), as well as with accountants (Reskin, 1989) and insurance adjusters (Phipps, 1990b).

Structural transformations affect black women differently. For instance, many clerical jobs are being eliminated just as black women are beginning to enter them in much larger numbers (Sokoloff, 1987b). Or, as salaried white male physicians abandon inner city "ghetto" hospitals, more jobs open up for black women (and men) physicians (and nurses) in previously unattainable positions (Lorber, 1985, 1987; Higginbotham, 1987). So, too, in female professions. Black women, who in the past might have had a chance to obtain only clerical work, may today have the chance to work as teachers and librarians. These changes provide very important opportunities for individual women. However, some of these jobs carry far less prestige and pay, and far more hazards than years ago when they were essentially dominated by white women (Dressel, 1987; Malveaux and Englander, 1987; Glazer, 1991).

In short, although the nature of the experience of black women in entering the professions is somewhat different from that of white women, the larger point is the same: individual effort is important but counts for less than structural factors *on a large scale*. This conclusion is buttressed by the work of Featherman and Hauser (1976), whose research showed that most upward mobility for individuals is accounted for by changes in the structure of occupations—for example, the growth of lower-level white-collar occupations since World War II.

A second problem is highlighted by Jacobs (1989). He argues that there can be substantial movement of individual women into male-dominated occupations; but even while these occupations appear to be opening up, there is a startling rate of attrition. Thus, although individual mobility into male occupations for women over the life cycle appears to be more common than was previously thought, change in the structure of gender segregation appears to be slow. Social-control mechanisms operate to keep the structure of the labor market gender segregated by pushing some women out while allowing other women in. Although Jacobs does not deal with the same dimensions in terms of racial segregation, I argue that not only the structure of gender segregation operates in society at large, but also the structure of race/gender segregation. Men's advantage in male-dominated professions is typically an advantage of white men of higher-level socioeconomic origins. Race and class are as important as gender in structuring the market; they are among the broader forces that impact on the lives of men and women as they enter or fail to enter the labor market.

A third problem inherent in focusing on individual change rather than on the broader structural context is that it ignores the fact that certain occupations into which women are entering may be in the process of resegregating. The principles of gender segregation or race/gender segregation may still be operative, but the composition of an occupation traditionally "thought of" as male dominated may be in the process of becoming female dominated. As I mentioned previously, this happened earlier in the century as clerical work and teaching became less entrepreneurial, more bureaucratic and lower paid. It may well be happening to accounting and psychology today. While the higher, more powerful levels of these professions may remain male dominated (as is the case for both clerical work and teaching), the nature of work in these occupations may be changing such that gender or race/gender composition of the occupation as a whole may be changing. This may not be a sign of desegregation but of resegregation: the entire occupation or a specific portion of it becomes dominated by a particular race/gender group differing from that traditionally identified with the profession. (For recent analyses of job resegregation, see Cohn, 1985; Reskin and Roos, 1990.)

Finally, recent research has shown that many of the studies completed in the 1960s and 1970s that made the case for individual mobility used statistics that were flawed (Hauser, 1992; S. Rytina, 1992). The United States may be a more open society than some, but the myth that hard work will be rewarded regardless of a person's racial/ethnic, gender, or class background is just that—a myth. Only a structural approach allows us to see why people from various groups are more or less likely to succeed in entering and rising in a given profession.

Even given all these caveats, something dramatic was happening on the occupational front during the 1960–1980 period. Opportunities for historically disadvantaged groups were on the increase. The number of professionals was growing, and larger numbers of women and minority men were among those counted at the higher levels of the professional hierarchy. The civil-rights movement of the 1950s and the women's movement of the 1960s led to affirmative-action mandates and equal employment opportunity legislation for women of all racial/

ethnic groups and for minority men. Given these structural changes, one might think that it would be relatively simple to assess the progress made by women and minority men; yet controversy rages over the extent of these changes. Who has benefited most, and in what ways, especially in the professions? Let us look at this controversy.

CONTROVERSY AND INTERPRETATION

The nature and extent of changes for disadvantaged groups is controversial. Has the expansion at different levels of the professions favored different race/gender groups? If so, in what ways? Have affirmative action and equal employment opportunity legislation helped disadvantaged groups more than white men? If so, how does this play itself out in different sectors of the professions for each of the race/gender groups? How do the advances of white women compare to those of black men and black women? Are black women "doubly advantaged" as some people argue, or are they "doubly disadvantaged" because of their race and gender statuses? Is gender no longer a key issue in the elite male professions? Is race "declining in significance" for those in the professions? Is "reverse discrimination" on the march? Just what is happening?

Gender and the Professions:
Theoretical Perspectives

Two competing views of the position of women in the professions have dominated the empirical and theoretical literature in sociology and economics. The first is known as *status attainment, human capital,* or *individual* analysis; the second as *occupational gender segregation, dual labor market,* or *structural* theory. Because both approaches tend to be located within the theoretical mainstream of social stratification theory, they necessarily provide a limited understanding of women in the professions. (For reviews of this literature, see Sokoloff, 1980; Fox and Hesse-Biber, 1984). Marxist theory and socialist feminist theory could present a broader perspective[17]—one that would stress the systems of capitalism, patriarchy, and internal colonization of minorities—but none of these alternative perspectives focus on professional women in any detail.[18] One exception is the recent work of black feminist scholars such as Higginbotham (1987), Higginbotham and Cannon (1988), P. Hill Collins (1990), and Malveaux (1981, 1985, 1990). Within their limits, then, what do the two primarily mainstream approaches have to tell us about the recent experience of women in the professions?

Supporters of the human capital/status attainment positions argue that women have made dramatic gains in the labor market since the upsurge of the women's movement and changes in legislation, both of which began in the 1960s. As early as 1972, George Hay Brown, then director of the Census Bureau, said in evaluating the 1970 census data on women: "Women in the seventies are *rapidly moving toward full equality*" (quoted in Rosenthal, 1972; my emphasis). The reasoning here is that the qualities people bring with them into the labor market (primarily their education, and secondarily their occupational training and experience and gender-role training) are the most important determinants of occupational success. So, if women can get the same education as men, both qualitatively (i.e., in prestigious fields at top-flight schools) and quantitatively (i.e., the same number of years of study), they should be able to achieve the same occupational status as men in general. In particular, they should be able to make their way into the higher-status, more privileged male-dominated professions, work their way up the ladder, and receive the same rewards. What is needed, the argument goes, is a resocialization of women to aspire to, educate themselves for, and train for more prestigious "male" occupations. The conclusion is that women's increased participation in the professions is largely due to their reaching the required levels of education and training and to changing their attitudes toward and behaviors associated with gender roles, children, and work commitment and continuity. In sum, if women succeed, it is because they have seized opportunities open to them that are similar to those open to men; if they fail, it is no one's fault but their own.

In the 1970s this position seriously began to be challenged by proponents of the second position—occupational gender segregation. This view holds that the problems women face in the labor market are due not so much to individual women's attitudes and qualifications as to the fact that the jobs and labor markets in which women are employed are organized to their disadvantage and segregate them from men. In other words, the locus of analysis is *structural*, not *individual*. Women are employed in sectors of the economy characterized by job instability, low capitalization, small profits, low wages, little advancement opportunity or job security, poor worker organization, and high turnover. In short, women are more likely to find employment in low-status, poorly paid, gender-segregated occupations such as clerical and service work. This is true as well in the professions in general and within male-dominated professions where women are not allowed to participate fully.

In the 1980s, proponents of this position expanded their analysis to argue that gender segregation takes many more forms in the workplace than previously acknowledged (for a review, see Reskin and Hartmann, 1986). In addition to occupational segregation itself, men and women in the same occupation are often employed in different industries or work for different employers. Establishment and industry segregation is common, and it occurs even when occupations are generally integrated. This is as true for the professions as for the labor force overall (Bielby and Baron, 1986). For example, women lawyers in the fastest-growing areas of in-house legal counsel are more likely to be recruited into financial services (less profitable, lower salaried, with more women employed in nonlegal jobs), while men are more likely to be recruited into in-house legal departments in more profitable manufacturing corporations (Roach, 1990). Of course, gender segregation is also tied to areas of specialization, with the more lucrative and more powerful being less accessible to women: for example, women lawyers are underrepresented in litigation (Epstein, 1983); women doctors, in surgery (Bowman and Gross, 1986).

In order to explain women's increased participation in high-status male-dominated professions, the proponents of the occupational-segregation position look to broader structural change in the economy and in the society. For example, they stress the importance of broad-scale social movements such as civil rights, the women's movement, affirmative-action legislation and policies, and occupational expansion, as well as occupational changes such as the increased emphasis on the importance of services in our society. But in order for women to participate more fully in prestigious occupations, most feminists would argue that women's socially defined responsibilities for domestic work and child care need to be restructured. Men, social agencies, and social services need to play a more equitable role in these traditionally privatized and female-oriented tasks.

However, structural theorists have argued that *despite* all these changes on both structural and individual levels, the amount of gender segregation overall and in the professions in particular has remained fairly constant throughout the 20th century.[19] Yet in the early 1980s, even ardent supporters of occupational gender segregation theory began pointing out that women in the more privileged sectors of the job market (professional and managerial) are doing much better in gaining access to these jobs than before and better than women in lower-status jobs (Burris and Wharton, 1982), or more specifically had done much better in reaping occupational rewards under Reagan-administration policies in the 1980s (Power, 1984).[20]

In sum, the human capital theory and the occupational gender segregation theory can be used to argue that there has been a significant numerical increase of women in the professions—the first by focusing on the individual and the second by looking at broader structural forces in society. However, neither adequately explains if and how this increase means genuine progress for black women and white women throughout the professional labor market. Both have paid insufficient attention to institutionalized racism, to the capitalist political economy, and to internalized oppression as these forces work in similar and different ways to affect the chances of black women and white women. In this study I attempt to show how black women and white women (and black men) have fared in the professions in the 1960–1980 period, and to place the data in an explanatory theoretical context.

Race and the Professions

The position of black men and black women in the professions should be evaluated in the context of greater polarization of blacks into the middle class and the "underclass" in U.S. society, and the dire reports of black men's loss of resources in poverty-stricken urban areas. Both conditions are said to be the product of the same economic conditions (Wilson, 1987). On the one hand, the civil-rights movement, the increasingly service-oriented, white-collar economy, and the growth of government and public-sector jobs have created unprecedented opportunities for educated blacks. A new black middle class was on the rise (Landry, 1987). On the other hand, the shift from a production to a service economy threatened to lock out uneducated, unskilled, and semiskilled people permanently. Deindustrialization and the loss of highly paid unionized jobs just as blacks (especially black men) were entering those markets led to massive dislocation of urban blacks. At the same time, comparatively well-educated, middle class blacks moved out of the previously economically varied central cities (Wilson, 1987).

Given these conditions, a debate has ensued about the progress of black professionals since the post–World War II expansion. One side argues that educated and trained blacks have done so well since World War II that they do not need "preferential treatment" in such programs as affirmative action. In fact, this group asserts, blacks are *hindered* by such policies because "qualified applicants suffer." They argue that "other people" say the black professional obtained the position only because of preferential treatment, not because of his or her merits. This devalues the qualified and capable blacks and creates tensions with whites.[21] Critics of this position would argue that given racial and gender/racial discrimination, this approach fails to consider the reality that the actual merits of a black person all too often are not recognized without the legal and moral muscle of affirmative action.

Black scholars on the other side of this debate argue that *despite* all the changes brought about by civil rights and affirmative action, the position of middle-class blacks in the job market is quite precarious. For example, black professionals are heavily dependent on employment by governmental agencies rather than within the free-market system. In a period of economic stagnation or contraction, then, the livelihood of middle-class blacks is in serious jeopardy (S. Collins, 1983). Moreover, despite greater integration of blacks into white society, racial stratification and segregation both on and off the job persist for black professionals and managers, as for most minority workers (Farley, 1984;

Landry, 1987; Gelman et al., 1988). Discrimination exists even for black professionals with more education and training than comparable whites (see, for example, L. Williams, 1991.) The occupational ghettoization of upper-level blacks (Higginbotham, 1987), the increasing number of suicides among high-level black professional women (McElroy, 1987), and the lack of acceptance or marginalization of many skilled and qualified blacks (Hesse-Biber, 1986) are just some of the reasons that proponents of this position question the degree to which discrimination has decreased against blacks, including black professionals. Once again, the decline in the significance of race in the experience and mobility of the black middle class is interpreted differently, depending on one's vantage point.

Gender and Race: Theories about Black Women and White Women in the Professions

White Women Have Made the Most Progress

In comparing the progress of black women and white women in the professions, two competing views likewise dominate: *white women have benefited more* versus *black women have benefited more*. According to the first position, it has commonly been argued that white women, particularly well-educated, middle-class white women, have been the major beneficiaries not only of affirmative action and the women's movement (see Rule, 1982; Hacker, 1984), but also of the specific policies of the conservative Reagan and Bush administrations (see Power, 1984). Thus, according to the Equal Employment Opportunity Commission (as reported in Rule, 1982), white women moved from holding a little more than 1 in 10 professional jobs (13.0 percent) in 1966 to holding almost one-third (31.6 percent) of all such jobs by 1979. In contrast, the percentage of black women increased from only 0.6 percent of all professionals to a mere 2.2 percent (and black men from 0.7 to 1.9 percent), hardly a challenge to the gains of white women. Moreover, given that 12 percent of the population is black, and that only 4 percent of all professionals are black, it is clear that blacks are greatly underrepresented. Those who assert that white women have the best chances to move up the occupational, professional, and corporate ladders also say that neither black men nor black women have gained very much, and that white males have been the major losers. To support this last point, they note that the white male proportion of the total professional labor force dropped from 83.5 percent in 1960 to 58.9 percent in 1979 (Rule, 1982).

In addition, while it may be the case that white women have made substantial gains, they have also been found to experience the effects of the "glass ceiling": they can go only so far up the professional/managerial ladder so that men continue to dominate in the higher reaches of the professions (e.g., see Skrzycki,

1990). Despite these limitations, glass is breakable: some white women will make it through the broken glass to top positions. Blacks, on the other hand, experience a "Lucite ceiling": Lucite is so strong that while you can see through it, you cannot break it like glass (Henriques, 1991). Therefore, black women (and black men) are not only restricted to middle-level professional and managerial positions, but they have even more diminished chances than white women to break through to the top.

In discussing the overall impact of affirmative action between 1968 and 1979 (based on unpublished Census Bureau data), Malveaux (1981) concludes that despite certain important gains made by black women,

> the gainers of so-called "affirmative action" in the period of 1972 to 1977 have been white women more than anyone else. The rates of change for both black men and black women have declined since 1972, whereas from 1968 to 1972 the major gains were made by black men as opposed to black women. The reasoning is simple. Race was stressed in the 1964 Executive Order; sex was added in 1972. So black men were brought into the workplace in so-called non-black jobs between 1968 and 1972, and the focus switched in a sense to women somewhat thereafter. (pp. 44–45)

Black Women Have Made the Most Progress

A second and more commonly held view in the mass media and some scholarly literature is that *black women have benefited more*. This position argues that not only have women done particularly well over the past quarter century in the professions, but black women have done the best. The giant strides made by black women are alleged to have led to greater equality between black women and white women. Thus one journalist reports that a Census Bureau study comparing 1970 and 1980 occupational data found that women and minorities made remarkable gains during the decade of the 1970s, and "black women seem to be the most mobile group of all. Confined mostly to menial jobs in the past, they [black women] made big gains in professional, service and blue collar work" (Herbers, 1983:1). This statement is backed up with data showing that between 1970 and 1980, black women lawyers increased *tenfold*, from 446 to 4,272. Likewise, an equally large rate of increase of black women occurred among psychologists, physicians, and computer operators (Herbers, 1983).

Those who say that black women have made the most progress look at economic gains as well as movement into the professions. They interpret income figures for black women as a whole in comparison to white women in supporting their point. The way the data are distorted to create the impression of black women's more advantaged position is described by both Almquist (1979) and Fox and Hesse-Biber (1984). For example, Fox and Hesse-Biber report that between 1939 and 1978, the median income of black women employed full-time, year-round (i.e., in all occupations, not just the professions) increased from 38 percent of white women workers' incomes to 94 percent. They point out how these data are used not only to show the progress of black women in relation to white women, but also to create the impression that "black women have an income advantage over black men because they have closed the gap on white women's earnings at a more rapid pace than black males have closed the gap on white males' earnings" (p. 165); that is, black men increased from only 45 to 74 percent of white men's incomes during the same time period. As Malveaux (1990) recently clarified, the extra burden that black women must contend with because of the disadvantaged labor-market experiences of their spouses or other members of their family unit is cleverly turned into a so-called "advantage." Moreover, not only has the income gap closed between black women and white women in general, but among professional, technical, and managerial workers, black women have been found to have somewhat higher earnings, on the average, than white women (Young, 1979). While Malveaux (1985, 1990) finds that these trends continued into the 1980s, she argues that the reason for black women's slightly higher earnings, especially in higher-status jobs, is due to their longer employment history (i.e, black women work more hours than white women) and the tendency for white women's employment to be less continuous (i.e., they are more likely than black women to take time off for child care and to work part-time).

In fact, argues Landry (1987:129), "Black females experience the double discrimination of being black and female. With white females, they suffer from occupational restrictions and income inequalities in a male-dominated market. When compared with white females, it becomes apparent that they also suffer from the additional handicap of a process that rewards black females and white females differently—frequently to their disadvantage. This is not always apparent from a comparison of incomes, as the average incomes of black middle-class females and white middle-class females are similar." In Landry's study, the average for black women was $9,843, for white women, $9,721. He continues, "The 'average' black female in my sample, however, was slightly older . . . , had two years more seniority, and had worked more years since marriage." Using education and occupation scores, one would "expect black females in the sample to exceed the average income of whites by far more than the $122 observed. . . . Indeed, if black females had experienced the same income allocation process as whites, their average incomes would be about $1,700 higher, or $11,376."

Black women's gains in the professions were not solely the result of affirmative action: both before and after significant affirmative-action legislation was implemented, black women entered professions at a faster rate than either black men or white women (Kilson, 1977). One study showed that black women increased their representation in the professions 3.5 times between 1966 and 1979, greater than any other race/gender group (Rule, 1982). Another study found that, while both black men and black women showed the greatest rate of change in the professions between 1968 and 1972, black women alone showed the greatest rate of increase in the professions between 1972 and 1977. The average annual rate of increase in professional/technical employment in the earlier period was 2.7; in the later one, it was 3.9. For black females it was as high as 7.0 in the 1968–1972 period and 10.6 in the 1972–1977 period (Malveaux, 1981:160, Table 3).

While neither Malveaux nor Rule draw such conclusions, these kinds of data have been used to support the hypothesis that because of their "doubly disadvantaged" status black women have been able to benefit twice from affirmative action, thereby outdoing all other disadvantaged groups, including white women and black men. Hacker (1986:32) supports this myth when he argues that in the mid-1980s "black women . . . have stronger representation than white women in professions and management." Even before the impact of affirmative action could be felt in the 1970s, black men, in particular, were said to be "devastated" psychologically and occupationally (Hare and Hare, 1970) because black women's double oppression was alleged to have led to their "unnatural superiority" over black men (Bernard, 1966).

This doubly disadvantaged status was sometimes referred to as the "twofer myth," a particularly popular explanation in the early 1970s for black women's achievement. According to this myth, employers had allegedly turned affirmative action to their advantage by hiring black women, thus gaining "two minorities for the price of one" (see Hernandez, 1981; Malveaux, 1981). The "positive effects of the multiple negative" status of black women have been argued specifically in the case of those few black women who have "made it" as successful professionals, including lawyers and physicians (Epstein, 1973; 1983).[22] Epstein contends that despite very real obstacles and barriers, successful black women in the professions are aided in their pursuits because the negative statuses of black and female combine either to cancel each other out or to create a unique position that is not devalued in the labor market. As several authors note, a number of *questionable assumptions* are embedded in the idea that successful black women have a double advantage: that black women experience less discrimination than black men, that black women benefit professionally due to an educational advantage over black men, that black women are somehow better prepared to cope with white male employers and white-controlled bureaucracies, that black women derive unusual motivational strength and ambition from their dual status, and that black women have an easier time finding jobs than black men do (Almquist, 1979; Fox and Hesse-Biber, 1984). (In addition, see Fulbright, 1985–86; Malveaux, 1990).

Once again, we are left with a confused picture of the comparative progress of black women and white women in the professions: one approach argues for larger gains by white women; the other, for the gains of black women over both white women and black men. Neither, however, uses white men, the dominant majority group, as a major standard against which to evaluate the achievements of black and white professional women in terms of their relationship to the production system, or their job tasks, power, right to make decisions, prestige, or income. Nor do they try to disentangle the dual impact of racial and sexual discrimination.[23]

In short, the foregoing theories fail to provide us with a clear understanding of who has benefited the most, especially in the coveted professions, given the economic, social, and political changes that burgeoned in the 1960s and 1970s. Moreover, we are left unprepared for the degree to which occupational segregation in the professions has persisted, and sometimes intensified, on the basis of both gender (Reskin and Roos, 1990) and race (Glenn, 1987; Higginbotham, 1987; Glazer, 1991).

INROADS AND INTERPRETATION

The Problem of the Half-Full or the Half-Empty Glass

Much of the controversy about how to interpret the progress of women and minorities since the heyday of the civil-rights and women's movements depends on whether one sees the glass as half-full or half-empty. All too often, only the most favorable aspects of aggregate data are stressed, and the glass is said to be half-full. The appearance of progress under these conditions can be downright misleading, if not incorrect. For example, between 1970 and 1980, women doubled their participation in several important male-dominated professions: as physicians, dentists, lawyers, clergy, and engineers, a not insignificant finding. In every case, however, an equally telling piece of information that compares women's position to men's is underplayed: in 1980 men overwhelmingly dominated these professions, holding 85 to 90 percent of these positions (USDL, Bureau of Labor Statistics, 1980; USDC, Bureau of Census, 1983a).

The overstatement of black women's progress in the male-dominated professions demands special consideration. Both numbers and percentages are given for the increased representation of black women in this privileged arena. That the number of black women increased about tenfold in such professions as law and medicine is of great importance. Yet these data must be placed in their proper context: even after these gains, black women were *less than 1 percent* of all lawyers or doctors in 1980. Their increased presence did not begin to challenge white male control of these professions. Thus to cite growth in such numbers to support the argument that black women have been the major beneficiaries of social movements from the 1950s on is simply wrong.

In addition to their *numerical* growth, the overall *rate of growth* of women in the professions has been high. Yet using the rate of growth to proclaim great progress for women can be just as misleading as using their numerical increase. Its importance has often been grossly overstated, since it is frequently based on the very small number of women who were in these jobs in the past. For the professions in general, the proportion of jobs held by black women multiplied more than 3.5 times between 1966 and 1979. For black men and white women, it increased only 2.5 times, while for white men the proportion of professional jobs decreased by 29 percent. However, despite these changes, black women still ended up with only 2.2 percent of all professional jobs in 1979 (as reported in Rule, 1982). It is obvious that the tenfold increase in the number of black women entering law and medicine is so high only because the base numbers at which the count for black women began was so outrageously low.

Studies using aggregate occupational data (e.g., the Census Bureau's three-digit detailed occupational category, which is most often used in gender segregation studies) severely underestimate the amount of gender segregation that exists within and between organizations. According to Bielby and Baron's (1986) important study of 400 California establishments or firms between 1959 and 1979, the more detailed the occupational categories used, the more segregation was revealed. In fact, using job titles specific to a particular firm or business led them to conclude that virtually all jobs are totally segregated. The index of gender segregation under these conditions is .96. That is, 96 percent of all women or men would have to change jobs for there to be an equal distribution of men and women in the labor force. Even though the literature shows a steady and steep decline in gender segregation in the professions since World War II, Bielby and Baron find that segregation in the professions is almost as extreme as in the overall labor force: the index of sex segregation is .94. Thus, they would argue, men and women in the same profession do not typically work in the same organizations; when they do, they typically are assigned different job titles, with different occupational opportunities and rewards.

Thus the use of percentage change or rates of change over time, or the incomplete use of the most favorable aspects of aggregate data, can lead to an interpretation that the glass is half-full rather than half-empty. In fact, I would suggest that both interpretations have some merit, but that they cannot be seen in isolation. Black women and white women may have indeed made gains, but they may simultaneously be even more segregated from white men than they were earlier.

The Problem of Winners and Losers

In addition to understanding the complexities of the half-full versus the half-empty glass, we need to understand what it means to ask "Who did best?" in the race for occupational mobility. Is it true that white men lost and women and minority men gained in the professions "at the expense" of white men, as one political scientist insists (Hacker, 1984)? This might be the case if the range and size of professional jobs remained the same over time. However, structural trans-formations in the economy, changes in the nature of work in individual profes-sions, and demographic shifts for each of the race/gender groups mean that the "winnings" of one or more disadvantaged groups do *not* necessarily equal "losses" for white men. Since the professions as a whole expanded during the 1960–1980 period, might it not have been a "win-win" situation, with white men gaining more of the better jobs in the professions than women and minority men?

Only by recognizing the possible influence of these structural changes on occupational mobility and equity can we begin to understand what "best" means when we ask, "Who did best in the fast-expanding professional arena of the post–civil rights and women's movement era?" This book allows us to do this by comparing all four of the race/gender groups with one another by using a *common base* that takes into account the changing structure of the population and the economy. Thus, instead of using many different measures of success unique to each race/gender group, I developed several measures of occupational mobility, but in such a way that each of the four groups can be compared along the same dimensions. This common metric allows us to see not only how each race/gender group does in comparison with itself over time, but also how the "gains and losses" of each of the race/gender groups compare with one another. Gains and losses for each group are stressed, not simply whether one group is ascendant over another. This is important precisely because the structures of the professions and the race/gender groups continue to change over time. Neither structure remains static, as the more traditional approach would argue; winning for one group does not necessarily mean losing for another group.

METHODOLOGICAL NOTE

Appendix 1, "Methodology," details some of the complex methodology used in this study to make data comparable across census years. However, for the data analysis that follows to be comprehensible to the reader, I would like to sum-marize several points here.

I used 1960 and 1980 census data made comparable to the 1970 detailed occupational census categories. This was necessitated by the fact that the occu-pational categories changed greatly over the time period between 1960 and 1980, particularly in the last census. There are, of course, methodological prob-lems in making the data comparable. (See Appendix 1 for a detailed analysis of the Census Bureau's changes in coding procedures, and for a description of the means by which I made the data comparable for the professional and techni-cal occupational categories across census years.) In reanalyzing the data, I categorized them by occupation, race (white and black), gender, and census years.

Given the complexity and dynamism of the changing occupational and demographic landscape, I have chosen to look at the professions in the following way: I distinguish the higher-status, more powerful, more highly paid *male-dominated professions* from the lower-status, less powerful, more poorly paid *female-dominated professions*. In addition, because not all of the male-dominated professions are equally powerful and able to establish the legitimacy of their claims to autonomy and self-control, I distinguished a group of *nonelite male professions* (for example, accounting and design) from the core or *elite male professions* (for example, doctors and lawyers).[24] In between the highly gender-segregated professions, a range of *nonsegregated, gender-neutral, or mixed* professions also emerges (for example, counseling, and personnel and labor relations). I also evaluate the mobility of women and minority men into the expanding areas of male-dominated, gender-neutral, and female-dominated *technical fields,* which generally require even less education and pay even more poorly than the professions. The result is a seven-category *intermediate level of analysis* of elite male, nonelite male, gender-neutral, and female professions; and male, gender-neutral, and female technical fields.

I have classified occupations as *male dominated* if they were 0 to 20 percent female in 1960; *gender neutral* if they were 20.1 to 60 percent female; and *female dominated* if they were 60.1 to 100 percent female.[25] This classification system remains the same throughout the analysis. That is, if an occupation was female dominated in 1960, it continues to be during the 20 years covered by this study. Thus the data do not tell the reader which occupations moved from being, say, female dominated to neutral or male dominated. Rather, they indicate the degree to which, for example, black women were able to move from female-dominated to formerly gender-neutral or male-dominated professions, in comparison to more advantaged population groups.

The following are the 30 largest professions and technical fields, classified by gender. (See Table 1.1) To be included as one of the large occupations in this study, the professional/technical field had to have at least 100,000 occupants in 1970, because analysis of individual small occupations was found to be very unreliable (see Rytina and Bianchi, 1984, for a discussion of size and reliability using these data). Appendix 2 contains a complete listing of all 94 detailed occupations.

In addition to stratifying occupations on the basis of their gender composition, I also look at the socioeconomic standing of each of the occupational groups. Both issues are important in evaluating not only the ability of women to enter more desirable male-dominated professions but also whether women of either race have made socioeconomic gains relative to (or, as some commentators argue, "at the expense of") white men and black men throughout the professions.

This approach takes into account the idea that gender controls the status of

TABLE 1.1   LARGE PROFESSIONAL/TECHNICAL FIELDS WITH THEIR NAM-POWERS OCCUPATIONAL-STATUS SCORES

Large Detailed Professions and Technical Fields	Nam-Powers Scores
Male professions	
Elite	
Lawyer	99
Physician	99
Nonelite	
Civil engineer	95
Electrical and electronic engineer	95
Mechanical engineer	95
Chemist	94
Engineer/nec*	94
Pharmacist	94
Industrial engineer	93
Accountant	89
Designer	89
Nonspecific college teacher**	87
Clergy	77
Gender-neutral professions	
Vocational and educational counselor	92
Personnel and labor-relations specialist	89
Computer programmer	89
Editor/reporter	86
Research worker	86
Secondary-school teacher	82
Painter/sculptor	77
Female professions	
Social worker	82
Librarian	75
Elementary-school teacher	73
Nurse	66
Prekindergarten and Kindergarten teacher	60
Teacher/nec	52
Male technical fields*	
Electrical and electronic engineer technologist	82
Drafter	80
Engineering and science technologist/nec	77
Female technical fields	
Clinical-laboratory technologist	70

Nec means not elsewhere classified.

**Nonspecific* means that the professor's specialty was not indicated in the census. This is a shifting, "grab-bag" category of college teachers who do not specify their fields: while only one-third of all college teachers were classified as nonspecific in 1960, this increased to two-thirds in 1980 (John Priebe, personal communication, 1986). Also note that while all detailed college-teacher categories are included in the seven-category intermediate-level analysis, none of the specified ones (e.g., sociology, physics, mathematics, economics,etc.) reached the criteria of 100,000 occupants in 1970 to be included in the more detailed analysis of the large professions/technical fields.

***None of the gender-neutral technical fields fulfills the criterion of at least 100,000 occupants in 1970 to be included among the large occupations in this study.

the occupation so strongly that it is dominant within the classification system, within which socioeconomic status is then determined. For example, when doctors are primarily white men, as has traditionally been the case in the United States, their status is higher than when they are predominantly female, as in the Soviet Union. Moreover, if all doctors were black women, we would anticipate that the linked variables of race and gender would be powerful determinants of the occupation's status.

In order to evaluate the progress of each of the race/gender groups up the socioeconomic hierarchy, I made use of the Nam-Powers (1983, Table A1) occupational-status scores. The scores for each occupation are determined primarily by the relative education and income levels of each of the detailed occupations.[26] The measure uses socioeconomic or class criteria, not status or prestige criteria.

Unlike other measures of occupational standing, the Nam-Powers scale is advantageous to my study for two reasons: first, while earlier studies were based wholly on the occupational experiences of men, the Nam-Powers scale is a measure developed specifically to include both women and men. Second, the occupational-status scores were developed for the 1970 occupational census categories, which are the basis for the occupational categories used in my study. (For a detailed discussion of their use, see Appendix 1, "Methodology.")

Professional and technical scores range from a low of 40 to a high of 99. Median occupational scores and the ranges for each of the seven intermediate occupational categories are contained in Table 1.2.

There is an inverse relationship between the percentage of women in the professional categories and the status of the category: the smaller the percentage female, the higher the occupational score. A slight variation occurs among the technical fields. In fact, as the median scores below indicate, male technical fields (79) rank higher than do female professions (73). This reflects, in part, the high status and higher income accorded male-dominated occupations in our society as well as the fact that several of the male technical fields had in earlier censuses been defined as professions (e.g., airplane pilot, radio broadcast announcer). Further, we should note the small number of detailed occupations contained in the neutral and female technical fields, two and four respectively. The scores for female and neutral technical fields, therefore, are less reliable than for the other categories.

While my major analysis focuses on the larger group of professions, I have also included the technical fields. As we saw in the discussion on "Just What Are the Professions?" on p. 9, until 1980 the Census Bureau did not differentiate technicians from professionals. Since I use the 1970 professional occupational categories, I have included technicians along with professionals in my analysis.

Because I use the categories of male-dominated, gender-neutral, and female-

**TABLE 1.2   MEDIAN SCORES AND RANGE OF SCORES FOR
INTERMEDIATE ANALYSIS OF PROFESSIONS AND TECHNICAL FIELDS
ON THE NAM-POWERS OCCUPATIONAL STATUS MEASURE**

Professions and Technical Fields	Median Score	Range	Number of Occupations
Male Professions	(95)	(71–99)	(51)
Elite*	97	96–99	23
Nonelite	94	71–95	28
Gender-Neutral Profs.**	91	49–99	33
Female Professions	73	40–93	12
Male Technical Fields	79	54–94	15
Gender-Neutral Tech. Fields	64	63–65	2
Female Technical Fields	69	64–70	4

*An elite profession is one whose Nam-Powers occupational status score fell above the median of 95 for male-dominated professions. A nonelite profession is one whose Nam-Powers status score was 95 or less.

**One would not expect the range of gender-neutral professions to go so high. Seven of the neutral professions could have been defined as elite according to the definition for male professions. All were very small and would not affect the results of the study. However, based on the gender composition, these occupations presented a problem. In the case of judge, for example (99 on the Nam-Powers scale, but coded as a gender-neutral profession because it is listed as between 20 and 60 percent female in 1960), one would have expected this to be an elite male profession. Several possibilities might explain this result: on the one hand, the percentage female may simply be wrong. However, it is also possible that in 1960, the number of female judges still reflected the growth of women in elite male professions that occurred earlier in the 1920s, and that this profession had not yet lost its more gender-neutral character (Bernard, 1971). Another possibility is that the types of judges included in 1960 and 1970 were quite different (more narrowly defined in 1970, but more broadly defined in 1960 and 1980), which certainly seems to be the case for the contrast between 1970 and 1980 (Dullea, 1984). Finally, the very small number of judges in the 120,000 to 125,000 subsamples on which 1960 and 1980 data were made comparable (see Appendix 1, "Methodology") may have improperly skewed the results.

As we will see, the range of Nam-Powers scores is much more reasonable with the 30 large professions/technical fields than with all 94. (Refer also to Table 1.1) This confirms the problems with very small occupational categories and reinforces the use of the 30 large occupations in the more detailed analysis.

dominated professions and technical fields, I am working with what sociologists call an *intermediate level of analysis*. This approach contrasts with the broader analysis of the professions vis-à-vis the labor force as a whole. I do perform finer analyses using the largest individual professions and technical fields—those that included at least 100,000 people in 1970. This is considered a more detailed level of analysis. Despite the fact that these detailed professions represent only one-third of the professional-technical occupational categories, they include almost 80 percent of all people in these occupations in both 1960 and 1980.

The data in my study permit us to draw conclusions only about the *occupational* level of analysis and the degree to which disadvantaged groups (defined in this study as white women, black men, and black women) were able to gain access to professional occupations traditionally dominated by white men, as well as to enter other occupations farther down the professional/technical hierarchy. As we will see, a considerable amount of this increased access was accomplished through the de-skilling and accompanying expansion of these jobs as well as through political pressure. The data reported here do not directly deal with the *job level* of analysis permitting a direct investigation of the changing nature of work in the professional and technical jobs themselves or how jobs are reorganized and distributed within a particular corporation, factory, government agency, or the like. However, my data in concert with other research support the conclusion that increased access to professional jobs in no way guarantees that disadvantaged groups would necessarily be better off. In fact, I have found, they can be simultaneously both better off *and* not better off: the glass is both half-full and half-empty.

In particular, the work of Bielby and Baron (1986), Reskin and Roos (1990), and Carter and Carter (1981) warns of the dangers of overlooking gender segregation within and across organizations, and especially *within* occupations that *appear* to have become gender integrated during the post–World War II period, especially since 1970. While Bielby and Baron and Reskin and Roos focus on a wide range of male-dominated occupations in the economy, Carter and Carter highlight this problem specifically for women in the professions. Moreover, a similar but more complex problem exists for black women and whether they were able to enter more desirable jobs traditionally held not only by men—black and white—but also by white women (see Malveaux, 1981, 1990; Malveaux and Englander, 1987; Higginbotham, 1987, 1988; Glazer, 1991).

There are four race/gender groups in this study: black women, white women, black men, and white men. Each group increases its numbers from two to four times in the professions and technical fields between 1960 and 1980. (See Appendix 1, "Methodology.") In order to make comparisons among and between the four race/gender groups, I developed two indexes: the *Index of Representation* and the *Index of Relative Advantage*. The first allows comparisons within each race/gender group; the second permits comparisons of one race/gender group with another. Both allow us to focus on the questions of *access* of each race/gender group (relative to the other groups) to different levels of the professional hierarchy *at a particular time* (in 1960 and in 1980) as well as change *over time* (between 1960 and 1980). The indexes are developed for the seven intermediate occupational categories (male-dominated, gender-neutral, and female-dominated professions and technical fields) as well as for each of the 30 large detailed occupations. Moreover, the indexes are constructed not only for the different decades but for each of the four race/gender groups. Using these measures, we are able to take into account structural changes and diversity in the four race/gender groups as well as throughout the professional/technical hierarchy.

The Index of Representation (Chapters 3 and 4) tells us how well a race/ gender group is represented in a particular profession or technical field in comparison to its overall representation in the labor force.[27] It corrects for the differences in population sizes of the different race/gender groups as well as the different sizes of occupations over time. In this way, everyone is put on a common metric, and the reader is not faced, for example, with answering the question, Is 3 percent a little or a lot of change for black women? Since black women are 5.3 percent of the labor force in 1980, if black women were 3 percent of a particular occupation, this measure tells us that black women were under parity and by how much, since 3% / 5.3% = 0.57. Parity (ratio = 1.00 in the index) occurs when the *expected* proportion of a race/gender group in a profession is equal to their *actual* proportion in the labor force. If the actual proportion of the group in the occupation is more than parity, the ratio is greater than 1.00; if the actual proportion is less than expected, the ratio is less than 1.00. (For another way to develop this type of measure, see Almquist, 1979.)

It is important to realize that the Index of Representation is a *conservative estimate* of movement toward equality for disadvantaged groups. (This is likewise the case for the Index of Relative Advantage.) As Barbara Reskin (personal communication, 1989) points out, the proportion of a group in the labor force is a conservative standard because higher proportions of all disadvantaged groups *would* work if they had a shot at better jobs, as do white men. The high labor force participation rate of white men reflects, in part, the superiority of the jobs available to them compared to unemployment. By the same token, the lower rates for blacks and women reflect their more limited alternatives. Thus, she argues, the index should be understood to be a conservative estimate of the level of representation one should expect for underrepresented groups in desirable occupations, and that achieving an index of 1.00 does not, in fact, reflect "true" parity.

In contrast, the Index of Relative Advantage (Chapters 5–7) is able to compare the progress of one group directly with the progress of another group. It does so by measuring how over- or underrepresented one race/gender group is vis-à-vis another race/gender group in the professions and technical fields. It can tell us, for example, how over- or underrepresented black women are, first, in relation to white women; then in relation to black men; and finally in relation to white men. This index controls for the differential distribution of each race/gender group in the professions as in the labor force overall. Here, for example, a ratio of 1.00 indicates parity of occupational distribution for black women in relation to the more advantaged race/gender group. A ratio of less than 1.00 indicates that black women are underrepresented, while a ratio of more than 1.00 indicates black women are overrepresented in comparison with the relatively more advantaged group. For example, in social work, a traditional female profession, black women's ratio in relation to white men is 4.99; in relation to white women it is 1.91; and in relation to black men it is 2.55. In every case, but most outstandingly in relation to white men, black women are far more likely than the other race/gender groups to be overrepresented in social work. In medicine, a heavily male-dominated profession, however, the ratios are quite different: 0.09, 0.53, and 0.34, respectively. Here black women are the most severely underrepresented in relation to white men; and although they are better off in relation to black men and white women, they are still poorly represented in relation to these other two disadvantaged groups as well.

In both the Index of Representation and the Index of Relative Advantage, change is represented by a move of at least 0.10 points in the index between 1960 and 1980. Perfect parity occurs at 1.00 points; any ratio from 0.91 to 1.10 thus indicates parity. The degree of over- or underrepresentation for both indexes is as follows:

	Overrepresentation	Underrepresentation
Slight	0.71–0.90	1.11–1.30
Moderate	0.41–0.70	1.31–1.60
Severe	0.11–0.40	1.61–2.00
Very Severe	0.10 or less	over 2.00

CONCLUSION

The remainder of this book is a more detailed explication of the points laid out in this introductory chapter. Chapter 2 provides a more in-depth look at the professions and the extent to which structural conditions have affected access to them by the four race/gender groups. Chapter 3 analyzes the actual "gains" and "losses" for the four groups between 1960 and 1980 by means of the Index of Representation. Chapters 4 through 7, the four "data" chapters, are each devoted to a single race/gender group; these chapters track the fortunes of these groups, both individually and relative to one another. Finally, Chapter 8 summarizes the earlier chapters and projects what the future is likely to hold.

By finding the right statistical tools and knowing how to use them, we can learn much from Census Bureau data about the fortunes of different race/gender groups in the United States. Within this context, this book is a preliminary effort in the project to understand how the massive economic and social changes that characterized the years between 1960 and 1980 affected the lives of black women and white women, especially in relation to the lives of black men and white men. I hope it provides a much needed baseline by which eventually to compare the censuses for 1990, a period of economic downturn, and 2000 to the progress made by women and minority men in the expansion era of the 1960s and 1970s. This project, therefore, should be seen as a beginning, not an end, as we move toward the 21st century.

Chapter 2

THE PROFESSIONS: STRUCTURAL CHANGE AND GROUP ACCESS

INTRODUCTION

In order to evaluate the progress of disadvantaged groups in the professions, one must appreciate the tremendous variety and changing nature of the professions themselves. They differ in status, income, size, rate of growth, history, and potential for change. These underlying structural conditions are strongly connected to their accessibility for different groups. Thus, just as the nature of the race- and gender-structured labor market has changed over time, so, too, has the rate at which each race/gender group has been able to gain access to the professions. Whether any disadvantaged group is able to gain jobs traditionally available to more advantaged groups is greatly affected by these underlying structural conditions. In 1960, for example, before economic and governmental expansion combined with the demands of the civil-rights and women's movements to create more job opportunities for disadvantaged groups, black women were only 6.9 percent of social workers (USDC, Bureau of Census, 1963). In 1980 structural conditions had changed access to the field sufficiently so that black women were now 13.4 percent of social workers (USDC, Bureau of Census, 1983). In this chapter I look at some of these underlying conditions by discussing basic changes in the size and composition of jobs in the professional labor market in the 1960–1980 period, as well as the relationship of each race/gender group to the total labor market overall.

INCREASED GROWTH IN THE PROFESSIONS:
HAS IT BENEFITED ALL GROUPS?

As the capitalist economy in the United States moved away from goods and toward service production, the professional labor force expanded enormously. Between 1900 and 1960, professional and technical workers increased from 4 percent to 11 percent of the entire labor force; by 1980 they made up as much as 16 percent. These increases are due, in large part, to the expansion of the health, education, research, and governmental sectors of the economy (Gartner and Reissman, 1973; Montagna, 1977; Amott and Matthaei, 1991).

Exactly what expansion of the professions has meant, both in terms of the kinds of jobs created and the work lives of those who fill them, is open to debate. Some have argued that jobs were created that required higher levels of education, training, and skills; allowed the worker more autonomy and input on the job; and led to greater satisfaction, personal growth, financial rewards, and job security (Parsons, 1939, 1970; Bell, 1973). Others have emphasized just the opposite: growth in the professions has been so large only because of the expansion of lower-level jobs, primarily in large bureaucracies (Braverman, 1974; Levin and Rumberger, 1983; Bluestone and Harrison, 1986; Dressel, 1987). Some have focused on the growth of technicians and auxiliary professionals such as paralegals (Birnbaum, 1971); others, on the expansion of increasingly more rationalized segments of the profession itself—like poorly paid family lawyers in regionalized or nationalized legal chains (Carter and Carter, 1981).

In the following analysis, I provide another way of looking at the growth of professional jobs by considering the professions and the technical fields in terms of their gender concentration.[1] This emphasizes the underlying gendered nature of the job market, which roughly correlates with the prestige and income of a given profession. For example, based on the Nam-Powers scale of occupational-status scores (on a scale of 1 to 100), the average score in this study for male professions is 95 in contrast to a lower figure of 73 for female professions. Not only status but also income varies with the proportions of men and women employed in a given occupation.[2] The evidence overwhelmingly supports the conclusion that male fields pay more than female fields (Bergmann, 1974; N. Rytina, 1982; England and Farkas, 1986; Catanzarite and Strober, 1988). It is no wonder that these gender-based income differences remain a key reason why women's groups criticize gender segregation.

According to my data, the number of jobs in the professions grew much faster than those in the labor force as a whole. Overall, between 1960 and 1980, the total number of professional and technical jobs more than doubled (from 7 to 15.3 million jobs), exhibiting a growth rate of 118 percent, as shown in Table 2.1. At the same time, the total experienced civilian labor force grew from just under 70 million to just over 100 million workers, a growth rate of only 45

TABLE 2.1   PERCENT (AND NUMBER) OF PROFESSIONS AND TECHNICAL FIELDS IN THE TOTAL LABOR FORCE AND GROWTH RATES, 1960 AND 1980

Professions and Technical Fields	(1) 1960 Percent*	(2) 1980 Percent*	(3) Numerical Change 1960–1980**	(4) Rate of Growth***	(5) Gr. Rate (Col. 4)/ ECLF Gr. Rate****
Male prof.	3.9 (2,733,398)	5.1 (5,182,739)	(2,449,341)	0.89	1.98
[Elite]	[1.2] [803,977]	[1.5] [1,502,771]	[698,794]	[0.87]	[1.93]
[Nonelite]	[2.8] [1,929,421]	[3.6] [3,679,968]	[1,750,547]	[0.91]	[2.02]
Neutral prof.	2.0 (1,427,199)	3.5 (3,508,024)	(2,080,825)	1.46	3.24
Female prof.	2.9 (2,040,727)	4.6 (4,663,945)	(2,623,218)	1.29	2.87
Prof. subtotal	8.9 (6,201,324)	13.2 (13,354,708)	(7,153,384)	1.15	2.56
Male tech.	0.9 (643,938)	1.4 (1,369,439)	(725,501)	1.27	2.82
Neutral tech.	0.1 (56,654)	0.2 (173,692)	(117,038)	2.07	4.60
Female tech.	0.2 (112,302)	0.4 (362,417)	(250,115)	2.23	4.96
Tech. subtotal	1.2 (812,894)	1.9 (1,905,548)	(1,092,654)	1.34	2.98
Prof. + tech. subtotal	10.1 (7,014,218)	15.1 (15,260,256)	(8,246,038)	1.18	2.62
ECLF*****	100 (69,671,049)	100 (101,303,879)	(31,632,830)	0.45	1.00

*Percent of prof/tech group out of all jobs in labor force in that year.
**Number of new prof/tech jobs.
***Rate of growth of prof/tech group between 1960 and 1980.
****Prof/tech group growth rate divided by ECLF growth rate.
*****Experienced Civilian Labor Force.

Percentages may not add up exactly because of rounding errors.

percent. Numerical growth was greater among the professions (7.2 million new jobs) than among the technical fields (1.1 million new jobs). But the professions were much larger than the technical fields at the beginning of the period. As a result, the percentage growth among the technical fields (134 percent) was somewhat larger than among the professions (115 percent).[3] (Another way of saying this is that the growth rate of the professions was 2.56 times that of the labor force, whereas it was almost 3 times the growth rate of the labor force for the technical fields. See Table 2.1, Column 5.)

Within the professions, the largest percentage growth occurred among the gender-neutral ones, and secondly among female-dominated professions. In contrast, among the technical fields, female-dominated occupations grew at the astounding rate of 223 percent, followed closely by the neutral occupations, which grew at 207 percent. In short, while in both professions and technical fields the male-dominated occupations grew two to three times faster than the total labor force (see Table 2.1, Column 5), the rate of growth was far greater in the neutral and female-dominated professions/technical fields than in the male-dominated ones. Given this growth, where was the expansion greatest?

Clearly, the numerical increase was greatest in the female-dominated professions, which gained 2.6 million new jobs. In fact, two occupations, elementary-school teaching and nursing, accounted for as much as one-fourth of all new professional jobs available during this period. (See Table 2.2.)[4] Male-dominated professions ran a close second, with 2.4 million new jobs. However, almost three-fourths of these new jobs were nonelite. Thus accountants and (nonspecific) college teachers show a far greater increase than lawyers and physicians. Although growth in the gender-neutral professions was not as great as in the female and male professions, these occupations experienced a substantial increase of 2.1 million new jobs. Interestingly, the increase of just over 1 million technical jobs occurred primarily in the male-dominated fields. What this means is that although the numerical increase in technical jobs was much smaller than among the professions, the new technical jobs were more likely than those in the professions to be in the higher-status, higher-paying male-dominated occupations.

As we will see in the following analysis, the uneven pattern of growth in the seven intermediate occupational categories is repeated in the 30 largest detailed professions and technical fields: some grew rapidly, some slowly, and some not at all.

AN INTRODUCTION TO THE DETAILED PROFESSIONS

Occupational growth has long been considered a structurally important factor in increasing job equity and occupational rewards (Blau and Duncan, 1967; Snyder, Hayward, and Hudis, 1978; England and Farkas, 1986). This view is supported by Jolly, Grimm, and Wozniak (1990) in their study of occupational desegregation in professional and managerial specialties between 1950 and 1980. They found that rapid growth was associated with women's entry into male fields and men's entry into female fields. However, declining occupational size was related to a gender-switching process in which a field left by men was entered by women.

Jolly, Grimm, and Wozniak defined those occupations that are average or above average in growth rates as *rapidly growing* professional/managerial jobs;

those jobs that have no or below-average growth as *slow growing;* and those jobs that decrease in growth rates as *declining.* Using these criteria, my data show that growth took place between 1960 and 1980 in all professional/technical occupations, except for some smaller occupations concentrated in college-teaching specialties.[5] A look at the 30 largest occupations (Table 2.2) shows the amount of growth for selected detailed professions. Throughout the book I will focus on these 30 professions/technical fields as a way of looking at important specific occupations that change over time. I chose these 30 large detailed professional/ technical occupations to avoid reliability problems in the smaller occupations with the smaller race/gender groups (i.e., black men and black women). (See Chapter 1.) Therefore, only detailed occupations with more than 100,000 people are included in this group.

Just as growth was uneven in the professions/technical fields overall, an analysis of the largest 30 of these occupations as shown in Table 2.2 tells us that growth within each of the major occupational groups was likewise uneven. In the elite male professions, law grew rapidly, medicine at a slower rate. In the nonelite male professions, growth was rapid in only three: accounting, nonspecific college teaching, and engineering/nec. Rapid growth was more prevalent in the remaining occupations than in male professions. Thus counseling, personnel and labor relations, computer programming, and research work grew rapidly among gender-neutral professions; social work, librarianship, elementary education, and prekindergarten and kindergarten teaching expanded at a high rate among female professions. Among the technical fields, rapidly growing occupations include electronics, engineering and science/nec, and clinical-laboratory work. All other large professions/technical fields grew at a slower than average rate.

In short, occupational growth was great among the professions and technical fields, but proceeded at different rates for the many professional and technical occupations. As we will see, this change was also experienced quite differently by each of the four race/gender groups.

GROWTH AND CHANGE FOR THE FOUR RACE/GENDER GROUPS

The preceding data have often been used by analysts to argue that the greatest job increases, both in the recent past and expected in the near future, are in the "best" (i.e., professional and managerial) jobs in society (see Enrenhalt, 1986; Greer, 1986). Moreover, since so many women have entered these jobs (see Table 2.3), it has also been argued that women have exceptionally good job prospects in the future. For example, given the changing composition of the

TABLE 2.2   NUMBERS OF NEW JOBS AND GROWTH RATES FOR 30 LARGE DETAILED PROFESSIONS/TECHNICIANS, 1960 AND 1980, WITH MEDIAN INCOMES

Large Detailed Professions and Technical Fields	1980 Median Income*	Total Numbers		# New Jobs	Growth Rate
		1960	1980		
Male professions					
Elite					
Lawyer	$25,505	203,305	470,847	267,542	1.32 rapid
Physician	$44,005	228,660	365,387	136,727	0.60 slow
Nonelite					
Civil engineer	$22,705	157,840	176,912	19,072	0.12 slow
Elect. + elect. engr.	$24,005	183,809	289,667	105,858	0.58 slow
Mechanical engineer	$24,005	160,697	189,630	28,933	0.18 slow
Chemist	$19,785	92,618	109,281	16,663	0.18 slow
Engineer/nec	$23,505	71,845	232,414	160,569	2.23 rapid
Pharmacist	$19,510	95,119	130,955	35,836	0.38 slow
Industrial engineer	$20,505	113,039	233,882	120,843	1.07 slow
Accountant	$15,005	490,019	1,075,111	585,092	1.19 rapid
Designer	$10,505	71,947	137,536	65,589	0.91 slow
Nonspecif. coll. tea.	$17,165	45,752	385,059	339,307	7.42 rapid
Clergy	$10,905	199,872	263,529	63,657	0.32 slow
Gender-neutral professions					
Voc. + ed. cnslr.	$14,005	31,926	171,789	139,863	4.38 rapid
Personnel + lab. rels.	$18,205	102,962	577,472	474,510	4.61 rapid
Computer programmer	$16,260	8,134	296,451	288,317	35.45 rapid
Editor/reporter	$12,070	102,131	209,140	107,009	1.05 slow
Research worker	NA	78,056	172,643	94,587	1.21 rapid
Secondary-sch. tea.	$13,605	562,424	802,286	239,862	0.43 slow
Painter/sculptor	$8,952.5	82,850	169,068	86,218	1.04 slow
Female professions					
Social worker	$11,965	92,006	396,878	304,872	3.31 rapid
Librarian	$10,095	75,456	172,344	96,888	1.28 rapid
Elementary-sch. tea.	$12,715	983,146	2,153,095	1,169,949	1.19 rapid
Nurse	$12,005	623,801	1,272,637	648,836	1.04 slow
Pre K + kinder. tea.	$4,505	69,024	168,404	99,380	1.44 rapid
Teacher/nec	$6,622.5	132,046	211,628	79,582	0.60 slow
Male technicians					
E + E engr. tech.	$16,005	108,740	269,348	160,608	1.48 rapid
Drafter	$14,005	216,013	296,463	80,450	0.37 slow
Eng. + sci. tech./nec	$13,375	107,488	273,647	166,159	1.55 rapid
Female technicians					
Clinical-lab. tech.	$11,005	57,840	215,098	157,258	2.72 rapid
Total big profs. + techs.		5,548,565	11,888,601	6,340,036	1.14 average
Total all profs. + techs.		7,014,218	15,260,256	8,246,038	1.18 average

*Adapted from Roos et al. (1990).
NA = Not Available

labor force, *Workforce 2000* suggests that women "will be rapidly entering many higher-paying professional and technical fields" between now and the year 2000 (Johnston and Packer, 1987:xx).

When one looks at the gender composition of these professional jobs, one finds that somewhat greater gains for women than for men have occurred in the professions overall (see Table 2.3). Between 1960 and 1980, women gained almost one-half million more new jobs in the professions than did men. In fact, since the percentage of women in all professions increased from 41 to 47.7 percent during these 20 years, one can argue that women were *more equally distributed* with men in professional occupations in 1980 than in 1960. These findings are similar to those of Ehrenhalt (as reported in Greer, 1986). On analyzing 50 selected professions, he found that women occupied just over 50 percent of these positions by 1986.

Although this was a period in which women's labor-force participation in general was rising, the increase of women in the professions (6.7 percent) was somewhat less than their increase in the total labor force (9.6 percent—see percentage change between 1960 and 1980 in Table 2.3). While the percentage of women increased relatively more slowly in the professions than in the total labor force, the reverse was true for the percentage of blacks in the professions. In the latter case, we need to ask what such an increase actually means: although one can justifiably call it a gain for blacks, it is so mainly because of the very small numbers of blacks in the professions in 1960 (compare gender and race categories in Table 2.3).

A look at the race composition of the changes in the professions between 1960 and 1980 reveals steady gains for black men and black women (see Table 2.3). Numerically, blacks increased from over 250,000 professionals, or 4.3 percent of all professionals, in 1960 to 1 million, or 7.5 percent, in 1980. Although this 3.2 percent increase translated into improved circumstances for almost 750,000 blacks, it is also true that the percentage of all professionals that blacks represented in 1980 was considerably less than the 12 percent that was their proportion of the population that same year (U.S. Bureau of Census, 1984). In contrast, whites gained almost 6.5 million new professional jobs, moving from under 6 million in 1960, or 95.7 percent of all professionals, to just under 12.5 million, or 92.5 percent, in 1980. In addition, among technicians, blacks increased only about 120,000, while whites increased just under 1 million.

As the share of professional/technical jobs expanded in the job market between 1960 and 1980, it did so at differing rates for each of the race/gender groups. And while women's growth expanded at a faster rate than that of men of their respective race, *all groups showed substantial numerical increases in each of the professions* (Table 2.4): there were 3.6 million more white men and 3.8 million more white women in professional and technical jobs in 1980 than

**TABLE 2.3   PERCENT GENDER AND RACE CATEGORIES IN PROFESSIONS AND
TOTAL LABOR FORCE, 1960 AND 1980; PERCENT CHANGE AND RATE OF
GROWTH, 1960 TO 1980**

	1960	1980	Percent Change 1960–1980	Rate of Growth
Gender category				
Professions				
Men	59.0	52.3	−6.7	
	(3,656,002)	(6,987,952)	(3,331,950)	0.91
Women	41.0	47.7	+6.7	
	(2,545,321)	(6,366,756)	(3,821,435)	1.50
Total	100	100		
	(6,201,323)	(13,354,708)		
Total labor force				
Men	67.5	57.9	−9.6	
	(47,003,541)	(58,642,368)	(11,638,827)	0.25
Women	32.5	42.1	+9.6	
	(22,667,508)	(42,661,511)	(19,994,003)	0.88
Total	100	100		
	(69,671,049)	(101,303,879)		
Race category				
Professions				
White	95.7	92.5	−3.2	
	(5,937,091)	(12,357,891)	(6,420,800)	1.08
Black	4.3	7.5	+3.2	
	(264,232)	(996,817)	(732,585)	2.78
Total	100	100		
	(6,201,323)	(13,354,708)		
Total labor force				
White	89.5	89.0	−0.5	
	(62,328,142)	(90,117,083)	(27,788,941)	0.45
Black	10.5	11.0	+0.5	
	(7,342,907)	(11,186,796)	(3,843,889)	0.52
Total	100	100		
	(69,671,049)	(101,303,879)		

in 1960. For blacks, the numerical increase was 538,000 more women and
313,000 more men. If we exclude the technicians, the growth among the professionals was as follows: 3.1 million more white men, 3.3 million more white
women, 481,000 more black women, and 252,000 more black men. Moreover,
while the growth rates for men (0.24 for white men, 0.29 for black men) and
women (0.88 for white women, 0.89 for black women) in the labor force were
similar, their rates of growth in the professions/technical fields were dissim-
ilar (white men = 0.86, black men = 2.95, white women = 1.50, black
women = 3.00).

In fact, if we compare each of the four groups' growth in professional and

TABLE 2.4 NUMBER OF NEW JOBS AND GROWTH RATES IN PROFESSIONS/ TECHNICAL FIELDS, AND IN LABOR FORCE, 1960–1980, FOR EACH RACE/ GENDER GROUP

Race/Gender Category	Professions/Technical Fields		Labor Force		Proportional Growth Rate*
	Number	Growth Rate	Number	Growth Rate	
White men	3,619,314	0.86	10,311,303	0.24	3.58
Black men	312,856	2.95	1,327,524	0.29	10.17
White women	3,775,591	1.50	17,477,638	0.88	1.70
Black women	538,277	3.00	2,516,365	0.89	3.37

*Growth in professions as a proportion of growth in total labor force.

technical occupations with their growth in total employment (see Column 5, Table 2.4), we can more easily see the overall variation in the impact of each group's growth in relation to the professions and technical fields. Thus we learn that black men's growth in the professions and technical fields was more than ten times their growth in the total labor force. This is in large part because of the incredibly small number of black men in the professions and technical fields in both 1960 and 1980. So a small numerical increase can mean a large rate of growth. Second, it is important to see that white men have a much lower growth rate, but one that was still the second-highest among all four race/gender groups. Contrary to expectations, white men showed remarkably high levels of increase throughout the professions and technical fields. Third, white women's increase in the professions and technical fields relative to their growth in the total labor force was the lowest of all race/gender groups. Again, the media would lead us to believe that the growth of white women was by far the greatest; but because of their high starting point in the professions in 1960 and their very high rate of increase in the total labor force between 1960 and 1980, they experienced far lower gains throughout the professions than expected relative to their overall labor force growth. Lastly, black women's growth rate was below both that of white men and black men, although higher than that of white women.

In the context of all these changes, however, it is important to emphasize that no group can be simply defined as a "loser": as the professions grow, there appears, overall, to be more opportunities for everyone. In 1980, after two decades of economic growth and social activism, a larger share of these new jobs went to groups "protected" under affirmative-action guidelines than was the case in 1960. Even so, a higher percentage of white men were in professional jobs in 1980 than in 1960. Thus, although the number of professional/technical jobs expanded, enabling each of the four race/gender groups to increase its representation in the professions considered as a whole, access to specific professional/ technical occupations was differentially available. In the following chapters we shall see in what ways and to what degree that access was stratified by race and gender.

CONCLUSION

The structural conditions underlying the professions and technical fields changed greatly during the 1960–1980 period, an era of rapid social change. These higher-status occupations expanded quickly, bringing about increased access for disadvantaged groups and majority men alike. However, growth was uneven across the four race/gender groups as well as within the different sectors and individual occupations that make up the professions and technical fields. These structural changes need to be kept in mind as we evaluate the degree to which increasing job equity occurs for disadvantaged groups throughout the professions. It is equally important to consider these broader structural changes in analyzing whether, and to what degree, white men's claims of being "unfairly edged out" of upper-tier jobs by women and minority men are legitimate.

Chapter 3 ———————————————————

"GAINS" AND "LOSSES" FOR
BLACK AND WHITE
MEN AND WOMEN IN THE
PROFESSIONS

INTRODUCTION

By 1980 women made up almost 45 percent of the employed in the United States and 60 percent of the newly employed, and were still increasing within the labor force. Given these trends, one political scientist asked, "Are the gains being made by women in the workplace coming at the expense of men?" (Hacker, 1984:1). In answering his own question with an unequivocal yes, Hacker argued that "among the most vivid cases of displacement [of men by women] are those in the upper reaches of the workplace" such as law, advertising, banking, and financial management (p. 2). That this decline was primarily among white men was established by Equal Employment Opportunity Commission data showing that white men were the only race/gender group to decline in the professions between 1966 and 1979 (see Chapter 1, p.18 "Gender and Race: Theories about Black Women and White Women in the Professions"). While white women gained the most, minority men and women were found to have made small but significant gains.

This chapter examines the changing patterns of access to the professions for black and white men and women by challenging two assumptions common in the literature. First, I ask whether the more general level of analysis obscures serious degrees of segregation in the professions. Thus I question whether using the general occupational category of "the professions" hides race/gender differences that occur at more detailed levels of analysis among the different professional occupations, say between lawyers and nursery-school teachers. Second, I question the use of a zero-sum approach to social change, where it is typically assumed that the size of the professions (i.e., the total number of jobs) remains the same, presumably leading to the "loss" of high-status jobs for white men and the simultaneous "gain" of these jobs by more disadvantaged groups. Instead, I use an index that reveals each race/gender group's proportional ability to gain access to professions in a changing occupational arena.

UNCOVERING THE DEGREE OF RACE/GENDER SEGREGATION

Table 3.1 displays the distribution of each of the four race/gender groups across the seven intermediate-range professional/technical occupational categories and shows how that distribution has changed over time. When we look at the percentage of each race/gender group (white men, black men, white women, black women) in the professions between 1960 and 1980, we see a favorable picture for disadvantaged groups: while white men show a steady decline, all other race/gender groups show a steady but small increase (Column 4).

According to my data, between 1960 and 1980, white men declined from 57.5 percent to 49.7 percent of all professionals, a decrease of 7.8 percent and the only decline among all race/gender groups. In contrast, white women increased 4.5 percent to be 42.8 percent of all professionals; black men increased 1.1 percent to hold a 2.6 percent share; and black women increased 2.1 percent to hold a 4.9 percent share. (For the technical fields, the very same pattern emerged, but in an even more intensified way.) This suggests that white men lost most, white women gained most, and black women did better than black men. This is precisely the interpretation often reported in the media and discussed in social-science research. However, if one compares the gains and losses of each race/gender group in the overall professions and technical fields (Column 4) with the gains and losses in the somewhat more detailed categories (though still intermediate level) of male-dominated, gender-neutral, and female-dominated professions and technical fields (Columns 1–3), a different picture emerges: many of the so-called gains for women and black men are diminished.

The Male Professions

It is misleading to generalize about white men's experiences in the *male professions* from their experiences in the professions as a whole. Although white men declined from just under three-fifths (57.5 percent) to about one-half (49.7 percent) of all professionals between 1960 and 1980 (Column 4), they maintained

TABLE 3.1 PERCENT OF EACH RACE/GENDER GROUP IN MALE, GENDER-NEUTRAL, AND FEMALE PROFESSIONS/TECHNICAL FIELDS AND IN TOTAL LABOR FORCE, 1960 AND 1980

Race/Gender Category	Professions						
	(1) Male Dom.	[1a] [Elite]	[1b] [Nonelite]	(2) Gender Neutral	(3) Female Dom.	(4) Total Profess.	(5) Total Labor Force
	1960						
White men	92.2	[94.5]	[91.2]	57.0	11.2	57.5	61.0
Black men	1.5	[1.5]	[1.5]	2.1	1.1	1.5	6.5
White women	6.2	[3.8]	[7.1]	38.7	81.0	38.3	28.5
Black women	0.2	[0.1]	[0.2]	2.2	6.6	2.8	4.1
	100	[100]	[100]	100	100	100	100
	1980						
White men	77.8	[86.9]	[74.1]	51.4	17.3	49.7	52.1
Black men	2.7	[2.2]	[2.9]	3.3	2.0	2.6	5.8
White women	18.1	[10.2]	[21.3]	41.3	71.3	42.8	36.8
Black women	1.4	[0.7]	[1.7]	4.0	9.4	4.9	5.3
	100	[100]	[100]	100	100	100	100
	Percent Change 1960–1980						
White men	−14.4	[−7.6]	[−17.1]	−5.6	+6.1	−7.8	
Black men	+1.2	[+0.7]	[+1.4]	+1.2	+0.9	+1.1	
White women	+11.9	[+6.4]	[+14.2]	+2.6	−9.7	+4.5	
Black women	+1.2	[+0.6]	[+1.5]	+1.8	+2.8	+2.1	

	Technical Fields			
	1960			
	Male	Neutral	Female	Total Techs.
White men	91.1	59.8	26.8	80.1
Black men	1.4	2.4	2.4	1.6
White women	7.2	35.7	66.2	17.3
Black women	0.3	2.1	4.6	1.0
	100	100	100	100
	1980			
White men	77.5	35.1	18.7	62.4
Black men	4.2	4.0	2.9	3.9
White women	16.6	52.4	71.1	30.2
Black women	1.8	8.5	7.3	3.4
	100	100	100	100
	Percent Change 1960–1980			
White men	−13.6	−24.7	−8.1	−17.7
Black men	+2.8	+1.6	+0.5	+2.3
White women	+9.4	+16.7	+4.9	+12.9
Black women	+1.5	+6.4	+2.7	+2.4

Percentages may not actually add to 100 because of rounding errors.

their prominence in the most coveted elite male professions by retaining 86.9 percent of those positions in 1980 (Column 1a). And even though they declined sharply from their almost total domination of the nonelite male professions, they still retained three-fourths (74.1 percent) of these jobs (Column 1b).[1] To be sure, disadvantaged groups made some small progress. Black men increased from 1.5 to 2.7 percent of the male-dominated professions (Column 1); white women tripled their representation, from 6.2 to 18.1 percent; and black women increased from 0.2 to 1.4 percent.

Earlier we saw that some reporters focused on the tenfold increase of black women lawyers in the 1970s without emphasizing that even with this increase, black women made up less than 1 percent of all lawyers. In the same way, some might focus on the high *rate of increase* for women and blacks in the professions: black men almost doubled (1.5 to 2.7 percent), white women tripled (6.2 to 18.1 percent), and black women experienced a sevenfold increase (0.2 to 1.4 percent) in the male professions. But these data make it ludicrous to argue that blacks or women have challenged white male dominance when white men held almost four of every five male professional jobs and almost nine of every ten elite male jobs in 1980.

The Gender-Neutral Professions and the Female Professions

Changes in the *gender-neutral professions* between 1960 and 1980 paralleled those in the male professions. White men declined 5.6 percent, from 57 to 51.4 percent (Table 3.1, Column 2), while the three disadvantaged race/gender groups showed small, but important, increases: white women, 2.6 percent (from 38.7 to 41.3 percent); black men, 1.2 percent (from 2.1 to 3.3 percent); and black women, 1.8 percent (from 2.2 to 4 percent). (The very same pattern emerged for the gender-neutral technical fields, but in an even more dramatic way.) Interestingly, it is in the traditional *female professions* that white men had their greatest increase: 6.1 percent (from 11.2 to 17.3 percent—see Column 3). This is the largest increase of any race/gender group in the female professions: black men increased 0.9 percent (from 1.1 to 2 percent), and black women increased 2.8 percent (from 6.6 to 9.4 percent). Only white women's presence in the female professions declined, by 9.7 percent (from 81 to 71.3 percent). (In contrast, among the lowest-status female technical fields, white men decreased from 26.8 to 18.7 percent and white women increased from 66.2 to 71.1 percent—see Column 3).

These results show how controversy can be generated about the meaning of a set of figures. When data are presented at the gross level, it is possible to make positive statements about the progress of disadvantaged groups. But when the data are disaggregated, interpretations may be far less positive. However, even these results may be distorted given that (a) each race/gender group is of a different size and entered the labor force at a different rate, and that (b) all professional occupational categories appear to be increasing but at different rates— that is, professions are changing in relative size, too. How, then, can we arrive at an accurate evaluation of the gains made by disadvantaged groups in the professions during the tumultuous years from 1960 to 1980?

THE NEED FOR A PROPORTIONAL INDEX OF CHANGE

A major problem with most gender-based analyses is that they are *ahistorical*— that is, they do not adjust for increases over time in the proportion of women in the labor force. For example, it is true that women constituted 41.0 percent of professionals in 1960 (see Table 2.3), and thus they were more represented in the professions than in the labor force as a whole (32.5 percent) *in that year.* Between 1960 and 1980, however, women's comparative position in the professions and in the labor force as a whole underwent a reversal: their entrance into the labor force was at a greater rate (9.6 percent) than their entrance into the professions (6.7 percent). This fact alone makes a considerable difference in any interpretation of women's position in the professions, let alone in the analysis of each race/gender group in the professional hierarchy. In short, gains for white women, as well as black women and black men, are misleading unless interpreted in the context of gains in the total labor force.

Further, we are faced with the added problem that theoretical assumptions are typically embedded in any method and are all too often unquestioned. This appears to be the case with the common way of expressing *percentage changes* for women and blacks in the professions. Thus the data show that white men declined over a 20-year period from 92.2 to 77.8 percent of all people in male-dominated professions, but these figures are simply interpreted as a large decline for white men (see Table 3.2, Column 1). However, these same male-dominated occupations have increased in size, and white men shared in that increase; thus the notion that white men "lost out" in the professions is misleading. The traditional method of looking only at percentage change is based on a zero-sum approach, which has two underlying and linked assumptions: that certain groups "win" and certain groups "lose," and that this must happen because the size of the professional category remains the same. These assumptions exclude the major social change that occurred throughout the 1960–1980 period, which, as we have seen, was partly responsible for large increases throughout the professions and, thereby, the possibility that everyone—including white men—would benefit.

The Index of Representation

Instead of relying on the static zero-sum model, I developed the Index of Representation, with which one can determine the proportionate share that each race/gender group has secured in the *changing* size of the professions within an *expanding* labor force. Thus the index holds the base population steady while making changes in relative occupational size visible. It also permits an evaluation of the changes in the representation of each race/gender group in the professional category in relation to its changes in the labor force as a whole. This index also takes into account the different sizes of the 94 detailed occupations in the seven-category occupational measure as well as the in-depth analysis of the 30 large detailed occupations.

The Index of Representation gives us a better understanding of whether disadvantaged groups have greater access to certain professions. It is similar to other measures used to study aspects of race and gender segregation (see Broom and Glenn, 1969; Treiman and Terrell, 1975). The index assumes that when the proportion of a race/gender group in a professional category is equal to its proportion in the labor force, parity of representation (1.00) has been reached. If the actual proportion of the group in the professional category is more than parity, the ratio is greater than 1.00; if the actual proportion is less than parity, the ratio is less than 1.00. So, for example, if women were 42.6 percent of the labor force in 1980 and 95.9 percent of nurses, the ratio was 2.23, which was much greater than parity. If they were 13.8 percent of lawyers, the ratio was 0.32, which was much less than parity. If they had been 42.6 percent of a particular profession, the ratio would have been 1.00, which would have been parity of representation.[2]

In short, past research using the zero-sum approach led people to look at the changing distribution of blacks and whites, women and men, throughout the professional labor force, by examining the proportion of each occupational category occupied by each race/gender group at a given point in time. This necessarily led to talk about "winners" and "losers" but gave no sense that the number of available professional jobs was expanding—and expanding at a faster rate than jobs in all other areas in the labor market. In contrast, the Index of Representation allows us to see how all groups may gain or lose, but does so against a set standard. Thus, instead of using the size of the occupation as the standard by which to develop percentage-point changes and thereby enter into a zero-sum approach to change, I use the Index of Representation to learn about the *proportionate share* of each race/gender group's participation in a *growing or shrinking occupation*.

Findings Using the Index of Representation

The *overall* figures for *1980* (Table 3.2, Column 4) suggest that all race/gender groups except black men were at or near parity in the professions. That is, they were represented in the professions roughly as much as they were in the overall labor force. Black men, however, were greatly underrepresented: their ratio was only 0.45, which means that they were less than half as likely to be in the professions as in the general labor force. A look at more detailed categories, however, reveals a very different picture from that given by the overall figures. In the elite and nonelite *male professions* such as medicine and accounting, respectively (Columns 1a and 1b), white men overwhelmingly outstripped all other race/gender groups: they were, respectively, 1.67 and 1.42 times as likely to appear there as in the total labor force. Of the three disadvantaged race/gender groups working in male-dominated professions (Column 1), black men (0.46) and white women (0.49) did equally well—both were moderately underrepresented, while black women did much worse (0.27). None of the three disadvantaged groups came close to their proportion in the total labor force. Gains were better for white men and worse for blacks (men and women) and white women in the elite than in the nonelite male professions. Clearly, while the disadvantaged groups had somewhat increased access to the male professions, they did far better in the nonelite ones such as accounting, design, and pharmacy, with black women showing the least-improved access.

White men and white women were virtually equally represented in the *gender-neutral professions* such as counseling and personnel work and in the total labor force in 1980, with ratios of 0.98 and 1.12, respectively (Column 2). Black men did somewhat better (ratio = 0.57) and black women did far better (ratio = 0.76) than anywhere else in the professions, although they were still slightly underrepresented. When we look at the *female professions*, however, we see that gender segregation held sway: women were almost twice as likely to be found there (as elementary-school teachers and nurses, for example) as in the overall labor force (ratios = 1.94 for white women; 1.78 for black women), while men were severely underrepresented (white men's ratio = 0.33; black men's ratio = 0.34).

In the *technical fields* in 1980, white men were the only group above parity: they were 1.2 times as likely to appear there as in the general labor force. This overrepresentation masks their highly variable representation in the gender-stratified and neutral areas: they dominated the *male technical fields* (such as drafting and engineering and science technology/nec) (1.49) but had ratios of only 0.67 and 0.36 in the neutral and female areas, respectively.[3] White women were slightly underrepresented in the total technical areas (ratio = 0.82), but this figure, which would seem to indicate something approaching equality, actually obscures the fact that they were heavily underrepresented in male fields (ratio = 0.45) and were concentrated in the neutral fields (such as radio oper-

TABLE 3.2   INDEX OF REPRESENTATION FOR RACE/GENDER GROUPS FOR PROFESSIONAL/TECHNICAL OCCUPATIONAL CATEGORIES, 1960 AND 1980

Race/Gender Category	Professions					
	(1) Male Dom.	[1a] [Elite]	[1b] [Nonelite]	(2) Gender Neutral	(3) Female Dom.	(4) Total Profess.
1960						
White men	1.51	[1.55]	[1.50]	0.94	0.18	0.94
Black men	0.23	[0.23]	[0.23]	0.33	0.17	0.23
White women	0.22	[0.14]	[0.25]	1.36	2.85	1.34
Black women	0.04	[0.03]	[0.05]	0.53	1.63	0.68
1980						
White men	1.49	[1.67]	[1.42]	0.98	0.33	0.95
Black men	0.46	[0.38]	[0.50]	0.57	0.34	0.45
White women	0.49	[0.28]	[0.58]	1.12	1.94	1.16
Black women	0.27	[0.13]	[0.32]	0.76	1.78	0.92
Changes in Index of Representation 1960–1980						
White men	−0.02	[+0.12]	[−0.08]	+0.04	+0.15	+0.01
Black men	+0.23	[+0.15]	[+0.27]	+0.24	+0.17	+0.22
White women	+0.27	[+0.14]	[+0.33]	−0.24	−0.91	−0.18
Black women	+0.23	[+0.10]	[+0.27]	+0.23	+0.15	+0.24

Race/Gender Category	Technical Fields			
	Male	Neutral	Female	Total Techs.
1960				
White men	1.49	0.98	0.44	1.31
Black men	0.22	0.37	0.37	0.25
White women	0.25	1.26	2.33	0.61
Black women	0.07	0.51	1.14	0.25
1980				
White men	1.49	0.67	0.36	1.20
Black men	0.72	0.69	0.50	0.68
White women	0.45	1.42	1.93	0.82
Black women	0.34	1.62	1.38	0.65
Changes in Index of Representation 1960–1980				
White men	0.00	−0.31	−0.08	−0.11
Black men	+0.50	+0.32	+0.13	+0.43
White women	+0.20	+0.16	−0.40	+0.21
Black women	+0.27	+1.11	+0.24	+0.40

ating) (1.42) and female areas (such as dental hygiene) (1.93). The pattern for black women was similar: their total ratio of 0.65 masks their concentration in neutral areas (1.62) and female fields (1.38).

The findings for black men are the most striking, however. Although their total ratio of 0.68 is almost identical with that of black women, and is less than that of white women, they appear to have moved the closest to parity of representation between 1960 and 1980 (Table 3.2, Column 4). In male-dominated fields they moved from a ratio of 0.22 to 0.72 (Column 1), and in gender-neutral fields from a ratio of 0.37 to 0.69 (Column 2).

The movement of black men into male technical fields (and the smaller movement of white women and black women into these areas as well) is a more important indicator of occupational mobility than movement into the female professions using traditional criteria. On the Nam-Powers scale of occupational-status scores, the median score for male technical fields is *higher* than the median score for female professions (79 and 73, respectively). So although the professions, in general, carry more status than the technical fields, in general, this is outweighed by the fact that what men control is more highly valued than what women control. In short, becoming an engineering technician is higher on the socioeconomic hierarchy than becoming an elementary-school teacher. However, despite the inroads that all three disadvantaged race/gender groups have made into the male professions and male technical fields, it is important to remember that white men continue to dominate both of these occupational arenas.

Using the intermediate analysis (i.e., the seven-category professional/technical variable), if we look at the *changes* in race/gender representation in the professions over the 20-year period, all race/gender groups appear to have moved toward greater parity of representation in most of the professions and technical fields vis-à-vis the overall labor force. But the degree of movement and the outcome as of 1980 contain both positive and negative strains.

The most striking finding is that white men *increased* from moderate to severe overrepresentation in the *elite male professions* (from 1.55 to 1.67) while maintaining their moderately high level of overrepresentation in the *nonelite male professions* (Columns 1a and 1b).[4] While all three disadvantaged race/gender groups increased their relative representation in the male-dominated professions (in large part because of the overall increase in the size of the male professions), they remained decidedly underrepresented compared to their proportions in the labor force as a whole. Despite this fact, blacks (men and women) and white women made their greatest absolute gains (0.27 to 0.33 points) in the lower-status, nonelite male professions such as accounting, designing, and nonspecific college teaching.

Blacks made similarly large gains in the *gender-neutral professions*. Black women's ratio increased from 0.53 to 0.76, and black men's from 0.33 to 0.57. White men were proportionately represented in these professions in both 1960 and 1980, while white women decreased their overrepresentation (from 1.36 to 1.12). The greatest change in the *female-dominated professions* was among white women: they decreased from being about three to two times overrepresented. Black women *increased* their overrepresentation from 1.63 to 1.78 times their proportion of the labor force, and both black men and white men showed small but important increases in the female professions (although they were still severely underrepresented). Finally, considering the overall *changes* between 1960 and 1980, black men and white women appear to have done better than black women in the professions, except in the gender-neutral professions, where black women make their greatest gains.

As for the *technicians,* even though white men showed no change in their moderately high level of overrepresentation among *male technicians* (ratio = 1.49), the other three race/gender groups made steady gains toward parity. In contrast, in the much smaller groups of *neutral* and *female technicians,* black and white women became increasingly or remained overrepresented. Finally, black men appear to have made the clearest moves toward parity throughout the technical fields, as they did in the professions.

In short, women and black men became more integrated into male-dominated and gender-neutral professions and technical fields, and men became more integrated into female-dominated professions (see also Burris and Wharton, 1982; Beller, 1984; Jacobs, 1986; Jolly, Grimm and Wozniak, 1990; Reskin and Roos, 1990). Yet, as we have seen, women's representation in the professions and technical fields has not grown as fast as their representation in the labor market; much of the growth for the disadvantaged race/gender groups is due to the overall increase in professional/technical jobs; and the most desired jobs of all (the elite male professions) are by and large still reserved for white males. In the lower-status but still desirable male-dominated technical fields, however, while white men have maintained their overrepresentation, black men primarily, but white and black women secondarily, have achieved greater access. This is quite important because, as we saw, the male technical fields have, on the average, higher scores on the Nam-Powers scale than the female-dominated professions.

CONCLUSION

There has been much debate over the progress of black women and white women and black men in the white-male-dominated professions. My data support the proposition that at general or aggregated levels of analysis, white men appear to lose and relatively disadvantaged groups seem to gain. But more detailed analyses that take into account the proportion of each race/gender group in the labor force result in modifying these hopeful interpretations.

While the proportion of white men declined from just under three-fifths to about one-half of <u>all</u> professionals between 1960 and 1980, it declined only slightly in the prestigious elite male professions. Moreover, when we control for shifts in the proportion of each race/gender group in the labor force vis-à-vis the professions, we find that white men in fact slightly <u>increased</u> their level of <u>over</u>-representation. (In the nonelite male professions, a similar process occurred, but with somewhat greater increases by women and black men.) It is thus misleading to conclude that white men "lost" their place in many of the most desirable jobs as a result of "gains" by blacks and white women, since the professional labor force expanded faster than the labor force as a whole. This is particularly true for white men in elite male-dominated professions: in 1980 white men still held almost 9 out of every 10 elite professional jobs, and three-fourths of nonelite male professional positions—that is, some of the most highly valued, best-paid jobs in our society.

The picture in the technical fields is somewhat more complex. White men maintained their moderately high level of overrepresentation in the male-dominated occupations. On the other hand, all disadvantaged groups, especially black men, made substantial increases in their moves toward parity in the male technical fields. Contrary to what happened in the professions, black women and white women either became or remained highly overrepresented in neutral and female areas by 1980. Thus women and minority men appear to have made more progress in the male technical fields than in the male professions.

Despite the relatively greater progress made by the three disadvantaged race/gender groups in the technical fields, to talk about "losses" experienced by white men appears inappropriate when the numbers of this group, as well as the other groups, have grown substantially in the professions and technical areas. This is *not* a zero-sum situation: any such gains by women and black men do *not* represent a direct loss for white men. And yet it is possible that an even more detailed analysis of the professional/technical data than I have presented in this chapter might reveal hidden levels of change that my relatively more inclusive analysis misses. For example, it might be that while white men maintained their moderately high levels of overrepresentation in male professions overall, they may have experienced an erosion of their dominance in individual male professions. If so, which ones? and why? If it happened, did it affect white women differently than black men and black women? If so, how?

Whatever the experience of white male professionals, they did not happen in isolation from the experiences of other major contenders in the professional labor market. While the markets are race and gender stratified, they are nonetheless interconnected. Throughout the rest of the book, I look at the various race/gender groups both in terms of their unique experiences in the professions and in the context of the other groups and some of the underlying structural conditions that shape the work lives of everyone in the U.S. economy.

Chapter 4

WHITE MEN: THE MORE THINGS CHANGE, THE MORE THEY STAY THE SAME

INTRODUCTION

White men are typically the group to whom black men and white women, but not black women, are compared in the labor force. Black women, here as elsewhere in the society, suffer a kind of "double jeopardy": as blacks they are judged against black men; as women, against white women. Given white men's prominence in the higher levels of the occupational hierarchy in general and the professions in particular, it is essential to know exactly where white men stand in the changing professional labor market.

As we saw in Chapter 3, reliance on general or gross statistics (i.e., using the professions writ large) can hide changes that have actually altered the professional landscape. An intermediate level of analysis of census data for 1960–1980 (i.e., using a seven-category occupational variable of male-dominated, neutral, and female-dominated professions and technical fields) revealed that, contrary to much of the media reportage and social-science literature, white men gained ground, instead of losing it, throughout the professions. In the most prestigious male professions, such as law and medicine, they even managed to dominate *more* in 1980 than in 1960. Despite this fact, one of the most hotly debated questions of the period was whether white men suffered from "reverse discrimination" in employment and admission to professional schools, which were the entry points to the elite occupations. Such discrimination allegedly existed across the board. As prospective students, blue-collar workers, white-collar workers, and managers alike, white men were often seen as victimized by society's attempts to rectify past injustices against white women and minority groups. As one recent headline loudly proclaimed: "Don't Forget the White Males" (Deutsch, 1991). It was widely believed that less-qualified individuals from these groups were chosen over more deserving white men. From a zero-sum perspective, this meant that white men were losing out.

In the professions, the case that aroused the indignation of some journalists and social commentators was that of Allan Bakke. In the early 1970s, Bakke, a white male, applied for admission to a dozen medical schools and was denied admission, including twice at the University of California's Davis campus. Charging reverse discrimination, Bakke took his case all the way to the U.S. Supreme Court. In 1978 the Court ruled in Bakke's favor, and he was admitted to medical school (Wilkinson, 1979).

If white men did in fact increase their hold on the professions, did "reverse discrimination" nevertheless exist in certain niches of the professional hierarchy? Would a more detailed analysis than that provided at an intermediate level of occupational categories reveal clear incursions by women and minority men into white men's protected domains?

In this chapter I look at the actual changes that took place for white men within individual detailed professional/technical occupations between 1960 and 1980. Because the data on the smaller detailed occupations are unreliable, I focus on the "large" professions—those with more than 100,000 occupants in 1970. With these data we can learn in which particular professions white men were able to increase their overrepresentation to the greatest degree and where, if at all, their numbers declined. Moreover, we can see which of the professions/ technical areas became desegregated, either because white men relinquished their dominance in male professions or because they moved into female professions. All of these processes may be obscured in analyses of more inclusive occupational categories.

NUMERICAL INCREASES AND GROWTH RATES

If one word had to be chosen to characterize the professions between 1960 and 1980, that word would be *growth*. All the race/gender groups benefited from this expansion of opportunity, but white men gained the most of all. (See Table 4.1.) They experienced a larger absolute (numerical) growth than any other race/gender group in the elite male, nonelite male, and neutral professions, as well as in the male technical fields. In other words, they strengthened their hold on the most desirable fields, which they already dominated. White women gained too, but in the less desirable areas that they already dominated. They increased more

**TABLE 4.I NUMERICAL GAINS BY EACH RACE/GENDER GROUP
THROUGHOUT PROFESSIONS AND TECHNICAL FIELDS, BETWEEN
1960 AND 1980**

	White Men	Black Men	White Women	Black Women
Professions				
Male	1,512,718	97,808	770,072	68,743
Elite	[546,016]	[20,924]	[122,522]	[9,332]
Nonelite	[966,702]	[76,884]	[647,550]	[59,411]
Neutral	987,784	85,074	898,576	109,391
Female	579,842	68,723	1,671,808	302,846
(Prof. subtotal)	3,080,344	251,605	3,340,456	480,980
Technicians				
Male	474,123	47,842	181,100	22,435
Neutral	27,064	5,568	70,754	13,652
Female	37,783	7,841	183,281	21,210
(Tech. subtotal)	539,970	61,251	435,135	57,297
Total change Prof. + Tech.	3,619,314	312,856	3,775,591	538,277
Total change in labor force	10,311,303	1,327,524	17,477,638	2,516,365

than white men (and black men and black women) in female professions and
neutral and female technical fields. Despite the increased numbers of women
and blacks in the professions and technical fields, white men did not decline in
absolute numbers. Even in the female professions, white men gained almost
580,000 new jobs.

In which fields did white men make their greatest gains? Table 4.2 allows us
to answer this question from two different vantage points: one based on raw
numbers (Column 2), the other based on percentage growth (Column 5). Focusing on numerical gains, the areas of most growth for white men between 1960
and 1980 in the male-dominated professions were among college teachers (nonspecific), lawyers, accountants, engineers/nec, and physicians, in descending
order. The single largest area of new jobs for white men was in a female-
dominated profession, elementary-school teaching, just as it was for *all* other
groups. White men also made large gains in two neutral professions, computer
programming and personnel and labor relations, and in two male-dominated
technical areas, as electrical engineering technicians and engineering and science technicians/nec. They made more moderate gains in all other professions/
technical areas except one: white men experienced a small but absolute decline
among chemists.

If we look at growth rates instead of numerical increases, the data displayed
in Table 4.2 tell a somewhat different story. While white men gained most numerically in male professions, their rate of growth was greatest outside the male
professions, with the exception of two lower-status (nonelite) ones: nonspecific

TABLE 4.2   TEN LARGEST-GROWING PROFESSIONS/TECHNICAL FIELDS FOR WHITE MEN, 1960–1980: NUMBERS AND GROWTH RATES

Increase Based on Raw Numbers			Increase Based on Percentage Growth		
	Largest Numerical Increase			Largest Percentage Increase	
(1) Occupation	(2) Number	(3) Percent	(4) Occupation	(5) Percent	(6) Number
Elementary school teacher	359,435	287.2	Computer programmer	3,314.7	192,797
Personnel + labor relats.	230,726	334.5	College teacher (nonspec.)	567.2	204,981
College teacher (nonsp.)	204,981	567.2	Personnel + labor relations	334.5	230,726
Lawyer	201,594	102.7	Elementary-school teacher	287.2	359,435
Accountant	199,707	49.0	Social worker	276.6	81,690
Computer programmer	192,797	3,314.7	Counselor	266.2	48,655
Engineer/nec	147,175	208.5	Nurse	234.3	31,364
Electrical-engineer techn.	127,431	126.0	Engineer/nec	208.5	147,175
Physician	104,274	49.9	Clinical-lab technician	204.9	30,930
Engineer + science techn/nec	93,171	103.9	Librarian	164.4	16,995

college teaching and engineering/nec. The greatest growth for white men was in the gender-neutral professions of computer programming and personnel and labor relations, followed by counseling. But half of the large occupations where white men grew the fastest was in the female professions/technical fields in the following descending order: elementary-school teaching, social work, nursing, clinical-laboratory work, and librarianship. Small numbers of white men in the female professions and technical fields in 1960 insured that relatively small numerical increases by 1980 translated into large percentage increases over time.

In short, white men show substantial numerical gains throughout the professions, especially in the male-dominated ones. However, one would not know this if their high rate of growth in the gender-neutral and female professions were emphasized instead. And despite this high growth rate, their numbers in 1980 were so small that there was little gender desegregation of female professions.

INDEX OF REPRESENTATION FOR THE 30 LARGE PROFESSIONS/TECHNICAL FIELDS

In Chapter 3 I described the Index of Representation, which I developed to compare the share that each race/gender group held in the professions to its share of the labor force. (This measure takes into account the different sizes and changing proportions of both the individual occupational categories and race/gender groups.) I used it to analyze the relatively more inclusive intermediate-level professional categories: male dominated, gender neutral, and female dominated. In this chapter I utilize the same procedure but apply it to each of the 30 large detailed professions/technical fields. I begin by obtaining the percentage of white men out of all men and women in each occupation in 1960 and in 1980. From these percentages, as shown in table 4.3, one would conclude that almost all of the large professions/technical fields became increasingly desegregated over the 20-year period, since the percentage of white men declined in all male and gender-neutral professions/technical fields. At the same time they increased in some of the female professions, such as elementary education (from 12.7 to 22.5 percent) and librarianship (from 13.7 to 15.9 percent). Despite these changes, the case for white male dominance of the top jobs in both 1960 and 1980 is demonstrated. Thus by 1980 both of the large elite (medicine and law) and more than half of the large nonelite male professions were 82 to 96 percent white men. Comparing white men's percentage in each of the large detailed professions to their percentage in the labor force gives us the detailed Index of Representation (Table 4.4).

Using the Index of Representation, we readily see that white men are overrepresented in high-status occupations and underrepresented in low-status ones. Thus in the male professions (and male technical areas), the pattern is for white men to maintain or increase their *over*representation; while in the much lower-status female professions (and technical areas), white men are very severely to moderately *under*represented. This was unequivocally the case in both 1960 and 1980.

Another way of looking at these data is to examine the degree to which white men move toward parity of representation over time as a measure of declining gender segregation. The Index of Representation reveals that white men failed to conform to the classic model of gender desegregation in 9 out of 11 nonelite male professions as well as the 2 large elite professions, law and medicine. Here white men either maintained or *increased* their moderate to severe levels of overrepresentation. (This same basic pattern repeated itself in the three large male technical fields: white men intensified or maintained their moderate to high levels of overrepresentation as electrical engineering technicians, drafters, and engineering and science technicians/nec.) This development was anticipated from the analysis of intermediate-level occupational categories of male, neutral, and female professions in Chapter 2.

What was not expected is that white men actually moved toward greater parity of representation in two of the nonelite male professions. In *accounting* and *design* white men decreased their overrepresentation and reached or nearly reached parity in the profession (i.e., their proportion in the detailed profession came closer to matching their proportion in the labor force).[1] Among lower-status male professions, then, there was a decline in occupational segregation. It could be that one area of increasing access for disadvantaged groups is in those expanding male-dominated occupations in which white men are reaching greater parity of representation. This could be related to the fact that these are two of the lowest paid of the large male professions—hence, less prestigious and therefore less desirable for the aspiring professional man.[2]

**TABLE 4.3   PROPORTION OF THE 30 LARGEST PROFESSIONAL/
TECHNICAL OCCUPATIONS HELD BY WHITE MEN, 1960 & 1980**

Large Detailed Professions/ Technical Fields	1960	1980	Difference 1960– 1980
Male professions	(92.2)	(77.8)	(−14.4)
Elite	[94.5]	[86.9]	[−7.6]
Lawyer	96.5	84.5	−12.0
Physician	91.5	85.8	−5.7
Nonelite	[91.2]	[74.1]	[−17.1]
Civil engineer	98.8	94.5	−4.3
Elect. + elect.engr.	98.6	92.3	−6.3
Mechanical engineer	99.3	95.7	−3.6
Chemist	91.0	76.8	−14.2
Engineer/nec	98.3	93.7	−4.6
Pharmacist	90.6	74.5	−16.1
Industrial engineer	97.6	82.1	−15.5
Accountant	83.2	56.5	−26.7
Designer	79.9	59.2	−20.7
Nonspecif. coll. tea.	79.0	62.6	−16.4
Clergy	91.1	88.7	−2.4
Gender-neutral profs.	(57.0)	(51.4)	(−5.6)
Voc. + ed.cnslr.	57.3	39.0	−18.3
Personnel + lab. rels.	67.0	51.9	−15.1
Computer programmer	71.5	67.0	−4.5
Editor/reporter	62.7	47.6	−15.1
Research worker	71.3	56.0	−15.3
Secondary-sch. tea.	48.2	41.0	−7.2
Painter/sculptor	70.4	51.8	−18.6
Female professions	(11.2)	(17.3)	(+6.1)
Social worker	32.1	28.0	−4.1
Librarian	13.7	15.9	+2.2
Elementary-sch. tea.	12.7	22.5	+9.8
Nurse	2.2	3.5	+1.3
Pre K + kinder. tea.	0.0	2.7	+2.7
Teacher/nec	29.8	29.1	−0.7
Male tech. fields	(91.1)	(77.5)	(−13.6)
E + E engr. tech.	93.0	84.9	−8.1
Drafter	93.1	79.3	−13.8
Eng. + sci. tech./nec	83.4	66.8	−16.6
Neutral tech. fields	(59.8)	(35.1)	(−24.7)
Female tech. fields	(26.8)	(18.7)	(−8.1)
Clinical-lab. tech.	26.1	21.4	−4.7
Percentage of white men in ECLF (experienced civilian labor force)	61.0	52.1	−8.9

TABLE 4.4   INDEX OF REPRESENTATION FOR WHITE MEN IN THE 30 LARGEST PROFESSIONAL/TECHNICAL OCCUPATIONS, 1960 & 1980

Large Detailed Professions/ Technical Fields	1960	1980	Difference 1960– 1980
Male professions	(1.51)	(1.49)	(−0.02)
Elite	[1.55]	[1.42]	[−0.13]
Lawyer	1.58	1.62	+0.04
Physician	1.50	1.65	+0.15
Nonelite	[1.50]	[1.42]	[−0.08]
Civil engineer	1.62	1.81	+0.19
Elect. + elect. engr.	1.62	1.77	+0.15
Mechanical engineer	1.63	1.84	+0.21
Chemist	1.49	1.47	−0.02
Engineer/nec	1.61	1.80	+0.19
Pharmacist	1.48	1.43	−0.05
Industrial engineer	1.60	1.57	−0.03
Accountant	1.36	1.08	−0.28
Designer	1.31	1.14	−0.17
Nonspecif. coll. tea.	1.29	1.20	−0.09
Clergy	1.49	1.70	+0.21
Gender-neutral profs.	(0.94)	(0.98)	(+0.04)
Voc. + ed. cnslr.	0.94	0.75	−0.19
Personnel + lab. rels.	1.10	1.00	−0.10
Computer programmer	1.17	1.29	+0.12
Editor/reporter	1.03	0.91	−0.12
Research worker	1.17	1.07	−0.10
Secondary-sch. tea.	0.79	0.79	0.00
Painter/sculptor	1.15	0.99	−0.16
Female professions	(0.18)	(0.33)	(+0.15)
Social worker	0.53	0.54	+0.01
Librarian	0.22	0.30	+0.08
Elementary-sch. tea.	0.21	0.43	+0.22
Nurse	0.04	0.07	+0.03
Pre K + kinder. tea.	0.00	0.05	+0.05
Teacher/nec	0.49	0.56	+0.07
Male tech. fields	(1.49)	(1.49)	(0.00)
E + E engr. tech.	1.52	1.63	+0.11
Drafter	1.53	1.52	−0.01
Eng. + sci. tech./nec	1.37	1.28	−0.09
Neutral tech. fields	(0.98)	(0.67)	(−0.31)
Female tech. fields	(0.44)	(0.36)	(−0.08)
Clinical-lab. tech.	0.37	0.41	+0.04

A somewhat different pattern emerges for white men in the gender-neutral professions: they tended to decrease their (over)representation. Among personnel and labor-relations specialists, editors/reporters, research workers, and painters/sculptors, white men either reached or maintained parity by 1980. In only one case, however, did white men become slightly *under*represented: as *vocational and educational counselors*. What is important here is that white men's decline in representation, even though not great (from 0.94 to 0.75), represents a genuine *loss* for white men. This appears to be the one profession in which white men could argue that they were being "edged out" by more disadvantaged groups.[3] Accordingly, it seems likely that counseling could be a place of increasing access for disadvantaged groups.

In contrast, in the neutral professions, white men's representation did not decline among *computer programmers*. In fact, in this they slightly increased their overrepresentation. During the 1960–1980 period, this profession expanded at the fastest rate of all the large professions/technical fields (see Chapter 2). This fact carries even greater weight when one realizes that computer programmers earn a high income for those in neutral professions. Given that rapid expansion is a structural condition providing for greater equity, it could be that disadvantaged groups have been able to gain greater access to programming, in part because white men's participation expanded along with that of women and black men.

Finally, the pattern for white men in the large female professions, which was repeated in the female technical fields, shows white men maintained their severe or moderate level of underrepresentation in all but elementary-school teaching. Here white men decreased their underrepresentation somewhat (from 0.21 to 0.43). Elementary-school teaching is the profession with the largest overall numerical increase between 1960 and 1980 with over 1.17 million new jobs. With such a large increase, were white men able to move toward parity as school-teachers because other race/gender groups were declining there or because the job expanded so much? Or were both things happening?

These questions cannot be answered by looking at white men (or any group) in isolation. In the remainder of the book, I compare black men and white women and black women *to white men* throughout the professional/technical hierarchy. Only by examining what was happening to all four race/gender groups is it possible to understand what was happening to any one of them.

CONCLUSION

During this period of economic growth and expanding opportunities for disadvantaged groups, white men continued to be the overwhelming majority in the most desirable and visible of the professions, the ones people think of when they say "profession." These consist primarily of the male professions, both elite and nonelite, including not only medicine and law, but also various engineering specialties. (This trend persisted for white men in the male technical fields too.) The only "losses" white men experienced were in the more moderate status professions, and only in a few of these. For example, the neutral profession of vocational and educational counseling was the only one of the big professions/ technical areas where white men actually lost out (i.e., became underrepresented) between 1960 and 1980. If one considers the move from moderate levels of overrepresentation to parity as a loss, then it could be argued that losses also occurred among the lower-status male professions of accounting and design. However, I would suggest this was not a loss for white men, but a readjustment of an imbalance that had historically favored them so that they came to occupy their fair share of the occupation—that is, they reached parity with their representation in the labor force. Given these changes, it is very clear that accounting and design became desegregated: by 1980 white men were no longer dominant. Perhaps the fact that these two occupations are among the lowest paid of the large male professions was a key element in their desegregation.

Desegregation does not happen only as a result of the influx of "outsiders" into desirable areas that have hitherto been closed to them. It occurs also when members of a more privileged group choose to enter the domain of a less privileged group. Specifically, white men began to move into one of the female-dominated professions: elementary-school teaching. This is probably related to the fact that the demand for teachers expanded greatly during this period. The over 1 million new jobs created a greater demand than could be filled by women, who traditionally entered this profession. But the fact that there were not enough women to fill the jobs was itself partly related to the changing opportunities experienced by white women, as we will see in a later chapter.

Chapter 5

BLACK MEN: AFFIRMATIVE ACTION OR REACTION?

INTRODUCTION

In the 1980s heightened concern was expressed over the decline of black men in professional and graduate schools as well as in college (Carter and Wilson, 1989; Daniels, 1989). This is a serious issue and deserves careful attention. The loss of these men will result in a significant decline in the pool of black male talent in the professions for decades to come.

In contrast, as we have seen, the 1960s and 1970s were regarded as a period of increased opportunities for educated and talented back men and women. Both groups expanded their tiny share of professional and technical jobs. Between 1960 and 1980, black men increased their proportion of both professional (from 1.5 to 2.6 percent) and technical jobs (from 1.6 to 3.9 percent), especially in male technical fields and gender-neutral professions. When looked at another way, however, the rise of black men in the occupational hierarchy was indeed dramatic: between 1960 and 1980, their growth in the professions was more than 10 times their growth in the total labor force, far greater than for any other of the four race/gender groups in the current study.

Unquestionably, the civil-rights movement and economic expansion were two key factors that opened up job opportunities for blacks in professional and managerial jobs in both government employment and major white corporations in the private sector (Freeman, 1976). William Julius Wilson (1987) specifically argues that changes in urban economies in conjunction with affirmative-action efforts lowered the racial barriers that had excluded qualified blacks. In addition, conservative black scholars argue that government intervention is no longer necessary, if it ever was, to protect employment opportunities for better-educated blacks. And because poor blacks are outside the reach of affirmative action, conservatives continue, it is totally unnecessary and should be abolished (Sowell, 1983, 1990; Loury, 1985; Steele, 1990).

On the face of it, this is a positive picture of the progress of black men in the professions throughout the 1960s and 1970s. But by itself, it is incomplete. Only by comparing black men's progress to that of white men will we be able to assess the degree to which racial barriers for black men were toppled during this period of affirmative action and economic expansion.

THE GROWTH OF BLACK MEN IN THE PROFESSIONS

The context necessary to understand black men's growth in the professions is the context of their decline in the labor force as a whole. According to Cummings (1983), in June 1983 a smaller percent of black men were employed or looking for work than in 1965. When only those able to find gainful employment in 1983 were included, Cummings found only 57.2 percent of all black men in the United States were accounted for. This is a tragic loss of labor power, economic resources, and self-esteem for the black community.

Despite this proportional loss in the labor force, my data show that black men had a net gain of 1.3 million jobs in the experienced civilian labor force between 1960 and 1980 (see Table 4.1). Of these, only 313,000 were in the professions/technical fields (with just over a quarter million in the professions). What this means is that just under one-quarter (23.6 percent) of all new jobs for black men were in the professions/technical fields. However, this is considerably less than for white men: more than one-third (35.1 percent) of all their new jobs during this period were in the professions and technical fields.

Out of the quarter million new professional jobs for black men, only 21,000 were in the elite male professions. They did much better in the nonelite male professions, with 77,000 new jobs. Their largest numerical increase was in the gender-neutral professions (85,000), and they showed a substantial increase in the female professions (69,000). Among the technical fields, more than three-fourths of black men's gains were in the higher-status, higher-paying male-dominated ones (48,000).

These data indicate that black men increased in the professions/technical fields, but not as much as white men. Progress has occurred for black men, but simultaneously, racial barriers to that progress persist. We can see both of these phenomena when we look at the detailed professions and technical fields in

which black men made their greatest *numerical* increases. Five of the top 10
occupations with the largest absolute increases were the same for black and
white men: elementary education, personnel and labor relations, accounting,
nonspecific college teaching, and computer programming. (See Table 5.1, Column 1). (As we will see, large increases in these professions tend to occur for
black women and white women also.)

Despite this similarity, the profile of the top 10 jobs for black and white men
is quite different. For black men, only two of these occupations were among the
male professions, and both were nonelite (accounting and nonspecific college
teaching). However, their numbers also increased substantially in *all three large
male technical areas* (electrical engineering technology, drafting, and engineering and science technology/nec). Fully one-half of their increase was in the
lower-status gender-neutral professions (personnel and labor relations, counseling, computer programming) and the female professions (social work, elementary education). In contrast, 7 of the 10 largest numerical gains for white men
were in higher-status, higher-paying male professions and technical areas, including both of the elite professions (law and medicine). (See Table 4.1.)

In addition to increases in absolute numbers of jobs, Table 5.1 displays the
occupations with the *fastest growth rates* (i.e., largest percentage increase) for
black men. While white men's rate of growth was high in some of the female
professions and technical areas (see Table 4.2), black men showed faster growth
rates in male professions, especially engineering specialties, and neutral professions (computer programming, counseling, personnel and labor relations, and
editing/reporting). For both groups of men it is important to remember that the
professions/technical areas with the fastest growth rates are precisely those in
which each group had the lowest starting point in 1960. Thus, although black
men seem to have grown fastest in engineering specialties, by 1980 the top 15
of 30 large professions/technical fields in which black men were most likely to
be employed did not contain a single engineering specialty. By 1980 only 2
percent of all engineers were black men.

A COMPARISON OF BLACK MEN AND WHITE MEN

In Chapter 4 we examined white men's representation in the various professions
in relation to their representation in the general labor force. This gave us a measure of the appropriate share of the profession white men "should" have had,
based on their share of the labor force. In most of the professions (especially the
highest-status, highest-paying male-dominated occupations), they held more
than their share. Since white men have dominated the professions, the inroads
that disadvantaged groups made into these occupations between 1960 and 1980
must be evaluated in comparison with the performance of the dominant group.

TABLE 5.1   TEN LARGEST-GROWING PROFESSIONS/TECHNICAL FIELDS FOR BLACK MEN, 1960–1980: NUMBERS AND GROWTH RATES

Increase Based on Raw Numbers			Increase Based on Percentage Growth		
	Largest Numerical Increase			Largest Percentage Increase	
(1) Occupation	(2) Number	(3) Percent	(4) Occupation	(5) Percent	(6) Number
Elementary-school teacher	30,971	237.7	Computer programmer	11,043.8	9,939
Personnel + labor relations	25,576	3,249.7	Counselor	3,254.5	9,204
Accountant	22,448	729.3	Personnel + labor relations	3,249.7	25,576
Social worker	20,171	526.7	Engineer/nec	1,114.8	5,454
Electrical-engineer techn.	11,718	548.5	Industrial engineer	1,077.1	5,346
Computer programmer	9,939	11,043.8	College teacher (nonsp.)	961.2	9,311
Drafter	9,819	436.8	Electrical engineer	731.4	6,768
College teacher (nonsp.)	9,311	961.2	Accountant	729.3	22,448
Counselor	9,204	3,254.5	Mechanical engineer	641.4	3,833
Engineer + science tech/nec	7,583	442.5	Editor/reporter	566.3	2,879

Thus, although it is true that black men were more likely to be employed as professionals in 1980 than in 1960, white men were even more so. The same is true for white women and black women, as we shall see in Chapters 6 and 7.

In order to understand how well a given race/gender group is represented in the professions, we need to make sure that the measures we use take into account the different size of each group in the profession and in the labor force and their differential growth rates when they are being compared to one another. In addition, we need to keep track of changes in the size of occupations and their differential growth rates. Otherwise, our results will be distorted.

Further, since I am concerned with whether or not the changing economic and political climate of the 1960s and 1970s did, in fact, increase disadvantaged groups' *access* to the professions, we need to determine the percentage of all black men in the labor force that have been able to enter a given profession (say accounting), not simply the percentage of all black professionals that are accountants. This must be compared with the percentage of all white male accountants out of all white men in the labor force. By creating a measure that uses both of these percentages, we are able to control for the different numbers of each race/gender group in the professions out of all members of that group, and their different rates of entry into the particular occupation. Any conclusions, of course, must be tempered by the realization that the percentages are often small, especially for black men and black women.

Thus to consider only the total population of professionals and technicians would not tell us the degree to which black men have been able to gain greater *access* to the professions, only where black men stand *once that access has been achieved or not.* In order to look at both access and ultimate achievement between 1960 and 1980, I developed the Index of Relative Advantage.

The Index of Relative Advantage works as follows: Divide the more disadvantaged group's percentage in an occupation (out of their total participation in the labor force) by that of the more advantaged group's percentage in that same occupation (out of *their* total participation in the labor force). If the index reaches 1.00, then there is parity of representation. If you wanted to apply this measure to black men and white men in, say, accounting, one would divide black men's percentage of accounting jobs by white men's percentage. (For a comparison of black men's and white men's percentages of the seven intermediate-range professional and technical categories, see Table 5.2) If the ratio is 1.00, then black men are equally likely to be represented as accountants out of all black men in the labor force as white men are likely to be represented as accountants out of all white men in the labor force. If black men were overrepresented in accounting (or any other profession) in comparison to white men, the ratio would be more than 1.00. If black men were underrepresented, the ratio would be less than 1.00.

AN INTERMEDIATE-LEVEL ANALYSIS
USING THE INDEX OF RELATIVE ADVANTAGE:
A COMPARISON OF BLACK MEN AND
WHITE MEN

Examination of the separate percentage increases of black and white men over the 20-year period indicates growth for both groups in the male, neutral, and female professions and in the overall technical fields. (See Table 5.2.) The question remains: was black men's increase better than, the same as, or worse than white men's? To answer this question, we look at the Index of Relative Advantage (Table 5.3). Here it becomes very clear that on the whole, throughout the professions/technical areas, black men moved toward greater parity with white men. However, the higher the status of the profession or technical field, the less likely black men were to have gained parity with white men.

When one looks at the progress of black men between 1960 and 1980 in relation to the progress of white men, one learns that black men moved from a ratio of 0.15 to 0.23 in *elite male* professions on the Index of Relative Advantage. Black men increased even more among *nonelites* (0.15 to 0.35), but despite their improvement remained severely underrepresented. In the fastest expanding *neutral* professions, black men moved from being severely to moderately underrepresented in relation to white men (0.35 to 0.58). And in the *female* professions black men remained essentially at parity (0.92 to 1.02).

TABLE 5.2   PERCENTAGE OF BLACK MEN IN PROFESSIONS/TECHNICAL FIELDS OF ALL BLACK MEN IN LABOR FORCE, 1960 AND 1980—COMPARED WITH WHITE MEN'S PERCENTAGE

	Black Men		White Men		Difference 1960–1980	
					Black Men	White Men
	1960	1980	1960	1980		
	(1)	(2)	(3)	(4)	(5)	(6)
Professions						
Elite Male	0.3	0.6	1.8	2.5	+0.3	+0.7
Nonelite Male	0.6	1.8	4.1	5.2	+1.2	+1.1
Neutral	0.7	2.0	1.9	3.4	+1.3	+1.5
Female	0.5	1.6	0.5	1.5	+1.1	+1.0
Profs. subtotal	2.1	5.9	8.3	12.6	+3.8	+4.2
Technical fields						
Male	0.2	1.0	1.4	2.0	+0.8	+0.6
Neutral	0.0	0.1	0.1	0.1	+0.1	0.0
Female	0.1	0.2	0.1	0.1	+0.1	0.0
Techs. subtotal	0.3	1.3	1.6	2.3	+1.0	+0.7
Profs. + techs. total*	2.4	7.2	9.9	14.8	+4.8	+4.9

*Percentages may not add up exactly because of rounding errors.

TABLE 5.3   INDEX OF RELATIVE ADVANTAGE FOR BLACK MEN IN COMPARISON TO WHITE MEN: INTERMEDIATE ANALYSIS

	Black Men/White Men		Difference 1960–1980
	1960	1980	
	(1)	(2)	(3)
Professions			
Elite male	0.15	0.23	+0.08
Nonelite male	0.15	0.35	+0.20
Neutral	0.35	0.58	+0.23
Female	0.92	1.02	+0.10
Technical fields			
Male	0.15	0.49	+0.34
Neutral	0.38	1.03	+0.65
Female	0.84	1.41	+0.57

In the *technical fields,* a slightly different pattern emerges. By 1980 black men had reached parity with white men in the neutral areas (0.38 to 1.03) and had become half as likely as white men to be employed in the higher-level male areas (0.15 to 0.49). Interestingly, in the lowest-status female technical areas, black men moved from a slight level of underrepresentation (0.84) to become moderately overrepresented (1.41).

In summary, although black men made overall gains in both the professions and the technical areas, their gains were greater the lower down the hierarchy these jobs are.

A DEEPER LOOK INTO THE DETAILED PROFESSIONS/TECHNICAL FIELDS

Black men appear to have achieved their greatest access, in comparison to white men's access, in professions and technical fields experiencing the largest *growth rates:*[1] counseling, personnel and labor relations, social work, and clinical-laboratory technology. (See Table 5.4.) In counseling and clinical-laboratory technology, they moved from being under- to overrepresented; and in social work, black men *increased* their overrepresentation. So, at the same time as black men increased their access to these three jobs, they experienced some form of increasing or new level of overconcentration in comparison to white men. At what point might we interpret this trend as one in which black men were becoming *re*segregated? Also, recall that counseling is the only profession in which white men decreased their "share" of the profession—that is, they became *more* underrepresented in the profession in 1980 than they were in 1960. And both social work and personnel and labor relations were among the largest expanding professions numerically. In short, *black men had increased access especially to jobs that experienced the largest growth rates,* some in which the numbers increased the most, as well as to the one profession in which white men were declining. Finally, not only are these lower-status jobs, but they also tend to be lower paying than those in the higher-status male professions (see Table 2.2).

The jobs in which black men were most likely to gain their greatest access in relation to white men were the jobs that blacks entered in increasing numbers during the years of civil-rights legislation and affirmative-action mandates. These include the occupations of greatest growth for black men in this study: counseling, personnel and labor relations, and social work, which "represent people-related as opposed to purely technical functions. The upheaval among blacks during the 1960s required skills which could be used to explain and alleviate black discontent" (S. Collins, 1983:375). These typically public-sector human-service jobs certainly fit well here.

However, black men's gains in human-services jobs did not necessarily continue. The situation in personnel and labor relations is instructive. It has been argued in the black community that blacks were hired in personnel as affirmative-action officers during the 1960s and 1970s (S. Collins, 1983, 1989; Fulbright, 1985–86; Deutsch, 1987; DiTomaso and Thompson, 1988). Often, these were black professionals diverted from other more prestigious professions

**TABLE 5.4   INDEX OF RELATIVE ADVANTAGE FOR BLACK
MEN IN COMPARISON TO WHITE MEN: DETAILED
PROFESSIONS/TECHNICAL FIELDS, 1960–1980**

Large Detailed Profession/ Technical Fields	1960 (1)	1980 (2)	Difference 1960–1980 (3)
Male professions			
Elite			
Lawyer	0.11	0.20	+0.09
Physician	0.21	0.28	+0.07
Nonelite			
Civil engineer	0.08	0.24	+0.16
Elect. + elect. engr.	0.05	0.26	+0.21
Mechanical engineer	0.04	0.22	+0.18
Chemist	0.18	0.43	+0.25
Engineer/nec	0.07	0.25	+0.18
Pharmacist	0.18	0.26	+0.08
Industrial engineer	0.04	0.28	+0.24
Accountant	0.07	0.38	+0.31
Designer	0.12	0.35	+0.23
Nonspecif. coll. tea.	0.25	0.39	+0.14
Clergy	0.69	0.50	−0.19
Gender-neutral profs.			
Voc. + ed. cnslr.	0.15	1.28	+1.13
Personnel + lab. rels.	0.11	0.80	+0.69
Computer programmer	0.15	0.46	+0.31
Editor/reporter	0.07	0.31	+0.24
Research worker	0.15	0.44	+0.29
Secondary-sch. tea.	0.55	0.55	0.00
Painter/sculptor	0.17	0.42	+0.25
Female professions			
Social worker	1.22	1.95	+0.73
Librarian	0.44	0.74	+0.30
Elementary-sch. tea.	0.98	0.82	−0.16
Nurse	1.36	1.28	−0.08
Pre K + kinder. tea.	9.44	2.43	−7.01
Teacher/nec	0.50	0.64	+0.14
Male tech. fields			
E + E engr. tech.	0.20	0.55	+0.35
Drafter	0.11	0.47	+0.36
Eng. + sci. tech./nec	0.18	0.46	+0.28
Female tech. fields			
Clinical-lab. tech.	0.86	1.52	+0.66

(Deutsch, 1987; S. Collins, 1989). As with other personnel jobs, these were staff positions with advisory capacity within an organization, not line positions with decision-making authority (Kanter, 1977; DiTomaso and Thompson, 1988). By the 1980s there was declining commitment to affirmative action, and many blacks in personnel found themselves either unable to move up in the corporation, or out of a job (L. Williams, 1985; Deutsch, 1987), to say nothing of the decline in the number of jobs in affirmative-action enforcement agencies themselves.

In addition to these major changes, several others should be noted. Black men made substantial gains (i.e., reached at least a low level of underrepresentation) as librarians. Moreover, they reached a moderate level of underrepresentation (and therefore improved in relation to white men) in at least one male profession (chemistry), four gender-neutral professions (computer programming, research work, painting/sculpting, and secondary education), and in all three male technical fields (electrical engineering technology, drafting, and engineering and science technology/nec). Black men made their *least progress in relation to white men* throughout the highest-status male professions, both elite and non-elite.

Finally, black men showed small "losses" in relation to white men in the clergy and elementary-school teaching, even though the ministry has always been a place of professional concentration for black men (Woodson, 1934; Kilson, 1977). As elementary-school teachers, black men were still well represented in comparison to white men by 1980, although not equally so (the ratio moved from 0.98 to 0.82 over the 20 years). This may be related to the increased number of white men entering teaching between 1960 and 1980 and to black men gaining somewhat greater opportunities elsewhere.

CONCLUSION

During the period of massive political and economic change in the 1960s and 1970s, black men increased their numbers and moved toward greater parity with white men throughout the professions/technical areas. However, the higher the status of the profession, the less likely black men were to be at parity with white men. In fact, among the large male professions, despite improvement in relation to white men, black men still remain severely underrepresented in both elite and almost all nonelite occupations. And even though the large growth rate in each of the five engineering specialties improved black men's representation, in these too they moved only from very severely to severely underrepresented in relation to white men by 1980.

Instead, it was precisely *outside* the higher-status, higher-paying professions that black men make their greatest gains in access in relation to white men. A look at the detailed occupational level reveals a clear pattern. Black men gained the greatest access to counseling, personnel and labor relations, social work, librarianship, and clinical-laboratory technology—all lower-paying gender-neutral and female professions and technical areas. All but librarianship were professions with the *fastest growth rates;* personnel and labor relations and social work were among the largest expanding numerically; and counseling was the only profession in which white men decreased their share between 1960 and 1980. Therefore, black men's gains in access were not an economic threat to white men because, according to these data, there was a large enough increase for *both groups.*

In addition, the first three of these professions—counseling, personnel and labor relations, and social work—fit the analysis developed by S. Collins (1983) that black men were recruited as part of the new black middle class into social-service jobs that served primarily black populations in an attempt to defuse social disruption among urban blacks. Heavily dependent on the federal government, these jobs are subject to political decisions rather than the usual market forces. Given the large federal budget cuts in the 1980s and even more so in the 1990s, black men in the professions may well lose out disproportionately unless special provisions are made to actively support and encourage minority participation.

Finally, in several of these occupations (counseling and social work, as well as clinical laboratory technology), black men not only increased their access, but became overrepresented in relation to white men. In a sense they became *more concentrated* than white men in these jobs. This raises the question whether, in fact, a form of resegregation of black men is occurring. Moreover, these data make it clear that while black men may gain greater *access* to a profession/technical field, they do not necessarily move toward greater *parity* with white men.

Chapter 6

WHITE WOMEN: MOVEMENT AND CHANGE

INTRODUCTION

In 1991, long after the era of economic growth and sociopolitical change had ended, more than a few white middle-class men still felt threatened by white women's alleged gains. Claiming that they were victims of "gender bias," men's-rights groups such as the self-appointed Greater Baltimore Commission for Men (Corey, 1991) and the national men's "warrior" or "wildman" movement (see Bly, 1990; Gabriel, 1990) sought to regain what they felt they had lost, both economically and politically as well as emotionally.

Yet how much change did economic expansion, feminist activism, and legislative gains of the sixties and seventies actually bring about for white women? How have they fared in the highest reaches of the professions? From one perspective, if we look at where white women were in the professions in 1960, they had nowhere to go but up. While they held a seemingly respectable 38.3 percent of all professional positions, they were actually concentrated in the female-dominated professions (81 percent) such as nursing and elementary education, which are among the lowest paid and lowest status of the professions. Among the elite male-dominated professions, they were only 3.8 percent. (See Table 3.1.) By 1980 these percentages had changed: white women had increased to 42.8 percent of all professionals; had decreased their concentration in the female-dominated professions to 71.3 percent; and had increased their share of elite male professional jobs to 10.2 percent. However, although these figures indicate some improvement, the basic profile remained the same.

In February 1986 the Bureau of Labor Statistics reported that women had made sufficient inroads throughout the professional labor force to gain the overall majority in nearly 50 professional occupations surveyed by the Census Bureau (Greer, 1986). This led a popular women's magazine to conclude erroneously that "for the first time ever, the number of women professionals equaled the number of men—heartening evidence of the steady headway women are making into traditionally *male* occupations" (McCrum and Rubin 1987:53, my emphasis). However, a closer look at the 50 professions would have revealed that the vast majority were not among the high-status "traditionally male occupations."

Another area of progress also needs to be studied carefully. Women have made steady inroads into the training grounds for professionals, the professional schools: their growth in professional schools has outstripped their growth in the professional labor force. In law school, for example, women increased from only 3.8 percent of all law students in 1963 to 8.5 percent in the 1970s, to one-third in 1980 (Epstein, 1983), and to 40 percent in 1988 (Weisenhaus, 1988). Some of the large, previously male-dominated law schools (such as New York University and Rutgers University) boasted a student body that has become 50 percent or more female ("Class of '86: . . .," 1986).

This has only added more fuel to the argument that barriers to established and protected male-dominated professions have been eroded by women. As Hacker has argued, "Among the most vivid cases of displacement [of men by women] are those in the upper reaches of the workplace. The proportion of women among graduate students has been increasing dramatically, providing stiff competition for young men who, a generation earlier, might have been all but certain of executive or professional careers. Between 1960 and 1983, the male proportion among lawyers declined from 98 percent to 85 percent" (Hacker, 1984:125). Yet despite these gains, the pinnacle of the legal profession—partnerships in law firms—is still largely white male. By 1987 women (mostly white women, at that) held fewer than 8 percent of partnerships at the top 250 firms in the country; and at that rate, by the year 2000 only 20 percent of partners will be women (Weisenhaus, 1988).

In medicine the situation is similar. In the 1989–1990 academic year, women were 37 percent of first-year medical students, and by the year 2020, they should be 25–30 percent of all physicians. But even within this elite profession, women M.D.s earn an average of 30 percent less than men (Altman with Rosenthal, 1990), probably because they are clustered in the less highly paid specialties. In 1986, 75 percent of female physicians were located in pediatrics, internal medicine, family practice, obstetrics and gynecology, and anesthesiology ("Women Doctors, by Specialty," 1990).

The occupational-segregation literature documents a significant decline in gender segregation in the professions after World War II, with the greatest changes occurring during the 1970s (Blitz, 1974; Fuchs, 1975; Burris and Wharton, 1982; Beller, 1984; Jacobs, 1984). As one scholar concludes, "[During the 1970s], a new pattern of female entry has emerged. Rather than continue to crowd into a limited subset of occupations, women are entering a wide variety of nontraditional occupations. These changes are most prominent at the white-collar level, especially among professional and managerial occupations. But little such change appeared for the blue-collar occupations" (Beller 1984:19). Unlike other previous researchers, Beller conducted separate analyses of whites and "nonwhites," which revealed greater declines in gender segregation in professional and managerial jobs for whites. These changes, she argued, were linked to desegregation in college majors. However, once again, the broad category of "white collar professional and managerial occupations" obscures an incredibly wide range of occupations, the majority of which do not qualify as elite male professions.

A second important obfuscation in the occupational-segregation literature is that most findings referring to "women" actually reveal the experiences primarily of *white* women, who dominate among women in the professions. In fact, in 1980 white women were 85 percent of all women in the professions, excluding Latina women (USDC, Bureau of Census, 1983a). This chapter and Chapter 7 clarify the progress of white women and black women in the professions and reveal contrasts between the two groups.

In this chapter I focus on two sets of questions. The first refers to the relationship of white women to white men in the professions. To what degree have white women been able to desegregate white-male-dominated professions? Have white women gained access to white-male-dominated professions as white men have gained access to white-female-dominated professions? Even if it does not make sense to talk about white men "losing" jobs or having them "taken away" by large numbers of white women, is there some way in which white women's "encroachment" into white men's traditionally protected domains bears any relationship to white men's perceptions of reality? Finally, is there any truth to the claim that white men have "encroached" upon white women in female-dominated professions?

The second set of questions concerns those claims in the media and scientific literature of the supposed gains of white women over black men. The belief that both black men and black women in the higher reaches of the occupational hierarchy have more difficulty than white women has been proclaimed in more than a few newspaper headlines: for example, "Blacks Believe White Women Lead in Job Gains" (in Rule, 1982). Likewise, Cortese's (1987) presentation at a professional sociology meeting charged that white women have been favored over black men: "Affirmative Action: Are White Women Gaining at the Expense of Black Men?"

CHANGES FROM 1960 TO 1980:
NUMBERS AND PERCENTAGES

Numerical Increase

Numerically, white women increased slightly more throughout the professions/ technical fields than did white men: almost 3.8 million new jobs compared to 3.6 million for white men. (See Table 4.1, Column 3.) And yet, because so many women entered the labor force between 1960 and 1980, this represents only one-fifth (21.6 percent) of all new jobs for white women. White men's gains in the professions were more substantial, as 35 percent of all their new jobs were in the professions.

As Table 4.1 makes clear, the largest number of new jobs for white women (1.7 million) were in the traditional female professions. Second were 900,000 in the gender-neutral professions. Of the 770,000 new jobs for white women in the male professions, the vast majority were in the nonelites. Only 123,000 more jobs in the elite male professions became available to white women during this 20-year period. In fact, they made greater numerical progress in male as well as female technical areas than in elite male professions.

Given this growth, where were white women concentrated in 1980? Consider the ten jobs with the largest numerical growth (Table 6.1, Column 1) for white women, and compare this list with those professions with the highest percentage growth rate for white women (Column 4). Half of the new jobs with the largest numerical increase were in female professions and female technical fields: elementary-school teaching, nursing, social work, prekindergarten and kindergarten teaching, and clinical-laboratory technology. The other half were located in gender-neutral professions (personnel and labor relations, secondary-school teaching, and computer programing) and nonelite male professions (accounting and nonspecific college teaching). All but two (prekindergarten and kindergarten teaching, and counseling) were among the 10 fastest-growing professions in the labor force overall. So unlike white men, white women were more likely to increase in professions in which the total number of jobs expanded the most, as was the case for black men.

Growth Rate (Percentage Increase)

Because white women were least often employed in male professions in 1960, this is where their strongest *growth rate* (i.e., their largest percentage increase) occurred. Seven of the 10 with the largest percentage growth were in male professions. However, their increase was not random, but tended to be concentrated in engineering specialties, as was also true for black men. White women also experienced high rates of growth in three gender-neutral professions (computer

TABLE 6.1   TEN LARGEST-GROWING PROFESSIONS/TECHNICAL FIELDS FOR WHITE WOMEN, 1960–1980: NUMBERS AND GROWTH RATES

Increase Based on Raw Numbers			Increase Based on Growth Rate		
	Largest Numerical Increase			Largest Percentage Increase	
(1) Occupation	(2) Number	(3) Percent	(4) Occupation	(5) Percent	(6) Number
Elementary-school teacher	658,888	85.5	Computer programmer	3,656.4	78,126
Nurse	531,919	93.3	College teacher (nonsp.)	1,424.0	115,500
Accountant	329,152	420.7	Industrial engineer	1,398.9	31,140
Personnel + labor relations	188,381	583.0	Lawyer	1,168.8	55,331
Secondary-school teacher	155,529	60.8	Engineer/nec	983.4	7,336
Social worker	153,101	293.2	Electrical engineer	727.8	11,514
College teacher (nonsp.)	115,500	1424.0	Civil engineer	601.1	4,202
Clinical-lab technician	103,507	268.3	Personnel + labor relations	583.0	188,381
Computer programmer	78,126	3,656.4	Counselor	518.8	66,524
Prekindgarten + K teacher	76,061	120.2	Mechanical engineer	506.7	2,823

programming, personnel and labor relations, and counseling), all of which expanded very rapidly over the 20-year period.

A Comparison with White Men

The Index of Relative Advantage

Just as other studies have shown, while the percentage of white men increased substantially in the professions as a whole over time, white women continue to be more highly concentrated than white men. (See Table 6.2.) So between 1960 and 1980, the percentage of white men in the professions and technical fields increased from 9.9 to 14.8, but the percentage of white women increased from 12.7 to 16.9. Because these percentages are based on the total number of white women and white men in the labor force, this does *not* necessarily mean that white women gained more professional jobs than did white men, but it does mean that both groups made progress relative to where they were in 1960. *Neither group "loses out"* in the professions/technical fields.

Yet when we break down the professions by gender concentration, it quickly becomes apparent that white men were more likely to be found in the male professions (7.7 percent) and white women in the female professions (8.9 percent). Less than one-half of 1 percent (0.4 percent) of all employed white women were represented in the elite male professions; and only 1.5 percent of all employed white men were found in the female professions in 1980. In both cases, this was an increase over time; in neither case was it very great.

In order to determine whether white women's increase was more or less than that of white men's, it is necessary to use the Index of Relative Advantage (see Table 6.3, Columns 1,2). (For an explanation of the index, see Chapter 5,"A

TABLE 6.2   PERCENTAGE OF WHITE WOMEN IN PROFESSIONS/TECHNICAL FIELDS OF ALL WHITE WOMEN IN LABOR FORCE, 1960 AND 1980—COMPARED WITH BLACK MEN'S AND WHITE MEN'S PERCENTAGE

	White Women		White Men		Black Men		Difference 1960–1980		
							White Women	White Men	Black Men
	1960 (1)	1980 (2)	1960 (3)	1980 (4)	1960 (5)	1980 (6)	(7)	(8)	(9)
Professions									
Elite Male	0.2	0.4	1.8	2.5	0.3	0.6	+0.2	+0.3	+0.7
Nonelite male	0.7	2.1	4.1	5.2	0.6	1.8	+1.4	+1.2	+1.1
Neutral	2.8	3.9	1.9	3.4	0.7	2.0	+1.1	+1.3	+1.5
Female	8.3	8.9	0.5	1.5	0.5	1.6	+0.6	+1.1	+1.0
Profs. subtotal	12.0	15.3	8.3	12.6	2.1	5.9	+3.3	+3.8	+4.2
Technical fields									
Male	0.2	0.6	1.4	2.0	0.2	1.0	+0.4	+0.8	+0.6
Neutral	0.1	0.2	0.1	0.1	0.0	0.1	+0.1	+0.1	0.0
Female	0.4	0.7	0.1	0.1	0.1	0.2	+0.3	+0.1	0.0
Techs. subtotal	0.7	1.5	1.6	2.3	0.3	1.3	+0.8	+1.0	+0.7
Profs. + techs. total*	12.7	16.9	9.9	14.8	2.4	7.2	+4.2	+4.8	+4.9

*Percentages may not add up exactly because of rounding errors.

Comparison of Black Men and White Men" pages 67–69). The index reveals thatwhile white women remained overrepresented in the total professional/technical category, by 1980 they were almost at parity with white men (the ratio moved from 1.28 to 1.14, while parity would be 0.90 to 1.10). However, even this masks the changes that both groups made over time, which only become more visible as the data are disaggregated.

The answer to the question, Did white women "take jobs away" from white men, especially elite male jobs? is emphatically no. In the *elite male professions,* despite all the remarkable changes that occurred between 1960 and 1980, there simply was not enough movement of white women *in relation to white men* for the index to reach the 0.10 point difference that would enable it to be counted as a change.[1] In 1980 white women were severely underrepresented. However, it is just as clear that white women showed important improvement in their move toward parity in the *nonelite male professions.* Here white women increased from being severely to moderately underrepresented in comparison to white men (the ratio moved from 0.17 to 0.41). (A similar change, although not as great, occurred in the male technical fields.)

In the *gender-neutral professions* we find an unexpected result: white women were moderately *over*represented in comparison to white men in 1960. While there was a decline in white women's overrepresentation by 1980, they did not quite reach parity with white men (the ratio changed from 1.45 to 1.14). In the *female professions,* the index shows an enormous decline in overrepresentation of white women (the ratio moved from 15.48 to 5.82). Despite that decline,

Table 6.3 INDEX OF RELATIVE ADVANTAGE FOR WHITE WOMEN IN COMPARISON TO WHITE MEN AND BLACK MEN: INTERMEDIATE ANALYSIS

	White Women/ White Men		White Women/ Black Men		Difference 1960–1980	
					White Women/ White Men	White Women/ Black Men
	1960 (1)	1980 (2)	1960 (3)	1980 (4)	(5)	(6)
Professions						
Elite male	0.09	0.17	0.59	0.73	+0.08	+0.14
Nonelite male	0.17	0.41	1.10	1.16	+0.24	+0.06
Neutral	1.45	1.14	4.17	1.97	−0.31	−2.20
Female	15.48	5.82	16.79	5.71	−9.66	−11.08
Technical fields						
Male	0.17	0.30	1.15	0.62	+0.13	−0.53
Neutral	1.28	2.11	3.38	2.05	+0.83	−1.33
Female	5.30	5.37	6.27	3.82	+0.07	−2.45
All profs. + techs.	1.28	1.14	5.39	2.35	−0.14	−3.04

white women were almost six times more likely to be in the female professions than were white men in 1980.

The picture of neutral and female technical fields was somewhat different from that of the neutral and female professions. White women became *increasingly over*represented in the gender-neutral technical fields, where they moved from 1.3 times to 2.1 times more likely to be found than white men. And in the female technical areas white women remained more than 5 times as likely as white men to be employed.

Ironically, throughout the professions, white men and white women moved closer to parity with each other in male and female as well as in neutral professions. Despite claims to the contrary, no one "took jobs away" from the other group. In the technical fields, though, white women appear to have increased their control over the neutral areas and to have maintained their fivefold overrepresentation in the female areas. Clearly, the lower levels of the technical labor force were becoming increasingly occupied by white women as compared to white men.

Movement and Change in the Detailed Occupations

The application of the Index of Relative Advantage to the 30 largest detailed professional and technical occupations unmasks several key trends. (See Table 6.4, Columns 1,2.) First, it becomes clear that white women not only improved generally in the *nonelite male professions* but actually reached parity or a low level of underrepresentation as *accountant* (0.41 to 0.95), *designer* (0.50 to 0.89), and *nonspecific college teacher* (0.48 to 0.73). In addition, white women

TABLE 6.4 INDEX OF RELATIVE ADVANTAGE FOR WHITE WOMEN IN COMPARISON TO WHITE MEN AND BLACK MEN: DETAILED PROFESSIONS/ TECHNICAL FIELDS, 1960–1980

Large Detailed Professions/ Technical Fields	White Women/White Men		White Women/Black Men		Difference 1960–1980	
	1960 (1)	1980 (2)	1960 (3)	1980 (4)	White Women/ White Men (5)	White Women/ Black Men (6)
Male professions						
Elite						
Lawyer	0.05	0.21	0.49	1.05	+0.16	+0.56
Physician	0.15	0.18	0.72	0.63	+0.03	−0.09
Nonelite						
Civil engineer	0.01	0.04	0.13	0.17	+0.03	+0.04
Elect. + elect. engr.	0.02	0.07	0.39	0.27	+0.05	−0.12
Mechanical engineer	0.01	0.03	0.21	0.12	+0.02	−0.09
Chemist	0.17	0.33	0.91	0.76	+0.16	−0.15
Engineer/nec	0.02	0.05	0.35	0.21	+0.03	−0.14
Pharmacist	0.18	0.42	1.00	1.61	+0.24	+0.61
Industrial engineer	0.04	0.25	1.02	0.89	+0.21	−0.13
Accountant	0.41	0.95	5.77	2.49	+0.54	−3.28
Designer	0.50	0.89	4.21	2.54	+0.39	−1.67
Nonspecif. coll. tea.	0.48	0.73	1.90	1.88	+0.25	−0.02
Clergy	0.05	0.09	0.07	0.15	+0.04	+0.08
Gender-neutral profs.						
Voc. + ed. cnslr.	1.50	1.68	10.30	1.31	+0.18	−8.99
Personnel + lab. rels.	1.00	1.04	9.32	1.31	+0.04	−8.01
Computer programmer	0.79	0.57	5.39	1.25	−0.22	−4.14
Editor/reporter	1.25	1.45	16.63	4.69	+0.20	−11.94
Research worker	0.80	0.95	5.45	2.18	+0.15	−3.27
Secondary-sch. tea.	2.02	1.77	3.68	3.23	−0.25	−0.45
Painter/sculptor	0.84	1.22	5.05	2.92	+0.38	−2.13
Female professions						
Social worker	3.79	2.61	3.10	1.34	−1.18	−1.76
Librarian	12.80	6.83	29.21	9.21	−5.97	−20.00
Elementary-sch. tea.	13.21	4.18	13.43	5.08	−9.03	−8.35
Nurse	91.33	34.87	67.27	27.33	−56.46	−39.94
Pre K + kinder. tea.	—	42.94	—	17.64	—	—
Teacher/nec	4.74	3.12	9.41	4.84	−1.62	−4.57
Male technical fields						
E + E engr. tech.	0.11	0.14	0.55	0.26	+0.03	−0.29
Drafter	0.13	0.28	1.26	0.61	+0.15	−0.65
Eng. + sci. tech./nec	0.37	0.57	2.05	1.23	+0.20	−0.82
Female technical fields						
Clinical-lab. tech.	5.48	4.37	6.37	2.88	−1.11	−3.49

moved from severely to moderately underrepresented as pharmacist (0.18 to 0.42) as well as engineering and science technician/nec (0.37 to 0.57) among the male technicians.

What is it about accounting, design, and nonspecific college teaching that allowed for such a remarkable move toward parity for white women in relation to white men? Several possible explanations emerge. The growth rate was very rapid in one (college teaching) and hovered about the average for the other two. Therefore, all had substantial room for new entrants. In addition, these three were the lowest paid of all nonelite male professions, except for the clergy. (See Table 2.2). Moreover, a look at the income changes between 1960 and 1980 reveals that both design and nonspecific college teaching experienced the greatest losses in income for women in comparison to men (see Table 6.5).

In short, it appears that white women were almost able to reach parity with white men in those expanding nonelite male professions characterized by relatively low status and low pay. This interpretation is supported by Reskin's (1989) study of accountants. Accounting expanded enormously between 1960 and 1980. According to my data, the almost 600,000 new accounting jobs were third only to elementary-school teaching and nursing. Because accounting was expanding so rapidly and the traditional labor supply of white men was not, "men did not resent women's entry because women constituted no threat: growth ensured that good jobs were plentiful, and within occupational segregation assured men's access to the best jobs" (p. 19). Moreover, as Reskin pointed out, accounting experienced this tremendous growth, in part, because of the changing nature of work in the profession: as large corporations expanded, their business functions became increasingly rationalized. This provided a larger number of more routinized opportunities in accounting that employers considered suitable for women. (See also Montagna, 1968.) In addition, small firms increasingly required accounting services as did individual taxpayers with the introduction of new tax laws. All these changes demanded more workers than the available pool of white men could provide.

In contrast, while white women substantially decreased their overrepresentation in each of the large *female professional/technical fields*, they never reached parity with white men. Therefore, no matter how much access white men had to female professions by 1980, white women maintained their "dominance" in this area even as they became significantly less concentrated. It should be clear that while some of this concentration was and continues to be by choice, much of it has occurred because of occupational gender segregation, which continues to channel women into lower-paid, lower-status professions and makes access to higher-level male-dominated professions difficult.

The more unexpected change took place in the *gender-neutral professions*. As stated previously, white women were moderately overrepresented in 1960 and declined to a low level of overrepresentation in 1980. Yet the more detailed analysis shows that in three of the seven large neutral professions, white women

TABLE 6.5 1960 AND 1980 INCOMES STANDARDIZED TO 1967 CONSUMER PRICE INDEX (CPI) FOR MEN AND WOMEN; WOMEN/MEN INCOME RATIOS; AND ACTUAL DOLLAR DIFFERENCE

Large Detailed Profession/ Technical Fields	Income				Women/Men Ratio		1980–1960 Income Difference	
	Men		Women					
	1960	1980	1960	1980	1960	1980	Men	Women
Male professions								
Elite								
Lawyer	$12,376	$11,747	$6,402	$5,267	0.52	0.45	–$629	–$1,135
Physician	16,662	20,252	7,395	7,292	0.44	0.36	3,590	–103
Nonelite								
Civil engineer	8,930	9,317	—*	5,478	—	0.59	387	—
Elect. + elect. engr.	9,941	9,771	6,294	7,292	0.63	0.75	–170	998
Mechanical engineer	9,709	9,722	—	6,488	—	0.67	13	—
Chemist	8,404	8,507	6,307	5,907	0.75	0.69	103	–400
Engineer/nec	9,936	9,722	—	6,178	—	0.64	–214	—
Pharmacist	8,386	8,507	5,519	4,781	0.66	0.56	121	–738
Industrial engineer	8,836	8,567	6,667	5,146	0.75	0.60	–269	–1,521
Accountant	7,695	7,586	5,108	4,457	0.66	0.59	–109	–651
Designer	8,624	6,887	5,389	2,513	0.62	0.36	–1,737	–2,876
Nonspecif. coll. tea.	8,616	8,104	6,689	4,254	0.78	0.52	–512	–2,435
Clergy	4,687	4,457	2,501	2,432	0.53	0.55	–230	–69

Gender-neutral profs.								
Voc. + ed. cnslr.	—	6,729	—	4,862	—	0.73	—	—
Personnel + lab. rels.	3,681	8,912	5,496	5,267	0.63	0.59	231	−229
Computer programmer	—	7,292	—	5,332	—	0.73	—	—
Editor/reporter	8,127	6,482	4,771	4,006	0.59	0.62	−1,645	−765
Research worker	—	—	—	—	—	—	—	—
Secondary-sch. tea.	7,132	6,563	5,557	4,862	.078	0.74	−569	−695
Painter/sculptor	—	4,862	—	2,432	—	0.50	—	—
Female professions								
Social worker	6,319	5,623	5,245	4,425	0.83	0.79	−696	−820
Librarian	6,089	5,267	4,673	4,052	0.77	0.77	−822	−621
Elementary-sch. tea.	6,351	6,482	5,138	4,846	0.81	0.75	131	−292
Nurse	5,168	5,899	4,316	4,862	0.84	0.82	731	546
Pre K + kinder. tea.	—	2,845	—	1,820	—	0.64	—	—
Teacher/nec	6,708	5,034	4,321	1,622	0.64	0.32	−1,674	−2,699
Male technical fields								
E + E engr. tech.	7,003	6,869	4,833	4,419	0.69	0.64	−134	−414
Drafter	6,848	6,077	5,280	3,933	0.77	0.65	−771	−1,347
Eng. + sci. tech./nec	6,709	6,462	4,710	3,850	0.70	0.60	−247	−860
Female technical fields								
Clinical-lab. techn.	—	5,382	—	4,218	—	0.78	—	—

Sources: 1960 data: USDC, Bureau of Census (1963), Table 30: pp. 396–415; 1980 data: Roos et al., 1990; Consumer Price Index data: U.S. Bureau of Census (1988), Table 729: p. 444.

* — = Data not available.

not only gained greater access but also *increased* their *over*representation (as counselors and editors/reporters) or *became over*represented (as painters/sculptors).[2] What might help to explain these changes?

While counseling expanded rapidly between 1960 and 1980, it is the one place where white men "lost out" in their share of the profession (see Chapter 4). It was also a place of tremendous expansion for black men in relation to white men during that same period (see Chapter 5). Perhaps the large increases in lower-level community and two-year colleges (Pincus, 1980) has created a demand for white women and black men (as well as black women; see Chapter 7) in vocational and educational counseling, while white men seek better alternatives elsewhere.

Although editing/reporting and painting/sculpting differ from counseling in that they grew at a slower than average rate and provided the lowest incomes among the gender-neutral professions (Table 2.2), they are similar in that the jobs appear to have become increasingly proletarianized. For example, Reskin (1990) provides a glimpse into this process for book editors. She describes how their jobs have declined in autonomy, creativity, and income, paving the way for increasing feminization of that occupation. The increasing ownership of publishing companies by outside interests and conglomerates both tarnished the industry's image and reshaped the editor's role. As job security declined and wages either failed to rise or declined, the number of qualified men looking for editorial careers decreased, and several female-dominated specialties in the field grew.

In short, as in the lowest levels of the nonelite male professions, white women appear to have gained in relation to white men in the neutral professions—but in occupations that were becoming less autonomous, more rationalized or de-skilled, and more poorly paid. Interestingly, the one neutral profession in which white women "lost out" to white men (i.e., white women became *increasingly* *under*represented in relation to white men) (0.79 to 0.57) is computer programming. It is probably not coincidental that this relatively new profession had the fastest growth rate of all professions between 1960 an 1980 and one of the highest incomes among the neutral professions (see Table 2.2).

To summarize, between 1960 and 1980 white women sharply decreased their overrepresentation in all large female professions and technical fields, although they remained very seriously overrepresented in relation to white men. To the extent that they were able to gain greater access to male-dominated professions, this clearly occurred *outside* the elite fields. However, white women made great strides in reaching or moving toward parity with white men in three nonelite professions: accounting, design, and nonspecific college teaching. In the large gender-neutral professions, white women were significantly more likely to become *over*represented as counselors, editors/reporters, and painters/sculptors. All of these professions in which white women made their greatest gains in access in relation to white men appear to be ones that were experiencing great changes: they were expanding at about average rates or better; and they were becoming more rationalized and less automous, and had low incomes for male and neutral professions. They became, in short, less desirable to white men.

A COMPARISON WITH BLACK MEN

The Index of Relative Advantage

To what degree did white women gain "at the expense" of black men? This question is just as misleading as the earlier one about threats to white men's dominance in elite male professions. The situation is far more complex than is implied by such a question. To be sure, some blacks have argued that white women have been able to make greater gains in the professions not only because of their greater access to a college education, but also because of their easier acceptance by white men who occupy powerful decision-making positions (Rule, 1982). In fact, it has been argued by some minority leaders that a real danger existed in that white women's attainments "would come at the expense of blacks and ethnic minorities and that white society would feel smug and righteous once they took care of their own women and granted them some privileges" (Babad, Birnbaum, and Benne, 1983:198).

It also has been argued that the women's movement of the 1960s and 1970s eclipsed the civil-rights movement of the 1950s, which had been both its catalyst and its model. As a result, white women gained at the expense of people of color—"particularly . . . the minority male" (Morris, as quoted in Cortese, 1987:4). In fact, Cortese (1987) argues, women have been able to gain access to economic markets dominated by white men, whereas black men have not. The problem for white women, he insists, is that of stratification—climbing up the ladder. In contrast, black men have the problem of gaining access to the ladder in the first place.

However, little in-depth analysis has been done to evaluate the belief that white women have gained at black men's expense. By using the Index of Relative Advantage to compare white women to black men in the professions/technical fields, it is possible to see how the two race/gender groups have fared.

The data displayed in Table 6.3, Columns 3 and 4, show that in 1960 white women were overrepresented, compared to black men, in the professions/technical fields overall (ratio = 5.39). They were especially overrepresented in the lower-status female professions (ratio = 16.79), the female technical fields (ratio = 6.27), and the gender-neutral professions (ratio = 4.17). Interestingly, the only area in which they were underrepresented in comparison to black men was in the elite male professions (ratio = 0.59).

By 1980 white women were still overrepresented in the professions and technical fields overall (ratio = 2.35), but were much less so. What this means is that in the 20-year period covered in this study, white women maintained their advantage, but it was a rapidly shrinking advantage: black men gained relative to white women, not the other way around. In short, the belief that white women gained at the expense of black men is unsupported by the data.

In the *elite male professions*, the one area in which they were underrepresented in 1960, white women made substantial progress toward parity with black men, although in 1980 they were still underrepresented (from 0.59 to 0.73). (In fact, white women actually reached parity with black men in the legal profession. See Table 6.4, Column 4.) However, in the lower-status *nonelite male professions*, white women remained slightly overrepresented in comparison to black men (from 1.10 to 1.16). Thus white women continued to show a slight racial advantage in these occupations over black men.

Given that the nonelite professions are typically male dominated, the perception on the part of black men that white women have had easier access is understandable from their vantage point. However, this conclusion should not be overemphasized, since white women were only very slightly overrepresented. More problematic is the fact that white women did so much better (i.e., were closer to parity) in both elite and nonelite male professions in relation to black men than to white men. This could be perceived as a disadvantage by black men when, in fact, white women were simply more equitably represented with black than with white men. If one's definition of equality is for each race/gender group to be distributed in a profession as they are in the labor force, then the changes documented here should be seen as positive, not negative. They are negative only if we assume that men, black or white, should dominate the higher-status, higher-paying male professions.

In contrast to their relative positions in the male professions, and contrary to expectation, black men were *under*represented compared to white women in the *male technical areas* in 1960 (ratio = 1.15). However, this reversed itself by 1980 (ratio = 0.62). At this later point, white women were moderately underrepresented. As stated earlier, in all other professions/technical areas, white women were very severely overrepresented in 1960, but this overrepresentation had decreased by 1980. Despite this decline, white women remain 2 to 3.8 times overrepresented in comparison to black men in all *gender-neutral and female professions and technical fields*.

In summary, the Index of Relative Advantage, as shown in Table 6.3 and elaborated on in Table 6.4, attests to the complex relationship between black men and white women throughout the professional/technical hierarchy. Simplistic approaches to this relationship can be both harmful and misleading.

A Detailed Occupational Analysis

The more detailed level of occupational analysis reveals several very important findings. (See Table 6.4, Columns 3,4.) First, in the male professions/technical areas, *white women "lost out"* (i.e., they became even more underrepresented in relation to black men) between 1960 and 1980 as *engineers* (electronic, nec, and industrial) and *chemists,* as well as in two of the three male technical areas (electrical engineering technology and drafting).[3] (In two cases, chemists and industrial engineers, white women and black men began at parity with each other; by 1980, white women had become slightly underrepresented.) These changes favoring black men in traditional male professions would have been lost from view without this finer level of analysis, although these trends should not be overdramatized: in 1980 black men still represented only a very small proportion of all engineers and chemists.

In some of the other nonelite male professions, white women maintained an advantage over black men, although it shrank (i.e., black men gained relative to white women, but had not achieved parity by 1980). Thus *white women may decrease their overrepresentation* by one-half as *accountants* (ratio moved from 5.77 to 2.49) and *designers* (ratio moved from 4.21 to 2.54) between 1960 and 1980. Yet in 1980 they *remained 2½ times over*represented in relation to black men. And in *nonspecific college teaching* (1.90 to 1.88), white women were likewise almost twice as overrepresented as black men in 1980. Despite black men's moves toward parity with white women, white women's greater advantage in these occupations may have been resented by black men, even though that advantage had *decreased* over time. However, the fact that these three nonelite male professions—*accountant, designer, and nonspecific college teacher*—are precisely where white men and white women reach parity with one another, but black men do not, means that black men are participating in fewer of the gains in these lower-status male professions.

The one nonelite profession in which white women might be said to have "taken over" from black men is as *pharmacist.* Here the index moved from parity in 1960 (1.00) to severe overrepresentation of white women in comparison to black men in 1980 (1.61). This is in line with Phipps's (1990a) analysis that men have declined in retail pharmacies as women have increasingly entered waged-labor, hospital-based pharmacies. That white women have gained greater access to pharmacy in relation to white men was demonstrated previously. However, why white women's gains in pharmacy are even more pronounced in relation to black men, according to my data, is unclear.

In each of the large *female professions and technical areas,* white women decreased their overrepresentation vis-à-vis black men yet remained very severely overrepresented in 1980. The one exception was in social work, where white women were only moderately overrepresented in 1980.

In the large *gender-neutral professions,* white women greatly decreased their overrepresentation in comparison to black men. Black men improved their representation, but did not come close to reaching parity with white women, except as *counselors, personnel and labor-relations specialists, and computer pro-*

grammers. As was discussed in Chapter 5, the important gains for black men in these professions and in social work reflect the positions in government agencies that opened up to black professionals as a part of the response to the urban riots of the 1960s.

SUMMARY

On the one hand, black men's sense that the "white system" has favored white women may be fueled by the fact that white women did better in relation to black men than in relation to white men. Between 1960 and 1980, not only did white women maintain high levels of overrepresentation in neutral and female professions/technical fields compared to black men, but they also did well in some of the male professions. This was true despite their substantial decline in overrepresentation with black men in the nonelite male professions and their slight underrepresentation in the elite fields. In the detailed occupations, white women actually reached parity with black men as lawyers. And in accounting, design, and nonspecific college teaching, as these jobs opened up more to disadvantaged groups, white women entered far more than black men.

On the other hand, black men were able to secure more nonelite male professional positions than white women in several engineering specialties as well as in chemistry. This trend also occurred in the elite profession of medicine. In addition, black men took the lead from white women in the male technical fields. Importantly, these jobs are higher status and higher paying than all the female professions/technical fields and most of the neutral professions where white women were in the lead over black men. And finally, white women's shrinking overrepresentation in the professions/technical fields overall means that black men gained relative to white women. Of course, neither came close to challenging the dominant group: white men.

CONCLUSION

After two decades of social ferment, to what extent had white women entered the male-dominated professions? By 1980 they had moved only slightly toward parity with white men in the elite occupations. Despite their increasing numbers, and newspaper headlines to the contrary, they remained severely underrepresented. This was not so in comparison to black men: white women made important moves toward parity in the elites, reaching equal representation with black men among lawyers in 1980. However, it is false to conclude either that white women have "taken jobs away" from white men in these most prestigious, most coveted of male professions or that they have "encroached" on black men's domain. Either statement assumes that just because men are *men* (whether white or black) they should have greater rights to these jobs. Parity of representation is the goal for all race/gender groups.

In contrast to the elite male professions, white women made far greater progress in entering some of the nonelites. The most outstanding instances are accounting, design, and nonspecific college teaching. Within the male professions, these jobs are low status, low paying, and had the greatest income loss for women between 1960 and 1980. They were marked by a decline in autonomy, decision making, and other aspects of control. In short, white women gained their greatest access in the male professions to jobs that were becoming less desirable to white men. However, even here white women did not "take over" these professions: rather, they reached parity with white men. These occupations have become gender desegregated among whites.

However, white women were always overrepresented in these three professions in relation to black men. And although they decreased their level of overrepresentation, white women still remained 2 to 2½ times more likely than black men to be accountants, designers, and nonspecific college teachers by 1980. While the argument that white women gained more from the sixties and seventies does not hold up (since they *decreased* their overrepresentation from about six to two times), black men's sense that things were better for white women than for them is understandable from their perspective, at least in these three professions.

On the other hand, black men gained greater advantages over white women in several of the higher-paying nonelite professions more traditionally associated with men. These include several engineering specialties and chemistry, almost half of the detailed nonelites, as well as medicine. The same is true for two of the three large male technical fields, electrical engineering technology and drafting. This is significant because male technical fields tend to pay more and to have higher status than all of the female and most of the gender-neutral professions/technical areas. In short, while white women did better than black men in certain of the nonelites, black men were overrepresented in comparison to white women in most of the large male professions and technical fields.

Between 1960 and 1980, did men enter the traditionally defined female professions? In general, throughout the remainder of the professions/technical fields, white women decreased their very high levels of overrepresentation in neutral and female occupations in relation to both white and black men; thus gender segregation in these occupations was on the decline. However, despite this, white women were still almost six times more likely than either group of men to be working in the female professions in 1980.[4] The only large detailed profession in which men (in this case, black men) came close to parity with white women was social work. In short, there is no evidence to support the argument that men—black or white—are encroaching on white women's domain.

What was the situation in the gender-neutral professions? To summarize, there were mixed gains for both white women and black men. Similar to what happened in Chapter 5 when black men were compared to white men, black men gained substantial access to employment as counselors and as personnel and labor-relations specialists (as well as social workers in the female professions) when compared to white women. These are some of the professions in the public sector to which the black middle class was recruited in an attempt to deal with burgeoning problems in the inner cities. In addition, black men made large gains in computer programing in relation to white women. Interestingly, this is the only detailed occupation in this study in which white women "lost out" to white men—that is, became increasingly more *under*represented when compared to white men. Computer programming had the fastest rate of expansion of all the professions/technical areas studied as well as one of the highest incomes in the neutral professions. In contrast, white women appear to have gained greater access to those neutral professions with lower incomes: editing/reporting, painting/sculpting, and counseling. We saw that white women reached parity with white men in nonelite male professions (accounting, design, and nonspecific college teaching) that were declining in autonomy and decision-making power, and were becoming more rationalized—in short, less desirable to white men. This, too, appears to be the case for the three gender-neutral professions where white women became increasingly overrepresented in relation to white men.

Chapter 7

BLACK WOMEN: BEYOND THE MYTH OF DOUBLE ADVANTAGE

INTRODUCTION

As affirmative-action requirements began to be enforced in the late 1960s and early 1970s, some members of the various race/gender groups began to feel threatened. Some white men who were not admitted to professional school or who were not hired in a desired professional or technical job blamed "the government" for seeing that these positions were filled with women or minority men. Some white women, aspiring to newly available slots that promised a chance at upward mobility, felt stymied not only by white men but also by competitors from minority groups. And some black men, upon failing to gain a desired position for which they were qualified, felt that not only white men but also women of all racial/ethic groups had received an unfair advantage.

But the race/gender group that was the object of most finger-pointing was black women. Because black women have both minority-group and female status, a myth sprang up, and was popularized by the media, that they have had a double advantage. The term for this supposed advantage is "twofer"—two for the price of one (Nelson, 1975; Malveaux, 1981). Supposedly, by hiring one black woman and counting her in two categories, professional schools and employers had found a way to comply with the letter of affirmative-action regulations while utterly violating the spirit of these regulations. Allegedly, successful black professional women had received the greatest benefit from these dubious practices.

What truth was there to black women's supposed double advantage? Eleanor Holmes Norton, former chair of the Equal Employment Opportunity Commission (EEOC), pronounced the twofer idea "totally fallacious": Norton explained that regardless of what a company or a school might try to get away with, no enforcement agency would give double credit for bringing in a black woman (Weathers, 1981).

In addition, the data fail to support the notion that black women gained tremendously in the professions at the expense of other groups. From one perspective, black women, even more than white women and, in some respects, black men, had nowhere to go but up. In 1960 they held only 2.8 percent of all professional positions—almost double the representation of black men, but many times below that of white women (38.3 percent) and white men (57.5 percent). However, just like white women, they were concentrated in the low-status, poorly paid female-dominated professions (6.6 percent), and were barely visible in the elite male-dominated professions (0.1 percent). In comparison, black men's tenuous representation in the professions was the reverse: higher in the elite male professions (1.5 percent) than in the female professions (1.1 percent). (See Table 3.1.)

By 1980 these percentages had improved somewhat—as, indeed, they had for all three disadvantaged race/gender groups. Black women now held 4.9 percent of all professional positions, which was still almost double the representation of black men. But though they had gained in all the gender-dominated professions, as well as in the neutral ones, they were still the most poorly represented race/gender group in the male-dominated professions, both elite and nonelite, and were still concentrated in the female-dominated occupations. (See Table 3.1.) Far from validating the belief that black women were doubly advantaged, these 20-year figures point out that they were if anything doubly *dis*advantaged. (For the concept of double disadvantage, sometimes called the "double whammy," especially in the black community, see Beale, 1970; Davis, 1971; Ladner, 1972; Weathers, 1981.)

THE INTERACTON OF RACE AND GENDER

Comparisons with White Women

Failure to look at the interaction of race and gender and its effects leads to a confusing and inconsistent view of black women in the labor force in general, and in the professions in particular. When the unique experiences of black women are not neglected, they are all too often said to be doing "better than" or to be successful "at the expense of" some other group. Let us look at some of these arguments.

The group to which black women have been most likely to be compared are white women. Typically, a comparison is made in their rates of increase in the professions over time. Only 1.5 percent of all black women, but 11.6 percent of all white women, were employed in the professions in 1910. By 1980 the proportion of black women almost equaled that of white women: 15.3 percent of black women and 17.4 percent of white women were in the professions. To be sure, the bulk of both black and white women's employment is in the female professions (Kilson, 1977; Wallace, 1980; Wilkie, 1985). What is all too often emphasized, however, is black women's *rate of increase,* which has far surpassed that of white women. Yet such growth has been possible only because black women began at such a low starting point.

In other types of comparisons between black women and white women, one is led to believe that black women are more "advantaged" than white women because of their better representation among blacks in the professions, especially higher-status fields such as medicine, law, and college teaching (e.g., Hacker 1984, 1986). Historically, black women always represented a larger proportion of the black professional community than white women did of the white community (Kilson, 1977), and this has remained true. For example, in 1980 almost one-quarter (24.0 percent) of all black physicians were women, while only about one-tenth (11.4 percent) of all white physicians were women. The difference was even greater among lawyers, where the figures are 31.4 percent for black women and 13.1 percent for white women (USDC, Bureau of Census, 1983a).

Although one can say that black women do better than white women, this is true primarily because black women are compared to the more disadvantaged group of black men, while white women are compared to the more advantaged group of white men. Not only does this picture inflate the perception of black women's mobility; it also fails to recognize the fact that it is black men's disadvantage in relation to white men that is key here, *not* black women's advantage *over* black men.

Comparisons with Black Men

Similarly, when comparing black women to black men, it has been argued that within the black population, discrimination against women has decreased much more rapidly than discrimination against men. Black women are said to have increased their occupational, educational, and economic status at a pace far greater than have black men (see, e.g., Szymanski, 1974; Fox and Hesse-Biber, 1984; Daniels, 1989). However, this approach also fails to take into account that black women are regarded as making such remarkable progress in comparison to black men in large part because they are actually compared with white women, a severely disadvantaged group—not with white men, the group with the greatest occupational/economic advantage and with whom black men are typically compared.

That black women's so-called privileged status in the job market is a threat to black men has been seriously argued in the past (Bernard, 1966; Moynihan, 1967; Bock, 1969; Hare and Hare, 1970). More recently, black women's success in education and the job market is said to be an important factor in the decline since the late 1970s of black men in college and in professional and graduate school as well as in the professions (Daniels, 1989). Thus, for example, concerned by the "displacement" of men by women in the job market, including the professions, Hacker (1984:128) suggests that "we already have had some glimpses of what can occur when women advance at a faster pace than men. Consider the [negative] experience of black Americans." He then goes on to describe the so-called greater opportunities and experiences of black women to the detriment of black men. To be sure, black men suffer tremendous burdens in the U.S. economy. Serious attention is required to deal with these problems. That, however, requires getting at root causes—the closing of inner-city factories, capital's demand for ever-cheaper labor, the outrageously high unemployment rates among blacks, and so on. It is both inaccurate and divisive to blame black women.

Comparisons with White Men

Finally, black women are rarely compared to white men. When they are, one of two stereotypes is put forth. Either black women are described as "having it made," just like white men, or they are charged with having displaced white men from the professions, particularly the most prestigious occupations.

What is the logic behind these apparently contradictory beliefs? The image that black women are a privileged group, as are white men, is usually based on income (Nelson, 1975; Bergmann, 1985; Malveaux, 1990). White men have the highest incomes, and black women have made greater relative gains in income than either black men or white women since World War II. However, it cannot be stressed too strongly that these income gains are *relative:* black women have come from an incredibly low starting point. It is also important, as we have seen, which race/gender comparison group is used. Too, there is an element of wishful thinking—that is, a positive image that the glass is half-full denies the reality that it is also half-empty.

The opposite image, that black women have gained in the professions at the expense of white men, stems from the fact that the "loss" of almost total control (i.e., percentage decline over time) in elite male professions for white men is described while the extraordinarily high *rate* of increase of black women is emphasized compared to where they were in 1960. This is part of the larger view that white men have been displaced by women and minorities, with minority women being the most advantaged of all. Thus, as we saw in Chapter 1, it was reported that between 1966 and 1979, white men's share of the professional job market fell by 29 percent while that of black women multiplied more than 3.5 times (Rule, 1982). At the same time, black women are said to have experienced enormously high rates of increase—as much as tenfold—in some of the most prestigious male professions (Herbers, 1983). This picture of white men's losses and black women's gains distorts the truth about black women's mobility and white men's loss of control, given that in 1980 black women represented less that 1 percent of all people in those elite male professions despite their tenfold increase.

In short, how we understand black women's progress in the professions depends in large part on the race/gender group to which they are compared. Moreover, the effects of race are not necessarily the same for men and women. Therefore, we must see the degree to which black men and black women have had similar or different experiences in their access to the professions. Likewise, the effects of gender are very likely to be different for white women and black women.

Rather than asking the polarized question, Are black women doubly advantaged or doubly disadvantaged? a comparison of black women with each of the other three race/gender groups allows us to ask a series of more meaningful questions: For example, have black women gained greater access to the more traditional elite male professions with privilege and power, or has their increase taken place primarily in categories of the professions that are less privileged? Have black women made inroads only or especially in areas that were "women's"—which, in practice, means that they had been reserved for white women? Have black women gained access to those professions only when white women were not entering at the same rate as in earlier decades? Have black women gained more access in professions in which black men were already well represented? Have black women been able to increase in professions in which white men began to show less interest? Have black women gained more access to the newest, fastest-growing, or largest expanding professions? Or have they gained access mainly in those professions experiencing a decline in automony or income?

A PROFILE OF BLACK WOMEN IN THE PROFESSIONS, 1960–1980

The most important facts to realize about black women in the professions are that (1) just as is the case with black men, their numbers in these occupations have been so small that any increase cannot come close to altering the white complexion of the professions overall; and that (2) they were so severely underrepresented in 1960 that their gains, although real, can easily be seen as greater than they actually were.

Black women gained more than a half-million new jobs in the professions/technical areas between 1960 and 1980. (See Chapter 4, Table 4.1.) Of these, 90 percent were in the professions and 10 percent in the technical fields. However, as with white women and black men, this represents a little over one-fifth of all new jobs for black women, even though the professions grew 35 percent overall during this time. Once again, these increases for the three disadvantaged race/gender groups were considerably less than for the most privileged group of white men, for whom more than one-third (35.1 percent) of the new jobs were in the professions/technical fields.

Within this growth of a half-million new professional jobs, black women gained less than 10,000 in the elite male professions. This is an incredibly small number that represents only 1.3 percent of all new elite male professional positions between 1960 and 1980, far less than black women's proportionate growth in the labor force. This is in contrast to the more than a half-million new elite male jobs gained by white men. And contrary to any suggestions that women "outdistanced' men in the black community, black women secured less than half as many new elite jobs (9,332) as black men (20,924).

Black women did better in the nonelite male professions, securing 59,411 new jobs. And, as was the case for white women, black women's greatest numerical increases occurred in female professions, with more than 300,000 new jobs. Their second-largest increase was in the neutral professions: there they gained almost 110,000 new jobs. And while black women gained only about 60,000 new jobs in the technical fields, it should be remembered that this number is six times greater than their gains in the elite male professions.

Given this profile of black women's occupational growth between 1960 and 1980, where were black women concentrated in 1980 in the professional labor market? Let us look at the top 10 jobs with the largest numerical growth and compare them with those professions with the highest growth rate for black women. (See Table 7.1.) In terms of the *number of new jobs,* as one might expect, black women were able to make gains in virtually the same professions as white women, with only one exception for each: black women increased in vocational and educational counseling, while white women increased in computer programming. Thus half of the top 10 largest new jobs for black women were in the female professions and technical fields (elementary education, nursing, social work, prekindergarten and kindergarten teaching, and clinical-laboratory technology). The other half were in gender-neutral professions (personnel and labor relations, secondary education, and counseling) and nonelite male professions (accounting and nonspecific college teaching). Eight were among the 10 fastest-growing professions in the labor force overall. So black women, like white women and black men, were likely to increase in professions where the total number of jobs had been expanding the most. This accords with

TABLE 7.1 TEN LARGEST-GROWING PROFESSIONS/TECHNICAL FIELDS FOR BLACK WOMEN, 1960–1980: NUMBERS AND GROWTH RATES

Increase Based on Raw Numbers			Increase Based on Percentage Growth		
	Largest Numerical Increase			Largest Percentage Increase	
(1) Occupation	(2) Number	(3) Percent	(4) Occupation	(5) Percent	(6) Number
Elementary-school teacher	120,655	163.2	Computer programmer	82,135.0	7,454
Nurse	81,175	212.9	Industrial engineer	6,682.7	2,673
Social worker	49,910	776.8	Personnel + labor relations	3,338.8	29,826
Account	33,784	2,662.6	Engineer/nec	3,019.0	604
Personnel + labor relations	29,826	3,338.8	Counselor	2,842.8	15,481
Secondary-school teacher	22,631	114.1	Accountant	2,662.6	33,784
Prekindergarten + K teacher	17,491	304.5	Lawyer	2,644.8	3,914
Clinical-lab technician	16,484	589.7	College teacher (nonsp.)	1,780.8	9,516
Counselor	15,481	2,842.8	Civil engineer	1,512.2	333
College teacher (nonsp.)	9,516	1,780.8	Drafter	1,467.0	2,391

much of the research that indicates blacks have been able to gain access to professional training and occupations that have expanded in numbers and have not threatened white male dominance (Blackwell, 1981; Landry, 1987).

Again, as one might expect, since in 1960 black women were the least likely of all race/gender groups to be employed in male professions, this is where their strongest *growth rate* occurred. Thus 6 of the top 10 jobs were in male professions, and 1 was in a male technical field. Black women also experienced high growth rates in 3 neutral professions: computer programming, personnel and labor relations, and counseling. Once again, black women's progress in the professions was almost identical to that of white women—the only difference is that white women's largest growth rates were concentrated in engineering (5 of the 7 male professions). Black women, however, did well in engineering (3 of the 7 male professions), but they "traded" 2 engineering jobs for accounting (a nonelite male profession) and drafting (a male technical field).

In sum, as with white women, while black women's growth rate was greatest in the male professions, the largest numbers of new jobs opening up to them between 1960 and 1980 were in the traditional female professions and technicians. This is dramatized by the data in Table 7.2. There we see that by 1980, black women had the highest concentration of new jobs among all four race/gender groups in elementary education, nursing, and social work. Thus, for example, social work, one of the fastest growing professions between 1960 and 1980 (with almost 305,000 new jobs), is where black women gained 2 1/2 to 3 times more new jobs (826 new jobs per 100,000 black women in the labor force) than did black men (327 new jobs per 100,000 black men) or white women (287 new jobs per 100,000 white women). This increased to almost 6 times for black women in comparison to white men (141 new jobs per 100,000 white men). In fact, as will become apparent, black women had the highest concentration of new jobs of all race/gender groups in each of the following professions and technical areas: the female occupations, in addition to elementary education, nursing, and social work, include library work, prekindergarten and kindergarten teaching, and clinical-laboratory technology; the gender-neutral professions include personnel and labor relations, and counseling. Not only were these large expanding occupations, they were also where black women made the greatest gains among all race/gender groups.

BLACK WOMEN AND WHITE MEN:
THE INDEX OF RELATIVE ADVANTAGE

A look at the Index of Relative Advantage (see Chapter 5, pp. 67–69) for black women in relation to white men throughout the professional/technical labor market (Table 7.3, Columns 1, 2) challenges the assertions that black women either "have it made," just like white men, or that they have displaced white men from the most prestigious professions. First, it is abundantly clear that in the *elite* male professions, black women made *no* discernible moves toward parity with white men: in 1980 as in 1960, black women were tragically and very severely underrepresented (the ratio moved from 0.02 to 0.08). It is important to remember here that some might argue black women made a fourfold increase in the elite male professions. However, I would argue this is a gross manipulation of statistics, when black women remain *very severely* underrepresented, not even being able to move to a level of severe underrepresentation, let alone parity, over 20 years of major social change.

While black women did better in the *nonelite* male professions, they were still severely underrepresented in comparison to white men in 1980 (the ratio moved from 0.03 to 0.23 over the 20 years). This same pattern held true in the male technical areas as well. In fact, examination of the large detailed male-dominated professions reinforces this finding. (See Table 7.4, Columns 1,2.) Black women remained severely or very severely underrepresented in all but two nonelites: in accounting and nonspecific college teaching black women became moderately underrepresented. This, too, was the pattern for one male technical field, engineering and science technology/nec. Thus, despite black women's high rate of increase as doctors, lawyers, psychologists, and the like, and despite whatever access they were able to achieve over time, black women did not begin to challenge white male control of these coveted positions. Nor did they catch

TABLE 7.2 PROFESSIONS/TECHNICAL FIELDS WITH GREATEST NUMERICAL GROWTH—FOR OCCUPATIONS WITH AT LEAST 100 NEW JOBS PER 100,000 PEOPLE IN THE LABOR FORCE

White Men		Black Men		White Women		Black Women	
Prof/Tech Fields	No. New Jobs /100,000 White Men in the Labor Force	Prof/Tech Fields	No. New Jobs /100,000 Black Men in the Labor Force	Prof/Tech Fields	No. New Jobs /100,000 White Women in the Labor Force	Prof/Tech Fields	No. New Jobs /100,000 Black Women in the Labor Force
Element.-sch. teach	623	Element-sch. teach	465	Account	697	Element-sch. teach	1,029
Personnel lab. rels	405	Personnel lab. rels	435	Personnel + lab. rels	429	Nurse	884
College teach–non	372	Account.	370	College teach–non	290	Social worker	826
Computer progrmer.	362	Social worker	327	Social worker	287	Account.	610
Lawyer	292	Elec. engr technic.	190	Computer progrmr.	204	Personnel + lab. rel	542
Engineer/nec	246	Computer progrmer.	170	Clinical-lab. tech.	186	Counselor	280
Elec.-engr technic.	195	Drafter	157	Counselor	148	Clinical-lab. tech.	261
Account.	191	Counselor	156	Lawyer	137	PreK + kindertea	232
Social worker	141	College teach–non	155	Engr + sci tech/nec	118	College teach–non	169
Engr + sci. tech/nec	135	Engr + sci tech/nec	121			Computer progrmer	138
Industr. engineer	104	Electrical engineer	111			Eng + sci tech/nec	131
Physician	101	Lawyer	104			Librarian	100
		Clinical-lab. tech.	102				

up with white women, who reached parity with white men in several of the nonelite male professions.

The one place where black women made very important and substantial increases toward more equitable access with white men was in the rapidly expanding *gender-neutral professions*. In Table 7.3, Columns 1 and 2, we see that black women moved from being moderately (0.57) to only slightly (0.77) underrepresented. And while they moved toward parity with white men in the *female professions*, black women were still more than five times as likely to occupy such positions in 1980. In both gender-neutral and female technical fields, it appears that black women became heavily overrepresented. Thus the professions/technical fields with the lowest status were where black women seemed to become heavily concentrated.

Examination of the large detailed gender-neutral and female professions/technical areas (see Table 7.4, Columns 1,2) expands our knowledge of this picture. In the gender-neutral professions, black women made dramatic increases in access to counseling, and personnel and labor relations, with more modest increases in most others (secondary education, research work, and editing/reporting). The female professions show a mixed pattern: social work and teaching/nec became *more* heavily black female, as did clinical laboratory work among the technical fields; librarianship, elementary education, and nursing moved toward parity with white men, with large black female overrepresentations remaining in 1980.

In short, black women neither "had it made" like white men in the elite male professions, nor did their large "rate of increase" there portend well for their final representation in comparison to white men. Where they, in fact, did do well in terms of gaining access appears most in the gender-neutral professions.[1] On the other hand, black women became over-represented or increased their overrepresentation in several of the lower-status or non-male-dominated professions and technical fields: counseling, secondary education, social work, teaching/nec, and clinical-laboratory work. Once again, not only were these some of the largest and fastest-expanding positions in the professions and technical areas, but they were also the public-service-oriented professions that S. Collins (1983) argued were the ones for which blacks were recruited to quell inner-city disturbances in the wake of 1960s' urban riots.

BLACK WOMEN AND BLACK MEN: THE INDEX OF RELATIVE ADVANTAGE

One of the most inaccurate and persistent arguments against black women is that they somehow have been able to secure better jobs than black men, in all areas

TABLE 7.3 INDEX OF RELATIVE ADVANTAGE FOR BLACK WOMEN IN COMPARISON TO WHITE MEN, BLACK MEN, AND WHITE WOMEN: INTERMEDIATE ANALYSIS

	Black Women/ White Men		Black Women/ Black Men		Black Women/ White Women		Difference 1960–1980		
	1960 (1)	1980 (2)	1960 (3)	1980 (4)	1960 (5)	1980 (6)	Black Women/ White Men (7)	Black Women/ Black Men (8)	Black Women/ White Women (9)
Professions									
Elite male	0.02	0.08	0.15	0.35	0.26	0.48	+0.06	+0.20	+0.22
Nonelite male	0.03	0.23	0.20	0.65	0.18	0.56	+0.20	+0.45	+0.38
Neutral	0.57	0.77	1.64	1.33	0.39	0.67	+0.20	−0.31	+0.28
Female	8.87	5.34	9.62	5.24	0.57	0.92	−3.53	−4.38	+0.35
Profs. subtotal	0.72	0.97	2.93	2.06	0.50	0.80	+0.25	−0.87	+0.30
Technical fields									
Male	0.05	0.23	0.32	0.46	0.29	0.74	+0.18	+0.14	+0.46
Neutral	0.52	2.40	1.37	2.33	0.41	1.14	+1.88	+0.96	+0.73
Female	2.59	3.84	3.06	2.73	0.49	0.71	+1.25	−0.33	+0.22
Techs. subtotal	0.19	0.54	0.99	0.96	0.41	0.79	+0.35	−0.03	+0.38

TABLE 7.4 INDEX OF RELATIVE ADVANTAGE FOR BLACK WOMEN IN COMPARISON TO WHITE MEN, BLACK MEN, AND WHITE WOMEN. DETAILED PROFESSIONS/TECHNICAL FIELDS, 1960–1980

Large Detailed Professions/ Technical Fields	Black Women/ Wh. Men		Black Women/ Bl. Men	
	1960 (1)	1980 (2)	1960 (3)	1980 (4)
Male professions				
Elite				
Lawyer	0.01	0.10	0.11	0.50
Physician	0.04	0.09	0.18	0.34
Nonelite				
Civil engineer	0.00	0.02	0.03	0.09
Elect. + elect. engr.	0.00	0.05	0.00	0.20
Mechanical engineer	0.00	0.02	0.05	0.07
Chemist	0.05	0.20	0.26	0.46
Engineer/nec	0.00	0.03	0.06	0.11
Pharmacist	0.02	0.17	0.14	0.67
Industrial engineer	0.01	0.14	0.13	0.51
Accountant	0.05	0.57	0.65	1.49
Designer	0.09	0.20	0.74	0.58
Nonspecif. coll. tea.	0.22	0.41	0.87	1.06
Clergy	0.04	0.04	0.06	0.07
Gender-neutral profs.				
Voc. + ed. cnslr.	0.45	2.36	3.05	1.84
Personnel + lab. rels.	0.19	1.01	1.80	1.27
Computer programmer	0.23	0.37	1.60	0.82
Editor/reporter	0.08	0.46	1.06	1.50
Research worker	0.24	0.67	1.61	1.53
Secondary-sch. tea.	1.09	1.27	1.99	2.32
Painter/sculptor	0.14	0.22	0.82	0.52
Female professions				
Social worker	3.26	4.99	2.66	2.55
Librarian	4.26	3.92	9.72	5.29
Elementary-sch. tea.	8.84	3.96	8.99	4.81
Nurse	42.62	26.28	31.39	20.60
Pre K + kinder. tea.	—	49.86	—	20.49
Teacher/nec	1.39	1.67	2.75	2.60
Male technical fields				
E + E engr. tech.	0.04	0.15	0.22	0.28
Drafter	0.01	0.11	0.11	0.23
Eng. + sci. tech./nec	0.10	0.44	0.57	0.96
Female technical fields				
Clinical-lab. tech.	2.77	4.13	3.22	2.72

Black Women/ Wh. Women		Difference 1960–1980		
		BlWomen/ White Men	BlWomen/ Black Men	BlWomen/ WhWomen
1960 (5)	1980 (6)	(7)	(8)	(9)
0.22	0.47	+0.09	+0.39	+0.25
0.24	0.53	+0.05	+0.16	+0.29
0.22	0.50	+0.02	+0.06	+0.28
0.00	0.74	+0.05	+0.20	+0.74
0.25	0.60	+0.02	+0.02	+0.35
0.29	0.61	+0.15	+0.20	+0.32
0.19	0.54	+0.03	+0.05	+0.35
0.14	0.41	+0.15	+0.53	+0.27
0.13	0.57	+0.13	+0.38	+0.44
0.11	0.60	+0.52	+0.84	+0.49
0.18	0.23	+0.11	−0.16	+0.05
0.46	0.57	+0.19	+0.19	+0.11
0.92	0.45	0.00	+0.01	−0.47
0.30	1.41	+1.91	−1.21	+1.11
0.19	0.97	+0.82	−0.53	+0.78
0.30	0.65	+0.14	−0.78	+0.35
0.06	0.32	+0.38	+0.44	+0.26
0.30	0.70	+0.43	−0.08	+0.40
0.54	0.72	+0.18	+0.33	+0.18
0.16	0.18	+0.08	−0.30	+0.02
0.86	1.91	+1.73	−0.11	+1.05
0.33	0.57	−0.34	−4.43	+0.24
0.67	0.95	−4.88	−4.18	+0.28
0.47	0.75	−16.34	−10.79	+0.28
0.63	1.16	—	—	+0.53
0.29	0.54	+0.28	−0.15	+0.25
0.40	1.06	+0.11	+0.06	+0.66
0.09	0.38	+0.10	+0.12	+0.29
0.28	0.78	+0.34	+0.39	+0.50
0.51	0.94	+1.36	−0.50	+0.43

including the professions. In fact, more than 25 years ago, Bernard (1966) labeled this a problem of the "unnatural superiority" of black women. This led
Nathan and Julia Hare (1970:66) to argue that "the positive virtues of being a
black woman—easier access to jobs and financial favors compared to black
men—have negative consequences in that they deprecate the black male." More
recently, Malveaux (1990) articulates a major problem facing black women as
one where some researchers attempt to turn a major disadvantage of black
women—that is, the labor-market disadvantage of *black men*—into a so-called
advantage—that is, the closer job status and incomes between black men and
women than between white men and women.

To be sure, historically black women's occupational alternatives have been
very limited. The one avenue out of poverty and being a maid or domestic
worker was higher education. However, in reality the position of black women
in the professions has been explained mostly by two facts: first, the vast majority
of black women have always been and continue to be employed predominantly
in low-paying, low-status teaching jobs. Second, the emphasis on the fact that
black women are better represented in high-level male-dominated professions in
the black community than are white women in the white community misses the
point that black women are still considerably less likely than black men to gain
access to these jobs: male privilege still operates here. Let us look at the data.

According to the Index of Relative Advantage, black women moved toward
parity with black men in the male professions between 1960 and 1980, but remained severely underrepresented in the elite (ratio moved from 0.15 to 0.35
between 1960 and 1980) and moderately underrepresented (ratio moved from
0.20 to 0.65) in the nonelite ones by 1980 (see Table 7.3, Columns 3,4). A
similar pattern occurred in the male technical fields. Thus, while they did significantly better in relation to black men than to white men in the male professions, black women in no way reached parity with black men in either group of
male professions. These findings are quite remarkable given the social scientific
and media support for the notion of black female advantage or superiority in the
black professional community.

On the other hand, a review of the large detailed professions *does* give us
some insight into those male professions in which black women *have* made
important gains in relation to black men. (See Table 7.4, Columns 3,4.) For
example, in nonspecific college teaching (0.87 to 1.06) and accounting (0.65 to
1.49), between 1960 and 1980 black women either reached parity or became
moderately overrepresented in relation to black men. In these two large expanding occupations, black women's access increased significantly. In several others,
black women became at least moderately (instead of severely or very severely)
underrepresented: this was true for pharmacy, industrial engineering, and chemistry, as well as for the elite profession of law. In contrast, the one place where

black women "lost out" was in design: here they became more underrepresented in relation to black men over time (the ratio moved from 0.74 to 0.58).

In sum, black women moved closer toward parity with black men than with white men throughout the male professions, although they *remained severely or moderately underrepresented*—that is, they did *not* reach parity with black men. On the other hand, when looking at large individual nonelite professions, we learned that black women became *more concentrated than black men* in the large expanding accounting profession while they "lost out" in design. And given that black women have become segregated in a number of occupations in which they had reached parity (as we shall see), is it probable that nonspecific college teaching—in which parity was reached in 1980—will become more heavily concentrated with black women over time? (This question also applies to the one male technical field, engineering and science technology/nec, in which black women reached parity with black men in 1980: the ratio moved from 0.57 to 0.96.)

Another set of trends emerged outside the male-dominated professions. As expected, black women decreased their high levels of overrepresentation in the *female professions* (from a ratio of 9.62 to 5.24) and in the *female technical fields* (from 3.06 to 2.73). (See Table 7.3, Columns 3,4.) Despite these changes, black women remained very severely overrepresented in comparison to black men. Unexpectedly, black women *started out* severely overrepresented in the gender-neutral professions in 1960 (the ratio was 1.64). By 1980 they had moved toward parity (the ratio was 1.33) and were more moderately overrepresented. What these findings tell us, then, is not that black women were increasing their access to the gender-neutral professions, but rather that black men were increasing *their* access in relation to black women in these occupations. On the other hand, it is the case that black women began and ended in a position of greater representation than black men in the gender-neutral professions.

In the *gender-neutral technical fields,* the trend was just the opposite. Here black women moved from being moderately to very severely overrepresented between 1960 and 1980 (from 1.37 to 2.33). In fact, it appears that in both the gender-neutral and female-dominated technical fields, black women were more concentrated than black men. Not so the male technical fields, where black women moved from being severely to moderately underrepresented over the 20 years (from 0.32 to 0.46).

Examination of the large *neutral professions* reveals two patterns in the black community that clearly segregated black men from black women. (See Table 7.4, Columns 3,4.) In secondary education (where the ratio moved from 1.99 to 2.32 between 1960 and 1980) and editing/reporting (from 1.06 to 1.50), black women became more concentrated than black men. In contrast, in computer programming (from 1.60 to 0.82) and painting/sculpting (from 0.82 to 0.52), black men became more concentrated than black women. As already noted, this same phenomenon occurred in two nonelite male professions: accounting, which became more heavily black female (from 0.65 to 1.49), and design, which became more heavily black male (from 0.74 to 0.58).

As these examples demonstrate, the more detailed analyses provide new insights into the occupational positions attainable by black women in relation to black men in the professions. In the first place, while black women did make moves toward parity with black men in the male professions, they did not reach equality with them. In no way are black women "superior to" or "more advantaged than" black men in either nonelite or elite male professions. Second, black women started out overrepresented in the neutral professions and decreased that overrepresentation over time. Third, within the black professional community, gender concentration or segregation appears to have *increased*—for both men and women. And fourth, black women appear to have gained and lost access in relation to black men in the smaller *technical-oriented*[2] gender-neutral (and nonelite male) professions such as computer programming, painting/sculpting, and accounting. This is in contrast to black women's gains to the largest-expanding *public-service-oriented* gender-neutral and female professions (such as counseling, personnel and labor relations, and social work) when compared to white men (and to white women, as we will see in the following analysis).

BLACK WOMEN AND WHITE WOMEN: THE INDEX OF RELATIVE ADVANTAGE

Black women do appear to have gained their greatest access throughout the professions in relation to white women—certainly much more than in relation to black men or white men.[3] However, this does not lead to the conclusion, as some have argued, that black women are more "advantaged" than white women or that black women are "doubly benefited" because of their race and gender statuses.

A review of the data on black women throughout the professional hierarchy between 1960 and 1980 in comparison to white women reveals a consistent pattern of increasing access. (See Table 7.3, Columns 5,6.) Thus in 1960 black women were only one-fourth as likely as white women to be working in *elite male professions*. By 1980 this improved to one-half as likely.[4] For the *gender-neutral professions*, black women moved to two-thirds as likely as white women to be employed; and in the female professions, black women increased from about half as likely to almost complete parity with white women in 1980. Similar trends occurred among the *technical fields*. On the one hand, then, black women increased their access overall in relation to white women throughout the professions. On the other hand, they did so in an inverse relation: the higher the gender status of the occupation, the less likely it was that parity was achieved. In these "intermediate-level" categories (from a high of elite male-dominated professions to a low of female-dominated technical fields), parity was reached only in the *female professions,* precisely where black women have always been most likely to be found. What is so interesting is that black women were substantially less likely than white women even to be in the female professions in 1960. So real progress for black women is that by 1980 they were at parity in the lowest-status professions!

A look at the detailed professions (see Table 7.4, Columns 5,6) reveals one further piece of important information in the gender-neutral and female professions: here it appears that black women not only gained increased access but became increasingly concentrated in several of them: vocational and educational counseling, social work, and prekindergarten and kindergarten teaching. The question arises: Were those professions where parity was reached by black women with white women in 1980 actually on their way to becoming overrepresented with black women? If so, we would have to add personnel and labor relations, elementary education, and clinical-laboratory work to the list of professions and technical fields in which black women were becoming increasingly likely to find work in comparison to white women. Clearly, this would represent an increase in the level of racial segregation among women.

The fact of black women's increasing concentration in some of the female and gender-neutral professions/technical fields leads us to ask: Were black women actually making these gains as white women either left these lower-status professions or did not enter them as much as before because of better opportunities elsewhere? A somewhat different analysis leads to the conclusion that this is probably the case. Earlier I made use of the Index of Representation (see Chapter 3, "The Index of Representation" p. 48). This allowed us to see the *proportionate shares* that each race/gender group secured in particular occupations as they changed in size in an ever-expanding labor force.

Such an analysis of the detailed professions can be found in Table 7.5 It shows us that black women made gains and/or became increasingly overrepresented in female professions/technical fields where white women were decreasing their "share" of the profession (i.e., were decreasing their level of overrepresentation in the profession in relation to the labor force as a whole) between 1960 and 1980. These included social work, librarianship, nursing, prekindergarten and kindergarten teaching, teaching/nec, and clinical-laboratory technology. This process also occurred in two of the gender-neutral professions, counseling and secondary education.[5] In addition, the male-dominated and gender-neutral professions in which white men decreased their share thus provided greater opportunities for white women: for example, accounting, design, and nonspecific college teaching (although college teaching did not quite reach the criterion for change) in the nonelite male professions and painting/sculpting in the gender-neutral professions.[6,7] In short, black women's increasing concentration in tra-

ditional female professions and some neutral professions appears related to the
better chances for white women in selected male-dominated and neutral professions where white men were decreasing their levels of overrepresentation. And
recall that, as was emphasized in Chapter 3, the fact that white women decreased
their overrepresentation should in no way be taken to mean they were not at or
above parity of representation in the profession as in the labor force.

In sum, it seems quite clear that black women were *not* more advantaged than
white women: they did not even reach parity with white women in the professions, except in the low-status female professions, where black women have
always been most heavily employed.[8] On the other hand, black women made
their best overall improvement in relation to white women (but not black men or
white men) throughout the professions/technical fields. However, they also
tended to become segregated (or overly concentrated) in some of the very same
public-service professions in which the black middle class was able to make
gains during the War against Poverty and the 1960–1970 era of affirmative-
action legislation, as was the case for black men.

Finally, the data suggest that not only did black women make their greatest
gains in relation to white women, but also that black women were able to make
these gains, in large part, because white women were not entering certain professions at the same rate in 1980 as they had in the past. Rather, white women's
opportunities appear to have expanded in some of the higher-status professions,
thereby "making room" for black women's increased access to and concentration
in the lower-status professions.

CONCLUSION

I conclude this chapter by answering the questions with which it began. First, it
does appear that black women gained access to and became overrepresented in
those professions that white women were not entering at quite the same high
rate as 20 years earlier. This included not only most of the large female professions (i.e., social work, librarianship, nursing, prekindergarten and kindergarten
teaching, teaching/nec), but several of the gender-neutral ones (counseling and
secondary education) as well as clinical-laboratory technology in the low-status
female technical fields. What this also means is that racial segregation (in the
sense of being shunted into certain places in the occupational hierarchy on the
basis of race; the occupations themselves do not necessarily become segregated)
between black and white women appears to have been on the *increase* in the
professions, even as black women made greater inroads into the professional/
technical labor force.

Second, these professions were primarily among the fastest growing with the
largest numerical expansion. So long as the occupation was expanding,
whites—both men and women—were not threatened by black women's greater

**TABLE 7.5   INDEX OF REPRESENTATION FOR DETAILED PROFESSIONS/
TECHNICAL FIELDS, 1960 AND 1980, FOR SELECTED OCCUPATIONS WITH
MORE THAN 100,000 PEOPLE IN 1970**

Large Detailed Professions/ Technical Fields	(A)* White Men		(B)** White Women		(C)*** Black Women	
	1960 (1)	1980 (2)	1960 (3)	1980 (4)	1960 (5)	1980 (6)
Male professions						
(Nonelite)						
Accountant	1.36	1.08	—	—	0.06	0.62
Designer	1.31	1.14	—	—	0.12	0.23
Coll. Tea-Nonspec.****	1.29	1.20	—	—	0.29	0.49
Male technical fields						
Engr + Sci Tech/nec****	1.37	1.28	—	—	0.14	0.57
Gender-neutral professions						
Voc + ed counselor	0.94	0.75	1.41	1.25	0.42	1.76
Personnel + lab rels	1.10	1.00	1.10	1.04	0.21	1.01
Computer programr	—	—	0.92	0.74	0.27	0.48
Editor/reporter	1.03	0.91	—	—	0.08	0.42
Research worker	1.17	1.07	—	—	0.28	0.72
Second-sch. teach	—	—	1.60	1.39	0.86	1.00
Painter/sculptor	1.15	0.99	—	—	—	—
Female professions						
Social worker	—	—	1.99	1.40	1.71	2.68
Librarian	—	—	2.87	2.08	0.96	1.19
Elem.-sch. teach	—	—	2.76	1.80	—	—
Nurse	—	—	3.21	2.35	1.50	1.77
PreK + kinder. teach	—	—	3.22	2.25	2.04	2.61
Teacher/nec	—	—	2.31	1.74	0.68	0.93
Female technical fields						
Clinical-lab tech	—	—	2.34	1.79	1.19	1.70

*Selected occupations in which white men decrease their share.
**Selected occupations in which white women decrease their share.
***Selected occupations in which black women increase their share.
****Although change is measured by a move of at least 0.10 points in the index, in this case the
 index moves only 0.09 points, but is included here because it is in the same direction as the change
 discussed.
—Not applicable.

access to these intermediate-level and lower-status professions. In addition,
counseling was the one profession in which white men actually decreased their
"share" of the occupation between 1960 and 1980: one could say that white men
"lost out" because they became increasingly underrepresented compared to their
proportion in the labor force overall. This was one of the places where black
women (and black men) moved from being underrepresented to being moderately overrepresented, while white women increased their overrepresentation in
this occupation.

Third, many of these professions were precisely the public-service professions
to which black men (although in somewhat fewer occupations than black

women) were found to gain access between 1960 and 1980. The demands of the civil-rights and women's movements were responded to. In particular, some social scientists have argued that these are the professions into which blacks were recruited to control the black inner-city disturbances of the 1960s. Because these jobs were (and still are) heavily dependent on public funds, middle-class black women's (and men's) employment has been subject to the prevailing political winds and can disappear at any time.

Fourth, black women did not seem to make gains in jobs where black men were already well represented. In fact, it appears that black women and black men tended to become increasingly segregated from one another in their professional employment. Moreover, while they were more likely to enter public-service helping professions when compared to whites (both women and men), black women were more likely to be found in technically-oriented professions such as accounting and editing/reporting when compared directly with black men. While black men were also employed in technically-oriented professions, men and women in the black community were employed in significantly different occupations: black women as accountants, editors/reporters, and secondary-school teachers, black men as designers, computer programmers, and painters/sculptors.

Finally, this analysis makes it abundantly clear that black women are not "more advantaged than" nor do they "take jobs away from" white men, black men, *or* white women. In the male-dominated professions, black women have done particularly poorly, especially in relation to white men, who remained firmly in control. While black women made important moves toward parity *outside* the male professions, it cannot be overemphasized that much of this greater access to the professions appears to have been a resegregation of black women into some of the lower levels of the professional hierarchy.[9] This development is not without its contradictions, since it means that many black women who had previously been unable to achieve professional jobs were increasingly able to do so—even if primarily in the female professions and technical fields to which black women have been traditionally relegated. Moreover, we must remember that black women did best in relation to all three race/gender groups in the gender-neutral professions—where their increasing access provided them with greater moves toward parity with the other three race/gender groups.

Chapter 8

THE HALF-EMPTY GLASS: CAN IT EVER BE FILLED?

TWENTY YEARS OF CHANGE: A SUMMARY OF WHAT HAPPENED IN THE PROFESSIONS 1960–1980

Introduction

The period between 1960 and 1980 was a time of remarkable change in the United States. The political and economic expansion of the post-World War II era was manifested, among other things, in a general increase in the sixties and seventies in what are considered to be the "good jobs"—particularly professional occupations. Not only were more of the prized jobs available, but the civil-rights and women's movements catalyzed legislation mandating that these jobs be open to everyone. My purpose in this book has been to investigate the degree to which black women and white women, in relation to black men and white men, were able to participate in these increasing opportunities in the occupational arena. To this end, I have explored the changes experienced by these men and women in the wide array of jobs available in the professional/technical labor force in the United States between 1960 and 1980.

What we have seen is that from one perspective, the glass was half-full by 1980; from another, it was half-empty. Although virtually all major groups in the society benefited from the economic expansion, there were other equally important but not so positive developments. These included the deterioration in job security, autonomy, promotion prospects, and real earnings for many jobs in the economy, including many of the professions. If we look at these changes in work processes and in professional/technical job rewards, questions are raised about the character of what first appeared to be increased opportunities for women and black men. For just one example, it is true that the disadvantaged groups of white women, black women, and black men all gained substantial access to what had been the white male-dominated professions of accounting, design, and nonspecific college teaching. But something else was happening to these professions. Even as they were opening to groups that had been excluded, these professions were in the process of losing their autonomy, relatively high status, and high-level job rewards. As their conditions of work deteriorated, white men moved on to other, more privileged occupations, leaving these deteriorating professions to groups that had heretofore been excluded from them.

In short, disadvantaged groups continued to have *less than equal opportunities;* and when they were offered better jobs, it was more than likely that these jobs were undergoing substantial changes, leading to their decline in attractiveness to the more privileged groups holding them. Although there was a new, much larger glass, many of the jobs contained within it in 1980 had deteriorated from what they had been in the smaller glass of 1960. Because the contents had changed over those 20 years, it becomes no simple matter to say whether by 1980 the glass was half-full or half-empty.

Occupations Providing the Greatest Access to Disadvantaged Groups

The period between 1960 and 1980 was one of rapid changes in the professions, not the least of which were changes in who occupied them. As the media consistently reported, women and minority men made definite progress in the professions, to some extent even in those customarily associated with white men. However, the media did not often report that white men participated in those gains as well, particularly in the most desirable male-dominated professions. While it is true that, over these 20 years of major social change, *disadvantaged groups* gained greater access to professional/technical occupations considered as a whole, when we look at these fields individually, we find that only *certain occupations* opened up significantly to women and minority men. And considering these occupations as a whole, race/gender hierarchies continued unchanged or reconstituted themselves with white men at the top of the professional/technical occupational ladder and black women at the bottom.

On the whole, white men retained dominance in the most desired professions as doctors, lawyers, engineers, and the like. A few male-dominated professions lower down the socioeconomic ladder created new opportunities primarily for white women, and secondarily for black men and black women; these included accounting, design, and nonspecific college teaching. Blacks, both men and women, did best in relation to white men *outside* male-dominated professions in such gender-neutral professions as personnel and labor relations, and vocational and educational counseling. Finally, the female-dominated professions/technical areas, typically the domain of white women, provided the greatest openings to black women, especially social work, prekindergarten and kindergarten teaching, elementary education, and clinical-laboratory work.

Increased Segregation and Increased Access

For all four groups of men and women, changes were channeled in several different directions throughout the professions simultaneously. Thus, while some occupations became integrated (i.e., each race/gender group became represented according to its percents in the labor force as a whole), most did not. Rather, they were primarily either preserved for white men or reserved for disadvantaged groups. In both cases, the occupations changed enough to provide openings to other groups, while remaining substantially segregated. Finally, another group of occupations appeared to have really opened up to disadvantaged groups, only to close again, trapping them in jobs that restrict disadvantaged incumbents to them—a form of group resegregation within occupations.[1]

As we have seen, out of the 30 large professions and technical areas[2] studied (which include about four-fifths of all professionals and technicians), very few occupations became *genuinely integrated*. This appears to have been the case for only three male professions: accounting, design, and nonspecific college teaching. (Even here white women moved the closest toward parity with white men; black men and black women were less able to close the gap.) All three of these occupations, even at the beginning of the period, were at the lowest end of the status and income range for male professions, and by the end of the period they had experienced serious deterioration in occupational advantage. Only one gender-neutral profession, personnel and labor relations, which had been a predominantly white occupation in 1960, became perfectly integrated over time for all race/gender groups. In short, most of the desired white male professions remained substantially segregated, with only very modest gains for disadvantaged race/gender groups.

In contrast to the overall increased access, some occupations remained or became increasingly dominated by white men. As we have seen, this is often obscured because an occupation can be preserved for the more advantaged group of white men and still allow women and minority men greater opportunities to enter it in those sectors white men deem as less desirable. This appears to have been the case throughout the elite and most of the nonelite male professions and male technical fields. In such a scenario, women and minority men in no way reach parity of representation with white men in the most desired of professional jobs, white men continue to have access to the "best" jobs, and white men do not "lose" such jobs to disadvantaged groups.

For example, as physicians, clergy, and engineers of many kinds, white men *increased* their overrepresentation in these professions in comparison to their representation in the labor force as a whole. Not only did these professions expand greatly during the period under study, but they also were able to include their traditional population of white men while allowing somewhat greater access to previously excluded groups. In short, as the glass expanded, so did the area allotted to disadvantaged groups. Yet the area reserved for white men grew even more! White men were able to retain or enter higher-tier, more autonomous sectors of these male-dominated professions, while black women, white women, and black men were able to gain access primarily to expanding numbers of routinized and more poorly paid jobs within the very same profession or technical field (see, e.g., Carter and Carter, 1981; Luxemberg, 1985; Robinson and McIlwee, 1989; Roach, 1990).

A major theoretical explanation for this set of circumstances was developed by Barbara F. Reskin and Patricia A. Roos in *Job Queues, Gender Queues* (1990). According to Reskin and Roos, job assignment is part of a "queuing" (i.e., ranking) system. Employers' preferences for workers and workers' preferences for jobs are both queued: "*labor queues* order groups of workers in terms of their attractiveness to employers, and *job queues* rank jobs in terms of their attractiveness to workers" (p. 29). This system determines who is hired in which positions: "employers hire workers from as high in the labor queue as possible, and workers accept the best jobs available to them. As a result the best jobs go to the most preferred workers, and less attractive jobs go to workers lower in the labor queue; bottom-ranked workers may go jobless, and the worst jobs may be left unfilled" (p. 30). Interestingly, this idea was first developed on the basis of race, not gender, by Thurow (1972).

Reskin and Roos apply these general principles to women and men in male-dominated jobs throughout the U.S. labor force during the approximate period of my study. Women are hired at the bottom of a given occupation and cannot move up until men abandon the positions at the top. During the 1970s, this movement accelerated due to a number of factors, including de-skilling of jobs (making them less desirable to men), changes in technology and work settings, declining wages and other rewards (autonomy, career prospects, etc.), the weakening of male labor unions, changing demand for workers, and affirmative-action policies. The result was an influx of women into jobs that men no longer wanted. Certain male occupations had undergone, in Reskin and Roos's phrase, "occupational feminization."

Let us extend their analysis beyond the two gender groups to the four race/

gender groups that I studied. As we have seen, white men in the professions either held on to their superior rewards or moved on to something better. Only when white men moved on from the top jobs (which had deteriorated in some way) could the three disadvantaged race/gender groups move up from the bottom. Likewise, although white women were clearly disadvantaged in relation to white men, they were more advantaged in relation to black women (and in some ways in relation to black men, although the picture is mixed).

In the higher-status professions, black men did not significantly improve their position relative to white men, but they were able to gain greater access relative to white women. This was true for most engineering specialties, chemistry, and medicine. Thus black men and white women became concentrated in *different* male professions, depending on the degree to which they were able to gain access. And as white women moved out of lower-status female professions and into higher-level gender-neutral and male professions, black women gained access to places from which they had previously been excluded by preferences for and by white women. Thus black women were last in line to be able to pursue their goals. It was only in those occupations or sectors of occupations that other groups deem less desirable that black women were able to gain access. And once in them, they tended to be trapped there, nominally professionals but unable to move out into other, more prestigious professions.

It is important to understand that even though other groups may filter into a given occupation, that occupation may remain heavily segregated (i.e., largely filled by a given race/gender group). This is true not only for the more prestigious occupations, but for the less prestigious as well. Thus, while all of the large female-dominated professions/technical fields showed significant declines in white women's overrepresentation in comparison to men, white women remained heavily overrepresented.

Although occupational gender segregation has persisted in the female fields, racial factors have also remained significant. Although the much larger numbers of white women ensured that they remained the numerical majority in these occupations, as certain of these fields declined in power, autonomy, and rewards, those white women that were able moved out and into the lower rungs of the male and gender-neutral professions. Black women thus moved into (i.e., became better represented in) social work, nursing, preschool and elementary education, and librarianship as these jobs became increasingly routinized, deskilled, and under male supervision and control (e.g., see Dressel, 1987). At the same time, once in them, black women tended to be restricted to these—and a very few other—professions. Because of their small numbers, however, black women (and black men) could simultaneously be channeled into a few fields and yet have no chance of ever becoming the numerical majority in them.

In sum, both gender and race/gender segregation operated in 1980 as well as in 1960, although the nature of the jobs as well as the exact race/gender composition changed. What did *not* change is that the most privileged occupations remained by and large reserved for white men, and the less privileged remained the province of black women, white women, and—to some extent—black men.

The Greatest Increases in Occupational Segregation, 1960–1980

Outside the already highly segregated male occupations, increased segregation occurred chiefly on the basis of race, although gender itself and race/gender were also important. For example, both black men and black women became overrepresented (in proportion to their share of the overall labor force) or increased their overrepresentation in comparison to white men as counselors, social workers, and clinical-laboratory technicians. However, these were also some of the very occupations in which black women were more heavily overrepresented than black men, when these two groups are compared. In addition, black women were also more likely to be overrepresented than white men as secondary-school teachers and teachers/nec. In short, while segregation was on the rise for black men and black women in certain gender-neutral and female professions/technical areas, it was more severe for black women than for black men.

Increasing segregation occurred also on the basis of gender; for example, in the profession of painting/sculpting. However, two other gender-neutral professions were already disproportionately occupied by white women in 1960: counseling and editing/reporting. Twenty years later, segregation in these occupations had intensified. Again, it is crucial to realize that some jobs became not just feminized, but "race/genderized." When black women and white women are compared, the following occupations moved from being overrepresented by white women to being overrepresented by black women between 1960 and 1980: vocational and educational counseling, social work, and prekindergarten and kindergarten teaching. Given the trend toward increased racial segregation among women, it is quite possible that those occupations in which black women finally reached parity with white women by 1980 will become increasingly occupied by black women. These occupations include a not insignificant number of middle- and lower-level large professions/technical areas: personnel and labor relations, elementary education, clinical-laboratory technology, and electrical-engineering technology.

As Reskin and Roos made clear in their analysis of gender, and as my study points out for race/gender as well, occupational segregation has continued to benefit primarily white men. However, we must also be careful to recognize the advances that individual members of disadvantaged race/gender groups have made. Opening up of professional and technical jobs has meant that some women and minority men have been able to get an education and use their skills to an extent that 20 years earlier would have been impossible. The irony, of course, is that most of these opportunities have come in the less prestigious occupations, and that many of the benefits of professionalism obtained 20 years previously have been seriously eroded. Thus the social and political conditions of professionalism have changed drastically—and often not for the better—in conjunction with the entrance of the previously excluded.

Access to the Elite Professions, 1960–1980

On the one hand, some members of the disadvantaged race/gender groups have indeed been able to enter the domain of white men. On the other hand, these fortunate individuals are just that—individuals—and their success, no matter how hard won and how well deserved, does not signify an advance for their group overall. For example, in the elite male profession of medicine, *black women* might have shown a threefold increase; but because their numbers were so small in comparison to white men, the fortunes *of the group* of black women hardly changed at all. Over the 20 years, black women physicians increased from 0.02 percent to 0.06 percent of all employed black women. Likewise, *black men* not only experienced enormous rates of growth in engineering specialties, but also increased their representation *in relation to white women* (thereby belying the claim that white women take important male-dominated jobs away from black men). Yet black men still represented only 2 percent of all engineers by 1980, far less than their 5.8 percent representation in the overall labor force. In short, despite the many changes in access to an occupation, that change may not be consequential in terms of the group's fortunes.

As we have seen, no matter what changes occurred in a profession, white men did not lose out. Instead, they maintained or increased their overrepresentation over time throughout most of the elite and nonelite male professions and male technical fields. So long as the occupation continued to expand, white men were able to take the best positions for themselves. Either women and minorities entered the lower-tier jobs in elite male professions, as other researchers have shown, or they gained access to occupations that themselves were the lower levels of the nonelite male professions, as my research has shown. In both cases, disadvantaged groups were faced with occupations that were deteriorating in quality and increasing in numbers while white men kept control of the best positions.[3]

A Structural Analysis of Increased Access to the Professions

As we have seen throughout this book, increased opportunities for women and minority men in the 1960–1980 period took place in professions that were undergoing substantial structural change. There are three major structural factors common to occupations that provided greater access: (1) increasing size, (2) decreasing status and/or deteriorating conditions of work, and (3) political pressure on behalf of disadvantaged groups.

Increased Size

One structural factor that correlates positively with increased job opportunities for disadvantaged groups is an increasing number of jobs in a given field. Women and black men were able to gain greater access, both inside and outside the male-dominated professions, to those occupations that expanded greatly in size. In some occupations, such as the nonelite male profession of accounting, expansion was so rapid that there were not enough white men to fill the new positions; thus all three disadvantaged race/gender groups were able to enter this field in large numbers. Other professions/technical areas where women and black men gained greater representation did not increase as much as accounting. Nevertheless, all increased the number of new jobs at a rate much faster than the average growth of most occupations.[4] Thus there were enough jobs so that white men (or white women in the female-dominated professions) could simultaneously increase their numbers and allow other groups in.

Low Status and Job Deterioration

Another important structural feature concerns the changing nature and conditions of work in those occupations that disadvantaged groups have been able to enter. As Reskin and Roos (1990:317) concluded in their study, "the structural change in queues that contributed most to women's inroads in the case study occupations . . . [was] men's reordering of the job queue. By downranking jobs in customarily male occupations, men abandoned them to women. It is this source of occupational feminization that seems most likely to contribute to *nominal* desegregation in the future." In my study, greater integration, as well as increased segregation, occurred in those professions in which working conditions and/or occupational rewards had been deteriorating over time. Most important, in the male professions, greater access for disadvantaged groups occurred mostly in the least desirable professions, if occupational status and level of income are used as criteria. For example, using the Nam-Powers (1983) occupational-status scores (described in Chapter 1), accounting, design, and non-specific college teaching had the lowest ratings and the lowest average incomes of all but one of the large male professions, the ministry.[5]

However, not only were these occupations less desirable to white men to begin with, but they became increasingly so over time. For example, design and non-specific college teaching experienced some of the largest drops in income for women compared to men between 1960 and 1980.[6] In addition, both historical and case-study analyses of accounting and college teaching have described the relationship between the deterioration of these professions in autonomy, control, skill requirements, working conditions, and income (in short, their proletarian-ization) and their increasing feminization.

A similar argument can be made about some of the occupations (especially in the gender-neutral and some of the female professions) that became increasingly segregated by race and gender. As was suggested earlier, the increase of blacks and white women in vocational and educational counseling may well have been related to the enormous expansion of two-year and community colleges in the 1960s. Many black, third-world, and poorer students of all racial/ethnic back-grounds were the first in their families to be able to go to college. The vast number of students requiring vocational and educational counseling mush-roomed. Counselors' caseloads expanded greatly, while the job itself became more narrowly focused and with fewer rewards than those traditionally asso-ciated with counseling well-to-do students attending elite colleges and universi-ties. The situation was similar for book editors: the decline in autonomy, creativ-ity, job security, and income paved the way for increasing feminization of that occupation.

Social work, a classic female profession, likewise became increasingly trans-formed after the mid-1960s as certain aspects of social-welfare work were au-tomated, intake procedures were separated from casework, income-maintenance activities were separated from the provision of social services, and jobs were reclassified, allowing larger jobs to be broken into smaller tasks and female workers to become increasingly less likely to control their own work process under the direction of male supervisors (Dressel, 1987). The de-skilling of social work has led not only to further subordination of women in the social welfare labor process, as Dressel argues; according to my data, it has also led to the access of black women to professional jobs previously held by white women.

In short, it appears that increased access to the professions for disadvantaged groups was largely related to the growth of a large number of jobs newly created in the professions that were deteriorating in power, prestige, income, and au-thority. This was true whether they were male professions (e.g., accounting, design, and college teaching) that became less desirable to white men; gender-neutral professions (e.g., editing/reporting and counseling) that were again, less desirable particularly to white men; or female professions (e.g., social work, and prekindergarten and kindergarten teaching) that were less desirable to white women, given other options available higher up the professional hierarchy. In each case, race/gender groups lower down the occupational hierarchy gained access to professions/technical arenas that favored groups deemed as less desir-able.

Political Pressures

A structural analysis also requires us to look at the ways in which race, gender, and class underlie the organization of basic social relations. How these social relations became transformed through political pressure from oppressed groups is part of the dynamics of change that led to the emergence of more women and the new black middle class in particular professions. So, for example, the growth of blacks in counseling, personnel and labor relations, and social work was not only part of the process of occupational proletarianization; it was also directly linked to the changes that emerged in the 1960s as government employed educated blacks in public-service occupations that served poor and black populations. At that time, poor and minority people were demanding more rights, services, and participation in the society. Also at that time, there were widespread riots and disturbances in deteriorating inner cities that were increasingly becoming ghettos for the black and third-world underclasses.

As earlier in U.S. history when racial segregation was legal, black professionals were able to provide services where whites would not go. This time, however, the new black middle class was more integrated occupationally into white society. Moreover, many blacks were hired by government or private corporations as affirmative-action officers in the 1960s and 1970s, only to be let go in the 1980s once the political and economic climate became less hospitable to blacks. These phenomena help explain the increasing segregation (or incredible overconcentration) of black men and women in such gender-neutral and female-dominated professions as counseling, social work, school teaching at all levels, and personnel and labor relations. That black women were overrepresented in these professions when compared to black men makes it clear that the forces of race and gender are intimately intertwined.

In short, political pressures clearly resulted in the growth of many of these jobs. This helps us to understand why these professions grew, why they grew using the labor of blacks and women, and why this growth did not represent a growth in power, earnings, or prestige to the extent that one would have expected.

In conclusion, certainly there was some integration of professions between 1960 and 1980, but it came about largely because of the growth and substantial change in character of the jobs themselves. Finally, many of these changes occurred because politically less powerful groups pushed for changes in the kinds of jobs and services they needed.

RACIAL AND GENDER SEGREGATION, 1980 TO THE PRESENT

The changes within professions have been so great that, in a sense, it no longer is adequate to talk about doctors or lawyers, engineers or pharmacists. The difference between a lawyer "working" the district court in a city like New York and the corporate counsel of a Wall Street firm, the difference between the pharmacist working for a multimillion-dollar research-based firm and one filling prescriptions in the local drugstore are so great that there well may be more that distinguishes the various positions *within* the professions than there are similarities. Increasingly the major aspect of the profession that they seem to share is the name. Likewise, a lawyer in a large, prestigious corporation and a vocational counselor in a public high school often share little more than the fact that they are both designated as "professionals."

While the degree of segregation seems high, even when we examine the detailed occupational data used in this research, it is clearly an underestimation of both gender and race segregation and stratification *within* an occupation. Several examples are pertinent here. Bielby and Baron (1986) studied gender segregation in occupations using firm-specific job titles. They found that even when men and women worked in the very same occupation, they were given different job titles, and were employed in different firms and geographic locations with different occupational opportunities and rewards. This held true for both professional and nonprofessional jobs. Despite women's increasing access to male-dominated jobs, the researchers concluded that gender segregation was continually being reestablished.

Likewise, Higginbotham (1987) argued that although more blacks may have found their way into professions traditionally associated with whites, they have been slotted into racially segregated positions. Thus during the 1970s, although more black men and black women were working as doctors and nurses, they were employed in public hospitals and municipal clinics as salaried workers servicing poor and minority populations. Such workers are "colonized" professionals. Higginbotham concluded in her study comparing black and white women in the professions that

> the patterns of employment for professional Black women must be discussed. Otherwise as we pass through the 1980s and into the 1990s, we will continue to find Black women teaching in public schools, nursing in public hospitals, and coping with heavy caseloads as social workers for the department of welfare. They will still be colonized professionals, caught in either public sector jobs or the few occupational opportunities in the private sector of the Black community. Maybe then researchers will cease to sing the praises of the tiny minority of Black women in formerly traditional male professions who are able to secure employment in the private sector. (1987:90)

Moreover,

> the minority of Black women who enter traditionally male professions also tend to be ghettoized in the public defender's office, city-run hospitals, dental clinics, and

minority relations for corporate firms. These patterns illustrate the persistence of racial stratification, even in the development of a Black middle class (1987:75).

Within the black community the degree of gender segregation and stratification is likewise evident. For example, in the traditionally male clergy, women numbered as many as one-third of all ministers in some of the historically black denominations in 1989 (Goldman, 1990). Yet black female clergy report they are unable to achieve pulpits of their own, which more recently has led them to open new churches on their own. While white female pastors said they have some similar problems in achieving major pulpits, black women clergy argued "that their plight was intensified by the fact that the church has traditionally been the primary vehicle for black men to exercise both religious and political power" (Goldman, 1990:28).

In science and engineering, another remarkable gender difference has emerged. In the mid-1980s, a landmark was reached when black women received, for the first time, more than half of all doctorates, including science and engineering, awarded to all black American citizens. However, only 6 percent of all science degrees awarded to black women were in the higher-paying and more prestigious areas of engineering, mathematics, and physical science. Black men predominated here. Black women's majority was in the less powerful and less lucrative life and social/behavioral sciences (Malcolm, 1989).

Ghettoization and Resegregation

Much of the literature on gender and race that emerged in the late 1980s and early 1990s began to discuss ghettoization of women into female enclaves and into lower-status, lower-paying segments of male professions. It also began to document the stratification of black women in relation to white women at all levels of the professional (and managerial) hierarchy in both female- and male-dominated professions.

Looking at gender segregation, Reskin and Roos and their colleagues (1990) reported on an important set of case studies on the feminization of male occupations. As we saw earlier in this chapter, they argued that the numerical increase of women in male occupations during the 1970s reflected both women's *ghettoization* in certain jobs within some of these male occupations (i.e., women held a restricted number of lower-level jobs) and the *resegregation* of others (i.e., men moved out and women became the majority). Genuine gender integration, they concluded, was indeed rare in the 1970s. The professions that experienced, first, ghettoization of women, then resegregation (i.e., became feminized) during this time included systems analysis, pharmacy, book editing, public relations, accounting and auditing, and reporting. Note that none of these are among the elite male professions. Thus, for example, among public-relations specialists, men were more likely to be promoted into public-relations management, while women ended up overrepresented as lower-level "communications technicians." Among pharmacists, men were more likely to be found in management positions in retail pharmacy and in research, while women were located in salaried hospital settings. Not only did women become ghettoized in public relations, the occupation also became resegregated. Retail pharmacy followed suit in the 1980s: women replaced men as the statistical majority in the occupation. Gender resegregation likewise occurred among book editors in the 1970s. Their analysis, they concluded, "does not offer a very rosy prognosis for desegregation, much less for genuine integration, during the 1990s" (p. 381).

Other research indicates that these trends continued beyond 1980. Blau (1989) found that by 1987, personnel, training, and labor relations; educational and vocational counseling; and public relations were among the male or gender-mixed professions that had become predominantly female. It appears that as male occupations change to permit women to participate, they often reach some kind of "tipping point" and become resegregated, only this time with women instead of men.

Lest one think that the elite male professions are exempt from these processes, it is important to recognize the continued ghettoization of women in newly expanding as well as older areas in law, medicine, engineering, and the like. This is in large part related to the increasing proletarianization of labor even in elite male professions. Thus even doctors, lawyers, and college professors are becoming more bureaucratized, with more outside interference in their monopoly over the profession. As Carter and Carter (1981) have argued, many of the tasks have become de-skilled in such a way that a split in the profession emerged between prestigious jobs with good pay, autonomy, and opportunity for growth and development, and a new class of more routinized, poorly paid jobs with little autonomy. This latter segment is unconnected by promotion ladders to prestigious jobs in the profession. And although this de-skilling process affects both men and women, Carter and Carter have predicted that "it is precisely in the newer, more routinized sector of professional employment that women's employment will be overwhelmingly concentrated" (p. 478). Thus the smaller upper tier of semiautonomous, highly paid jobs will continue to exist, will continue to be male dominated, and will maintain institutional barriers that make access from the newly created routinized jobs difficult to achieve.

Recent examples in law, medicine, and engineering are becoming plentiful. In-house corporate legal counsel is the fastest-expanding segment of the legal profession. Women lawyers are more likely to be recruited as in-house legal counsel in financial services (which is lower salaried, with more women employed in nonlegal jobs as well) than into more profitable manufacturing corporations (Roach, 1990). In medicine, increasing bureaucratization combined with declining profitability, entrepreneurial potential, and social status to weaken men's involvement in medicine and open up certain sectors to women (Luxenberg, 1985; Nesbitt, 1986; Leslie, 1987). Likewise, one study concludes that in engineering, even when women and men are virtually identical in educational qualifications and time on the job, and have similar occupational attitudes, women are less likely than men to hold high-status jobs in design or management:

> The men outrank women in structural arenas where the profession of engineering itself flourishes—where authority relations are least bureaucratic, growth and technical innovation are greatest, and engineers have the most status and power (i.e., in electrical engineering and high tech firms). Women achieve equality with men where there are resources specifically designed for them (affirmative action), where the work of engineers is most routine, the power of engineers is relatively low, and the work place is most bureaucratic in structure (i.e., in mechanical engineering and aerospace). That is, opportunities for women appear greatest where the power of engineers is offset by other forces. (Robinson and McIlwee, 1989:462–463)

At the highest levels of the professional and corporate world, we have only recently recognized that despite all the changes women have made, only a minuscule number are able to reach the top, even with the passage of time (Schafran, 1987). Thus *Fortune* asked, "Why Women Still Don't Hit the Top" (Fierman, 1990) in a survey of 4,012 people listed as the highest-paid officers and directors of the 1,000 largest U.S. industrial and service companies. Only 19 women—less than 1 percent—were identified among the more than 4,000 executives. Structural barriers, as well as stereotyping and discrimination, are among the impediments cited to advancement. In the legal profession, although women increased from 2.8 percent of all partners in the 250 largest firms at the beginning of the 1980s, by 1989 they were less than 1 in 10 (9.2 percent) of the partners in these top firms (Jensen, 1990; see also Stille, 1985; Weisenhaus, 1988). Even when women lawyers are not limited to the "mommy track" (Kingson, 1988), they ". . . Aren't Yet Equal Partners" either (Goldstein, 1988; Menkel-Meadow, 1987–88). And women may well be better able to become partners—even in top law firms—precisely when these partnerships become less desirable (Cowan, 1992). Even in more typically female professions such as education, school superintendents have usually been men. Today that still continues to be the case. For example, in 1988 only 3.8 percent of all superintendents of independent school districts and 6.2 percent of dependent school districts in New York State were women (Rush, 1989).

The continued domination of white men in top positions where professionally trained people are likely to be employed throughout the economy is repeated today in almost every study cited: the centers of power surrounding the president in the White House and the Cabinet (Dowd, 1991); the Federal Reserve, the government's most influential economic policy-making institution (Crustinger, 1990); top executives in the defense industry (Hyde, 1989); managers and professionals at the upper reaches of the corporate world (Silver, 1990; Skrzycki, 1990); deans and heads of departments in medical schools (Altman, 1988) as well as chief executives of national medical organizations (Hilts, 1991); scientists elevated to the rolls of the National Academy of Sciences (Angier, 1991); partners in prestigious law firms (Weisenhaus, 1988; Brenner, 1990; Jensen, 1990). The list goes on. Not only do white women fail to reach top positions throughout executive and professional domains—the proverbial "glass ceiling" is reached—but, as much of this same research shows, this situation is much worse for minorities—both men and women.

Segregation and Stratification: Black Women in the Professions

Recent research has likewise suggested that segregation and stratification within professions for black women have continued to rise, and have had a distinctive impact on this race/gender group. Specifically, there are two somewhat contradictory aspects of increasing opportunity for black women. The first is the degree to which opportunity has changed from one generation to another. The second is the degree to which, in any one generation, people can make choices among the full range of jobs available in the economy. In the first case, there certainly have been changes for black women: it makes a tremendous difference that one can now become a social worker or an accountant rather than a secretary or a cleaning woman. In the second case, there is virtually no difference: black women are no more free to choose among the wide array of different sorts of work now than they were a generation ago. If they were, black women would not be concentrated in the lowest levels of the professional/technical labor force, nor would they have to wait for better jobs until white women are able to find better opportunities themselves outside the traditional female professions.

Studies have consistently shown that black women are concentrated in different jobs than white women throughout the labor force, including the professions (Almquist, 1979; Wallace, 1980; Malveaux, 1981, 1985, 1990; Westcott, 1982; Dill, Cannon, and Vanneman, 1987; Amott and Matthaei, 1991). Black women are primarily overrepresented in occupations outside the professions—more so than white women. And within the professions, black women are concentrated in far fewer jobs than white women.

For example, in 1980, among the top 40 occupations in which black women were overconcentrated, the only professional/technical jobs were social worker, prekindergarten and kindergarten teacher, dietitian, and licensed practical nurse. In contrast, white women, although overrepresented in these occupations, were also heavily concentrated as librarians, health professors, home-economics professors, registered nurses, dental hygienists, occupational therapists, speech therapists, and health-record technicians (Dill, Cannon, and Vanneman, 1987).[7] The fact that black women have become more highly concentrated in a few female professions/technical areas while white women have found employment in a wider variety is important for at least two reasons: first, for the greater limitations placed on black women; second, because the occupations in which black women are concentrated tend to pay so much less than those in which white women are concentrated (Dill, Cannon, and Vanneman, 1987).

Although there are very few detailed occupational studies that have compared black and white women in the professions, there have been a larger number of popular and scholarly articles on blacks in management, some of which have focused on black women. The degree of racial segregation and stratification is apparent throughout this literature. For example, Malveaux (1981) pointed out that black women are more likely to be management trainees at McDonald's franchises than at more financially and socially well-off corporations. Further, Malveaux reports on a survey of several elite universities and their M.B.A. programs between 1975 and 1980, which found that no black women were on "fast tracks" and no black women were hired at management jobs paying more than $40,000. This was in sharp contrast to white men, black men, and white women, who were able to find first jobs in these categories. Almost a decade later, in 1988, black women constituted only 2 percent of all managers in companies with at least 100 employees.[8] Moreover, once in the door, the few black women managers suffered from isolation, lack of mentors, and stereotyping. They reported they were usually the only black women in management, were bypassed for promotions, and were relegated to staff positions that were not on the fast track and thus were vulnerable to corporate streamlining (Alexander, 1990). The continuing level of discrimination against black women once they have gained access to managerial and professional jobs persists. This is also documented in other recent studies that include black women managers (Fulbright, 1985–86; Nkomo, 1986; Alston, 1987; DiTomaso and Thompson, 1988; and S. Collins, 1989). Recently opportunities for black women to gain entry to the upper echelons of corporate America also have been recognized. So, too, have the very significant barriers (King, 1988; Silver, 1990).

The detailed studies of black women and white women in the professions have indicated that because of discriminatory barriers in the private sector and the fact that black women are clustered in female occupations in the public sector, black teachers, counselors, and librarians are more likely to be dependent on public funding than whites employed in the private sector (Higginbotham, 1987). Exposure of even this level of segregation does not get at the race/gender stratification *within* schools, hospitals, and libraries. For example, in 1984 the U.S. public-school system remained highly segregated, with nearly two-thirds of black youngsters attending predominantly minority schools (Fiske, 1987). It is hard to imagine that black women have been able to find teaching jobs in higher-income white school districts in numbers that are anywhere near parity with their representation in the educational system. Moreover, even in the more poorly

funded minority schools, whites—men and women—have been able to secure
the higher level and more supervisory positions. Similar results have been found
in nursing (Sacks, 1984; Malveaux and Englander, 1986; Hine, 1989; Glazer,
1991) and social work (Dressel, 1987).

It seems logical that the expansion of a new field, such as computers, for
example, would open opportunities to previously excluded groups. However,
Glenn and Tolbert (1987) found that even when racial/ethnic minority women
have been able to secure jobs in computer occupations, they are more likely to
enter the lower ranks of the computer hierarchy and to experience wage discrimination. While most of their earnings disadvantage was due to their concentration
in lower-level occupations outside the professions, at each level of the hierarchy,
race and gender discrimination led to their receiving lower wages. This was true
among professional and technical computer analysts and programmers as well
as "nonprofessional" computer operators, repairers, and data-entry keyers.

Although even less research has been done on black women lawyers, doctors,
dentists, college professors, veterinarians, clergy, and the like, one case study
of the careers of 238 black women lawyers is instructive (Simpson, 1990). This
small number represents a full 5 percent of the national population of black
women attorneys. After a minimum of five years in practice, black women attorneys were primarily employed in government (59 percent), rarely in law firms
(13 percent). Even when black women from elite law schools are compared with
white men from elite law schools, their ability to find entry-level jobs in prestigious law firms is severely circumscribed. The type of law school one attends is
crucial to a lawyer's career, since it determines where, when, and with whom
one practices law and ultimately the level of income. However, only 35 percent
of the black women lawyers Simpson studied were originally recruited into law
firms. Most found their first jobs in government. This is in sharp contrast to an
earlier, more localized study of white male lawyers in Chicago: Heinz and Laumann (1982) found that 69 percent gained their first jobs in large law firms.
The elite law school does not play the same role for black women as it has for
white men.[9]

Despite the image of law firms vying with one another and paying dearly for
"the few qualified blacks," Simpson found that most of the women left jobs only
to be recruited into other jobs at entry-level positions—a lateral move. And
while promotions peaked early in their careers, the women were trapped at low
levels even in the government. They had reached the proverbial "glass ceiling"—that is, they had encountered a barrier that was not apparent until they
ran into it. Those working in law firms were not promoted out of entry-level
positions. It seemed clear to these women that their race, gender, or a combi-
nation of both limited their mobility in the organizations in which they worked.
Half believed they were not assigned prestigious cases that could lead to promotion.

My own research findings dovetail with Simpson's. Preliminary interviews with black and white women attorneys in a large mid-Atlantic city indicated that even when blacks were recruited into prestigious law firms, they tended to be deployed to a branch of the firm that was located in the black community. The women were sure that this segregation of black attorneys—women and men— severely limited their career prospects.

THE PARADOX OF PARTIAL CHANGE

The expansionist era of the 1960s and 1970s led to greater opportunities for disadvantaged groups in the professions. White women who previously might have been clerical workers, schoolteachers, and social workers now had greater possibilities of entering lower-level college teaching and accounting. Black men who might have been laborers and factory assembly-line workers had more chances to work as vocational and educational counselors and affirmative-action officers. And black women, whose futures might have encompassed domestic or manufacturing work, were better able to seek employment as clerical workers, schoolteachers, counselors, and social workers. In each case these jobs outearn the ones left behind and provide better working conditions, job opportunities, and life chances. From this perspective, the glass is not half-empty but half-full.

All too often we forget that these jobs are ones that white women, black women, and black men are proud of, jobs that they have struggled both individually and collectively to get and that they find fulfilling. Thus, even if given the opportunity to enter elite male professions, many black women (just like many individuals in any race/gender group) might well prefer to be teachers, counselors, and social workers. In addition, some of these women are able to rise to the position of agency heads in their particular professions. In so doing, they occupy positions that are usually expected to be filled by men (Gilkes, 1980, 1982).[10]

White women college teachers may well be happier in academia than in the faster-paced, profit-oriented world of law or medicine. Black men counselors working with teenagers in high school may prefer these jobs over more desk-oriented engineering jobs. The problem for many of these men and women is that they are neither adequately respected for the jobs they do, paid high enough wages, nor provided with the many job benefits and the security that characterize the more "elite" jobs and that they often desperately need.

Moreover, much of the upward mobility experienced by black men and women and white women is all too often grounded in a system that has simultaneously reshaped these professions so that they no longer provide the same resources and rewards that they did in the past to white men. A further look at the data, then, leads us to see that the glass is half-empty. As we have seen, the jobs themselves often have deteriorated in pay, autonomy, and opportunities.

This, then, is the *paradox of partial change:* groups of individuals may experience upward mobility in the professions precisely as the professions themselves are being downgraded in different ways. Moreover, just as integration of disadvantaged groups occurs in some professions, there is the simultaneous phenomenon of increasing segregation. Again, the glass is *both* half-full and half-empty.

Increasing segregation by race and gender occurs not only on the basis of the particular profession or specialties within them, but also in terms of the geographic location and populations served. As was discussed earlier, much of the mobility of the new black middle class has been based on the servicing of poor and minority populations that had previously been unserved or underserved by white professionals. Much of this employment is highly dependent on government funding, not the "free market." These are hard-won gains for blacks, and yet dependency on government funding makes them more vulnerable to the winds of political change. This is of particular relevance in the 1990s as the downturn in the economy has left many government agencies, as well as private-sector jobs, subject to large numbers of layoffs, (e.g., see Bartlett, 1991; Hinds, 1991; Kilborn, 1991; Mid-Atlantic Bureau of Labor Statistics, 1991; Nasar, 1992).

Thus, in the context of a changing economy and political pressure exerted by oppressed people, the social forces of class, race, and gender, while allowing for impressive gains for disadvantaged groups, have simultaneously created conditions that have led to increasing segregation by race and gender. Now, in the 1990s, in a shrinking economy and in a climate that is increasingly hostile to affirmative action, men and women, blacks and whites, are divided on a variety of levels. This is complicated all the more by the fact that those who appear to have benefited the most have been the relatively more privileged women in the white community and the relatively better-off men and women in the black community. This has created breaches among women (professional and managerial versus those in lower-status and lesser-paying traditionally female jobs or women who work primarily in the home) and among blacks (professional and managerial versus those in less-desired and rewarded jobs, unemployed, or not in the labor force). This fragmentation is *not* inevitable. The need now is to respect each other's uniquenesses and contributions, while developing strategies and coalitions to work toward a genuinely humane, just, and egalitarian society.

TOWARD THE FUTURE; BUILDING COALITIONS FOR CHANGE

As we have seen, three major factors were important to the expansion of opportunities for disadvantaged race/gender groups between 1960 and 1980: an expanding economy that created new jobs, a politically liberal and socially activist

climate that encouraged such legislation as affirmative action, and both sponta-
neous and organized pressure from below, as seen, for example, in the civil
rights and women's movements. In the 1980s and continuing into the 1990s,
none of these factors have continued to operate to the same degree as they did
earlier. A bleak economic situation, coupled with the socially conservative policies of the Reagan and Bush administrations, has made it far more difficult to
attempt to remedy past race and gender discrimination through finding, nurtur-
ing, hiring, and promoting talented women of all racial/ethnic backgrounds and
minority men.

The Economic and Political Climate

Since 1990, the U.S. economy has been in the most recent of its 8 post-World
War II recessions. Seeking to maintain their profits, U.S. businesses have laid
off workers and eliminated jobs—some of them permanently, subcontracted out
other jobs to people who can be even more quickly hired or dismissed, and
moved many of their operations overseas to take advantage of cheap nonunion-
ized labor pools in impoverished countries. While we typically think of these
changes in terms of manufacturing, the same trends are occurring in the service
industries today, affecting professional as well as "nonprofessional" workers
(Lohr, 1991; Nasar, 1992). The recession, the deterioration of good jobs, plus
the job flight abroad have had a devastating effect in the United States: unemployment has increased, membership in labor unions has declined, and members
of all race/gender groups, but most particularly the disadvantaged groups, fear
that their opportunities for mobility have gone up in smoke.

The economic and political climates are tightly interconnected. In the early
1990s, efforts to achieve even modest civil-rights legislation have been stymied
by a backlash, primarily from white men who fear what they call "quotas." The
debate over the civil-rights bill in 1990–1991 (a bill attempting to restore civil-
rights legislation negated in the 1980s during the Reagan administration that
President George Bush continually vowed to veto in the early 1990s, but ultimately signed when passed in a weakened form) epitomized the struggle between white male elites who hoped to hang on to their positions of power and
profits and members of disadvantaged groups who hoped for some legal affir-
mation of their right to escape second-class citizenship. This situation is even
more complicated by the fact that relatively more privileged groups at each level
of the occupational hierarchy try to hang on to their privileges, particularly in
harsh economic times.[11]

Meanwhile, the most recent data on black and white men and women in the
professions tell us that although white men, black men, and white women have
increased their representation in the professions, it has been at a much slower
rate than in the 1960–1980 period. And black women have actually lost ground
(Swinton, 1990). To reverse this trend so that at least some important gains in

mobility can be made by majority and minority women and minority men, the 1990s require a newer, more intensive set of policies, including those of affirmative action, that are strongly enforced. Given a political/economic climate that is clearly hostile to affirmative action and other liberal policies, how might such policies be generated and effectively used?

Direct Action through Coalition Building

The third factor that operated in the 1960s and 1970s was pressure from, among others, minority groups and white women. Although their protests were directed at overcoming discrimination on multiple levels, two major demands were for job opportunities (often in government) and affirmative-action policies. Often the different pressure groups did not work in coalition and their various demands were not coordinated. In an expanding economy and a supportive political climate, working in genuine coalitions may have seemed less necessary. Now, in a shrinking economy and a hostile political climate, there is ever more reason for understanding how oppression operates specifically in relation to each group and working in coalitions to overcome those oppressions. Women and men from different racial/ethnic and class backgrounds must not only struggle around different oppressions but come to terms with at least some of these differences. This point is clearly stated by Malveaux (1990:229), who says that the "heart of the matter" between black women and white women is that

> white women who experience gender-based economic discrimination are the mothers, daughters, sisters, and wives of the patriarchs who have also institutionalized racial discrimination against Black people. Black women experience an economic oppression that has a basis in both race and gender. For white women to assume an alliance between themselves and Black women without taking matters of race and family (and thus, Black men) into consideration is a mistake. Too frequently this mistake characterizes feminist theory, scholarship, activism, and policy development.

If, as Malveaux and others (e.g., Dill, 1983; Jordan, 1985; Ramazanoglu, 1989; Daly, 1991) say, the danger is that some well-meaning but naive white women may assume a "sisterhood" that is not so easily come by, there is another more invidious danger as well. Malveaux also questions "whether powerful [white] women want to bend the rules so that society will accommodate a few more of them, or whether they want to change society's rules so that far more women [and disadvantaged men] will have access to power" (p. 229).

The difficulties involved in building coalitions between white women and black women are not the only such barriers to overcome: gender, class, and racial/ethnic differences on all levels make the process of working together difficult. In a climate of shrinking economic opportunity, it is all too easy for such differences to heighten animosity and competition for scarce resources not only between black and white professional women, but between women from different class and ethnic backgrounds as well.

Nevertheless, there have been recent examples of coalitions between disadvantaged groups: the Rainbow Coalition, in which blacks and whites, Latinas/os, Native Americans and Asians, women and men, worked for Jesse Jackson's 1988 presidential campaign; the coalitions of racially and ethnically diverse populations in inner cities fighting for a better education for all their children (Dill, 1983); the expansion of racial diversity in local antirape movements to provide many of the much-needed services to battered and abused racial/ethnic minority women in poor communities (Matthews, 1989); and so on.

Such models can be adapted to the kinds of efforts that were successful in the 1960s and 1970s, as all the while new and better models are developed. In the 1990s, group pressure is needed once again to end race, gender, and class discrimination that perpetuates occupational segregation, lack of advancement, and low pay. Pressure is also needed to open up and create new government positions (especially policy-making positions) to members of minority groups and to women. But this time it is even more essential for the various disadvantaged groups to work together. If they do not, it will be all too easy for those who control the economic and political institutions to use divide-and-conquer tactics, to parcel out a few prestigious positions to members of one group and not another. As Bonnie Thornton Dill, a black feminist scholar, suggested almost a decade ago:

> While analytically we must carefully examine the structures that differentiate us, politically we must fight the segmentation of oppression into categories such as "racial issues," "feminist issues," and "class issues." This is, of course, a task of almost overwhelming magnitude, and yet it seems to me the only viable way to avoid the errors of the past and to move forward to make sisterhood a meaningful feminist concept for all women, across the boundaries of race and class. For it is through first seeking to understand struggles that are not particularly shaped by one's own immediate personal priorities that we will begin to experience and understand the needs and priorities of our sisters—be they black, brown, white, poor, or rich. When we have reached a point where the differences between us *enrich* our political and social action rather than divide it, we will have gone beyond the personal and will, in fact, be "political enough." (1983:148)

If the disadvantaged race/gender groups can learn to respect one another's diversity, different historical conditions, and different needs, as well as their own personal and structural positions of absolute and relative advantage and disadvantage, then such coalitions can come about. If not, then little is likely to change.

APPENDIX I: METHODOLOGY

Many methodological issues were discussed in earlier chapters where appropriate in order to assist the reader in understanding the procedures I used to carry out this research. In this Appendix, I discuss (1) the comparability of detailed occupational categories across three census years, (2) the distribution of each of the four race/gender groups across these newly constructed comparable occupational categories, (3) a factor to correct for those individuals who did not report their detailed occupation, and (4) a factor to correct for the undercount of particular race/gender groups in the labor force.

MAKING 1960, 1970, AND 1980 CENSUS CATEGORIES COMPARABLE

At the time this research was carried out, there was no way to directly compare the detailed occupational categories of the U.S. Census between 1960 and 1980 because of the many changes in coding procedures over the years. In this section I describe, first, the ways in which the three census years are different from one another and the problems this generated in trying to compare data across census years. Second, I specify how the occupations were made comparable across the three census years. Third, I present the means by which I recalculated the four race/gender groups for 1960 and 1980 for each of the comparable professional and technical occupational categories. Although my focus is on the professions, the procedures developed can be applied to other occupational categories.[1]

DIFFERENCES IN OCCUPATIONAL CODES ACROSS
THE THREE CENSUS DECADES

The occupational categories in the 1960, 1970, and 1980 censuses were coded quite differently.[2] Between 1960 and 1970, the occupational-classification system was expanded from 297 detailed (three-digit) categories to 441. By 1980 the 441 detailed occupational categories within 12 broad[3] groups were expanded to 503 categories within 13 broad groups. Over the three censuses, the number of detailed professional/technical occupational categories increased from 84 to 123 to 127.[4] However, even though the number of categories in the professions/technical fields is more similar between 1970 and 1980 than 1960 and 1970, the reclassification itself was far greater between 1970 and 1980.

The differences between the ways in which the three census years were originally coded can be found in Priebe, Heinkel, and Greene (1972) for 1960 and 1970, and in USDC, Bureau of Census (1983a) and Bianchi and Rytina (1984) for 1970 and 1980. First, 1960 and 1970 are more similar than 1970 and 1980 in the way in which data were coded for the different detailed occupations. They differ primarily in the fact that in 1970, larger categories (especially large residual categories or growth categories) were split into two or more detailed occupational categories. For example, while all computer-related workers were located in the large residual category of "professional, technical, kindred worker/not elsewhere classified" in 1960, in 1970 they were separated into three distinct professional computer categories: computer programmers, computer systems analysts, and computer specialists/nec.

Second, several professional occupations were downgraded by the Census Bureau to technicians between 1960 and 1970. For example, airplane pilots, surveyors, drafters, radio operators, and embalmers were considered professions in 1960 but technicians in 1970.

By 1980, though, there were not only changes such as those that occurred in 1970, but an added and difficult problem for researchers in that detailed occupations were often shifted from one broad category to another. Accountants as well as personnel and labor relations workers were in the professional category in 1970 but were classified as managerial in 1980. In contrast, sales engineers were shifted from the professional category to sales. This problem is compounded by the fact that some occupations were split into several different detailed occupations, which were then placed in different major categories of the entire occupational-classification system. For example, the 1970 professional occupation "foresters and conservationists" branched out into seven different 1980 codes, of which one was classified as management, two as professions, and four as service occupations in 1980.

In addition, a certain degree of both upgrading and downgrading of occupations occurred. For example, computer programmers were downgraded from professions in 1970 to technicians in 1980. On the other hand, licensed practical nurses were upgraded from the service category to technicians.

STANDARDIZING TO 1970 OCCUPATIONAL CATEGORIES

Because data exist by which to compare 1960 to 1970 (Priebe, Heinkel, and Greene, 1972) and 1980 to 1970 (USDC, Bureau of Census, 1986a, 1986b), 1960 and 1980 detailed occupational-census categories were recoded to match, or were standardized to, those of the 1970 census, despite some necessary loss of detail.[5]

A set of "double-coded" data were used in each of the two comparisons. That is, the gaps or differences between the 1960 and 1970 classification systems were bridged through a sample of 100,000 records from the 1960 census in which people in the experienced civilian labor force were assigned both a 1960 and a 1970 code (i.e., were "double-coded") (Priebe, Heinkel, and Greene, 1972). The data from this double-coded sample consist of a cross-classification of 1960 and 1970 detailed occupational codes and permit one to see how the 1960 codes may be followed through to their 1970 code destination. They also give us the proportion of men or women in the 1960 code that would have been included in the 1970 code. This tells us how much of the 1960 occupational category would have been included in the 1970 occupational category.

A similar procedure was used to compare 1970 and 1980 census data: in this case, however, a sample of 125,000 cases was double-coded and reordered so that we can follow the reclassification of 1980 occupational codes into their 1970 code destination (USDC, Bureau of Census, 1986b; see also Rytina and Bianchi, 1984, for further clarification). This, too, includes the proportion of men or women in the 1980 code that would have been included in the 1970 occupational category.[6]

An example of how this reclassification might operate can be seen with *accountant,* which was classified among the professions in 1960 and 1970 (Tables A.1 and A.2), but among managers and administrators in 1980 (Tables A.3 and A.4). In 1970 the detailed-occupation accountant (occupational code 001–Tables A.1 and A.2, Column 1) included four different 1960 occupation categories: accountant and auditor (occupational code 000), statistician and actuary (occupational code 174), agent/nec (occupational code 301), and clerical and kindred worker/nec (occupational code 370) (Column 2). Thus, while the vast majority of those classified as accountants in 1960 were also accountants in 1970, we are able to take into account those who in 1960 (e.g., statisticians and actuaries, agents/nec, etc.) were classified elsewhere, but in 1970 were now considered accountants (Column 3).

Similarly, when comparing 1970 and 1980 (Tables A.3 and A.4), we learn that the 1970 occupation of accountant (occupational code 001) (Column 1) branched out into five different 1980 codes: financial manager (occupational code 007), accountant and auditor (occupational code 023), inspector and compliance officer, except construction (occupational code 036), and bookkeeper, accounting and auditing clerk (occupational code 337) (Column 2). The first four are managerial categories, the last one clerical. As Column 3 then indicates, while almost all 1980 accountants and auditors would have been classified accountants in 1970, that was also the case for almost one-fifth (19.245 percent) of the other financial officers for the men (Table A.3) and just under half (47.059 percent) of all other financial officers for the women. (Table A.4)

The limitations of the double-coding method have been discussed in Rytina and Bianchi (1984). Briefly, 100,000 cases (in the 1960–1970 comparison) or 125,000 cases (in the 1970–1980 comparison) is not a large number when analyzing very small detailed occupations. This poses problems of reliability, especially as we break down our analysis by race/gender group. This is particularly problematic when looking at black men and black women because of their small numbers in the professions. On the other hand, the fact that my study analyzes only individual detailed occupations with at least 100,000 people in 1970 or combines all occupations into a seven-category professional/technical hierarchy minimizes some of these problems. Finally, there is also an unknown amount of error in the double-coding operation.

HOW THE FOUR RACE/GENDER GROUPS WERE RECALCULATED FOR 1960 AND 1980 CENSUSES TO MAKE USE OF THE 1970 OCCUPATIONAL CATEGORIES

The ultimate goal was to convert 1960 and 1980 professional/technical occupational categories to those of 1970, separately for each race/gender group (white men, black men, white women, black women). To accomplish this goal, I allocated into the 1970 detailed occupational codes (as found in USDC, Bureau of Census, 1975 [Table 2]) all the people in the 1960 or 1980 census who belong there. I did this by using two different sets of data for each of the 1960 and 1980 census years. I designated these as (1) the *occupational summary data* and (2) the *conversion data*.

The *occupational summary data* consist of the *numerical distribution* of black women, white women, black men, and white men (and total men and total women) in the detailed occupational categories of the experienced civilian labor force. For 1960 (see Tables A.1 and A.2, Columns 4 and 6) this can be found in USDC, Bureau of Census, 1963 (Table 3); for 1980 (see Tables A.3 and A.4, Columns 4 and 6) this can be found in USDC, Bureau of Census, 1983 (Table 2).

The *conversion data* consist of the *percentage of men and women* who would have been classified in the 1970 occupational codes in 1960 (Tables A.1 and A.2, Column 3) (or 1980–Tables A.3 and A.4, Column 3) in order to make 1960 (or 1980) occupational codes consistent with those of 1970. For the 1960–1970 comparison, this is based on a sample of 100,000 cases from the 1970 census that estimates the percentage of the 1960 occupational category that went into the 1970 occupational code (see Tables A.1 and A.2, Column 3) (Priebe, Heinkel, and Greene, 1972). For the 1980–1970 comparison, this is based on a sample of 125,000 cases from the 1970 census that estimates the percentage of the 1980 occupational category in the 1970 occupational code (see Tables A.3 and A.4, Column 3) (USDC, Bureau of Census, 1986a, 1986b). I made use of both of these publications to come up with the number of men (Tables A.1 and A.3, Columns 5 and 7) and the number of women (Tables A.2 and A.4, Columns 5 and 7) in 1960 (or in 1980) who would have been classified in a particular profession in 1970.

Tables A.1 to A.4 provide an example for *accounting* of how the numbers change for each of the four race/gender groups when 1970 occupational categories are used instead of 1960 (Tables A.1, A.2) or 1980 (Tables A.3, A.4). In these figures, Columns 1, 2, and 3 refer to the *conversion data;* Columns 4 and 6 refer to the *occupational summary data;* Columns 5 and 7 are the *actual numbers* used in this study once the procedures (spelled out in this Appendix) are applied.

Because the conversion data have only the "percentage of men and women" and not the "percentage of men and woman *by race,*" I applied the "percentage of men" and the "percentage of women" separately to blacks and whites in this study. This assumes the same gender distribution of blacks and whites in an occupation, which may not, in fact, be the case. For example, there may be more (or fewer) women among blacks in elementary-school teaching than among whites. However, comparability of the data has not been assessed for race by the Census Bureau because of the small sample in some occupational categories (Priebe, personal communication, 1986). Moreover, in my study, I am assuming the comparability developed for men and women can be applied to black and white men and women separately because the numbers of each race/gender group are controlled for by applying the percentages in the conversion data to the actual numbers (in the summary data) for each race/gender group in the census, and therefore percentage distributions in each detailed occupational category.

Because of the complexity of the procedure, I shall give an example of how one detailed occupational category, *accountant and auditor*, was transformed to become comparable across all three census years for each of the four race/gender groups. First I will look at the steps to convert 1960 to 1970 occupational categories and get the number of people in each race/gender group in 1960 who would have been in the 1970 occupational category of accountants. Then I will look at this same procedure for the 1980 census.

Converting 1960 to 1970 Occupational
Categories for Black and White Women and Men:

In converting the 1960 category of accountants and auditors to that of 1970 (accountants), my goal was to allocate into 1970 code 001 (accountants) all the people in the 1960 census who belong there. (See Tables A.1 and A.2.) The problem, however, is that while all accountants and auditors (occupational code 000) in 1960 were allocated into accountants (occupational code 001) in 1970, portions of several other occupational categories in 1960 were likewise assigned to category 001 in 1970: statisticians and actuaries (occupational code 174), agents/nec (occupational code 301), and clerical and kindred workers/nec (occupational code 370). The question in each case is how many were so allocated. To answer this, I employed the following procedures.

I located the percent of each of the 1960 components of the 1970 accountant occupational code (occupational code 001) that were in that 001 code, separately for men and women (Tables A.1, A.2, Column 3). The 1960–1970 conversion data tell us that 100.0 percent of 1960 code 000 (accountants and auditors) went into 1970 code 001 (accountants), both for men and for women. Likewise, for men, 6.25 percent of 1960 statisticians and actuaries (occupational code 174), 1.807 percent of 1960 agents/nec (occupational code 301), and 1.166 percent of clerical and kindred workers/nec (occupational code 370) went into 1970 code 001 (accountants). For the women, 100.0 percent of accountants and auditors as well as 0.077 percent of clerical and kindred workers/nec went into 1970's code 001 (accountant). (There are no cases of female statisticians and actuaries or agents/nec in the 100,000 sample.)

I then calculated the number of white men, black men, white women, and black women separately in 1960 who would have been in the 1970 code 001 (accountant). By using white males as the example, we can see how this was done. From the *occupational summary data* we know there were 390,596 white male accountants and auditors in 1960 (Table A.1, Column 4). Therefore, I multiplied the 1960 number (390,596) by the percentage of that code in 1970 for men (100.0 percent), which yielded 390,596 white male accountants and auditors who should be recoded into the 1970 code 001 (accountants). I continued this procedure for 1960 codes 174 (statistician and actuary), 301 (agent/

TABLE A.1 AN EXAMPLE OF THE CONVERSION OF 1960 DATA CATEGORIES TO 1970 DATA CATEGORIES: MALE ACCOUNTANTS

(1)* 1970 Occupation Code	(2)* 1960 Occupation Code	(3)* Male Percent of 1970 Code	(4)** White Male 1960 Data	(5) Converted White Male 1960 Data	(6)** Black Male 1960 Data	(7) Converted Black Male 1960 Data
Accountant (001)	Acct. & audit. (000)	100.000	390,596	390,596	2,417	2,417
	Statistic & actuary (174)	6.250	13,910	869	285	18
	Agent/nec (301)	1.807	130,267	2,354	1,720	31
	Cler. & kindred/ nec (370)	1.166	1,167,361	13,611	52,512	612
	Totals			407,430		3,078

*Source: Priebe, Heinkel, and Green, 1972. (Refers to *conversion data*.)
**Source: USDC, Bureau of Census, 1963. (Refers to *occupational summary data*.)

TABLE A.2 AN EXAMPLE OF THE CONVERSION OF 1960 DATA CATEGORIES TO 1970 DATA CATEGORIES: FEMALE ACCOUNTANTS

(1)* 1970 Occupation Code	(2)* 1960 Occupation Code	(3)* Female Percent 1970 Code	(4)** White Female 1960 Data	(5) Converted White Female 1960 Data	(6)** Black Female 1960 Data	(7) Converted Black Female 1960 Data
Accountant (001)	Acct. & audit. (000)	100.000	76,931	76,931	1,217	1,217
	Statistic. & actuary (174)	0.000	6,376	0	141	0
	Agent/nec (301)	0.000	28,189	0	782	0
	Cler. & kindred/ nec (370)	0.077	1,700,269	1,309	67,353	52
	Totals			78,240		1,269

*Source: Priebe, Heinkel, and Greene, 1972. (Refers to *conversion data*.)
**Source: USDC, Bureau of Census, 1963. (Refers to *occupational summary data*.)

nec), and 370 (clerical and kindred workers/nec). Thus I multiplied 13,910 × 6.25% = 869 for code 174 (statistician and actuary), 130,267 × 1.807% = 2,354 for code 301 (agent/nec), and 1,167,361 × 1.166% = 13,611 for code 370 (clerical and kindred workers/nec) because a portion of the white men in each of these 1960 codes needed to be recoded into the 1970 code 001 (accountant). After calculating these numbers, I summed to arrive at the number of white men (390,596 + 869 + 2,354 + 13,611 = 407,430) in 1960 belonging in the 1970 code 001 (accountant).

This very same procedure was repeated separately for black men, white women, and black women. The end result was the total number of each race/

gender group in 1960 who would have been accountants (occupational code 001) according to the 1970 occupational-classification scheme.

Converting 1980 to 1970 Occupational
Categories for Black and White Women and Men.

In this case I allocated into 1970 code 001 (accountants) all the people in the 1980 census who belonged there. (See Tables A.3 and A.4) Again, while the majority of accountants in 1980 (occupational code 023) were assigned to accountants (occupational code 001) in 1970, some people assigned to "nonaccountant" categories in 1980 belonged in code 001 (accountant) in 1970. This includes financial managers (occupational code 007), other financial officers (occupational code 025), inspectors and compliance officers, except construction (occupational code 036), and bookkeeper, accounting, and auditing clerk (occupational code 337). I needed to find out for each case how many there were. I located the percentage of each of the 1980 components of the 1970 accountant code (001) separately for men and women, multiplying the appropriate percentage by the number of white men, black men, white women, and black women separately in the 1980 census, summing these component numbers for the 001 code (accountants) separately for each race/gender group.

In Tables A.3 and A.4 we learn the percentage of each of the 1980 components of the 1970 accountant code (001) that went into that 001 code. This conversion table tells us (Column 3) that 2.933 percent of 1980 code 007 (financial managers) went into 1970 code 001 (accountants) for men and 8.571 percent for women. Likewise, for men: 96.841 percent of 1980's accountants and auditors (occupational code 023) went into 1970's code 001 (accountants), 19.245 percent of the financial officers (occupational code 025), 11.574 percent of inspectors and compliance officers, except construction (occupational code 036), and 10.594 percent of bookkeepers, accounting, and auditing clerks (occupational code 337). A separate set of percentages apply for women.

I then calculated the number of each race/gender group separately in 1980 who would have been in the 1970 code for accountants. I continue my example with white men. According to the occupational summary data for 1980 (Columns 4 and 6), there were 266,814 white male financial managers in 1980. Therefore, I multiplied this 1980 number by the percentage of that occupational code in 1970 (266,814 × .02933 = 7,826). Thus 7,826 white male financial managers needed to be recoded into 1970 code 001 (accountant). This procedure was again followed for 1980 codes 023—accountants and auditors (.96841 × 577,147 = 558,915), 025—other financial officers (.19245 × 209,877 = 40,391), 036—inspectors and compliance officers, except construction (.11574 × 115,431 = 13,360), and 337—bookkeepers, accounting and auditing clerks (.10594 × 169,795 = 17,988) because a portion of the white men in each of these 1980 categories needed to be recoded into 1970 code 001 (accountants).

TABLE A.3   AN EXAMPLE OF THE CONVERSION OF 1980 DATA CATEGORIES TO 1970 DATA CATEGORIES: MALE ACCOUNTANTS

(1)* 1970 Occupation Code	(2)* 1980 Occupation Code	(3)* Male Percent of 1970 Code	(4)** White Male 1980 Data	(5) Converted White Male 1980 Data	(6)** Black Male 1980 Data	(7) Converted Black Male 1980 Data
Accountant (001)	Finance. mgrs. (007)	2.933	266,814	7,826	6,882	202
	Accts. & audits. (023)	96.841	577,147	558,915	23,476	22,734
	Other finance. ofcrs. (025)	19.245	209,877	40,391	7,498	1,443
	Inspector & compliance ofcer., except construction (036)	11.574	115,431	13,360	9,186	1,063
	Bookkeeper, acctg. & audtg. Clk. (337)	10.594	169,795	17,988	13,231	1,402
	Totals			638,480		26,844

*Source: USDC, Bureau of Census, 1986b. (Refers to *conversion data*.)
**USDC, Bureau of Census, 1983a. (Refers to *occupational summary data*.)

TABLE A.4   AN EXAMPLE OF THE CONVERSION OF 1980 DATA CATEGORIES TO 1970 DATA CATEGORIES: FEMALE ACCOUNTANTS

(1)* 1970 Occupation Code	(2)* 1980 Occupation Code	(3)* Female Percent of 1970 Code	(4)** White Female 1980 Data	(5) Converted White Female 1980 Data	(6)** Black Female 1980 Data	(7) Converted Black Female 1980 Data
Accountant (001)	Financ. Mgr. (007)	8.571	119,376	10,232	6,050	519
	Acct. & audit. (023)	99.614	333,755	332,453	30,892	30,773
	Other Finance. Ofcrs. (025)	47.059	164,928	77,613	11,074	5,211
	Inspect. & compliance ofcr., except Construct. (036)	0.000	21,861	0	4,756	0
	Bookkeeper, Acctg. & Audtg. Clk. (337)	0.513	1,580,754	8,109	70,187	360
	Totals			428,407		36,863

*Source: USDC, Bureau of Census, 1986b. (Refers to *conversion data*.)
**Source: USDC, Bureau of Census, 1983a. (Refers to *occupational summary data*.)

After calculating these numbers, I summed to arrive at the number of white men (7,826 + 558,915 + 40,391 + 13,360 + 17,988 = 638,480) in 1980 belonging in the 1970 code 001 (accountant).

This procedure was repeated separately for black men, white women, and black women. In the end, I had the total number of each race/gender group in 1980 who were accountants (occupational code 001) according to the 1970 occupational classification scheme.

CORRECTION FACTOR FOR NONRESPONSE CASES

In each of the three census years, people who did not indicate their occupations (i.e., nonresponse cases) were allocated (i.e., distributed) by the Census Bureau differently. In 1960 there was one overall "nonresponse" category for the entire detailed occupational system (USDC, Bureau of Census, 1963). In 1970, each of the 12 major occupational groups in the labor force had a separate nonresponse or "allocated" category (USDC, Bureau of Census, 1975). For the professions it was "professional/technical/kindred workers—allocated." In the current study, the "professional/technical/kindred—allocated" category in 1970 has been eliminated from the analysis. Thus 1960 and 1970 are comparable in having *no* allocated or nonresponse categories in the professions.

In 1980 a completely different procedure was applied by the Census Bureau: all nonresponse cases were distributed *throughout* the 503 detailed occupational categories (USDC, Bureau of Census, 1983a). In order to correct for this difference, I had to *subtract* these nonresponse cases from each of the professional/technical detailed occupational categories in my study. I did this by multiplying the number in each detailed occupational category in the 1980 census by a factor of 0.9509164. This correction factor was derived by comparing the distribution of all persons in the professional and technical labor force before and after allocation procedures were carried out (USDC, Bureau of Census, 1983b). However, it should be clear that these data are available only for the employed population. My study, in contrast, includes the experienced civilian labor force. Therefore, while this correction factor is the best available (John Priebe, personal communication, 1987), it would have been better if it had been based on the experienced civilian and not the employed labor force.

Population

In the final analysis, after the procedures were applied to make the 1960 and 1980 data comparable to 1970 occupational categories, and "nonresponses" were corrected across census years, we find that blacks in professional and technical work increased between 1960 and 1980 from 286,000 to 1.14 million;

TABLE A.5   NUMBERS OF BLACKS AND WHITES, WOMEN AND MEN, IN 1960, 1970, 1980 PROFESSIONS AND TECHNICAL OCCUPATIONS, USING DATA MADE COMPARABLE ACROSS CENSUS YEARS*

		1960	1970	1980
Whites				
	Men	4,213,960	6,370,637	7,833,274
	Women	2,514,625	3,999,719	6,290,216
	Total	6,728,585	10,370,356	14,123,490
Blacks				
	Men	105,942	219,860	418,798
	Women	179,691	354,446	717,968
	Total	285,633	574,306	1,136,766

*Correction factor for nonresponse cases included here.

whites, from 6.73 to 14.12 million. While black men and black women show a higher rate of increase in the professions and technical areas (a quadrupling of their representation) than white men and women (a doubling and tripling, respectively), this is largely based on the much smaller numbers with which blacks began. (See Table A.5.)

CORRECTION FACTOR FOR UNDERCOUNT OF RACE/GENDER GROUPS IN THE EXPERIENCED CIVILIAN LABOR FORCE

Two indexes were developed in this book: the Index of Representation (which compares a race/gender group's representation in a particular profession with its representation in the labor force as a whole) and the Index of Relative Advantage (which tells how well represented one race/gender group in a particular profession is in comparison to another race/gender group in that profession). Both indexes use in their calculations figures for the experienced civilian labor force as a whole, separately for each race/gender group. This is a problem because, according to the Census Bureau, there was a gross undercount of blacks, both men and women, in the total population (and therefore in the labor force overall) in each of the three census years.[7] It was highest for black men (the undercount for black men of all ages ranges from 8.8 to 10.6 percent for each of the three census years); half as high for black women (3.1 to 6.2 percent); and much lower for white men (1.5 to 3.0 percent) and white women (0 to 2.4 percent). In this study, I applied a correction factor to the data for the *experienced civilian labor force* in order to minimize the distorting effect of this gross undercount of blacks, particularly the men, in the population. Separate correction factors were developed for each race/gender group for each census year. I am indebted to Gregory Robinson from the Census Bureau for his help in this effort.

TABLE A.6   NUMBERS OF BLACKS AND WHITES, WOMEN AND MEN, IN 1960, 1970, 1980 IN THE EXPERIENCED CIVILIAN LABOR FORCE, USING DATA MADE COMPARABLE ACROSS CENSUS YEARS*

	1960	1970	1980
Whites			
Men	42,501,080	45,768,440	52,812,383
Women	19,827,062	26,838,833	37,304,700
Total	62,328,142	72,607,273	90,117,083
Blacks			
Men	4,502,461	4,828,431	5,829,985
Women	2,840,446	3,733,343	5,356,811
Total	7,342,907	8,561,773	11,186,796

*Correction factor for undercount of race/gender groups included here.

In the undercount correction factor, for each race/gender group for each census year separately, I estimated the number of people in (1) the Census Bureau's estimated population of the census between the ages of 15 and 64 years old and (2) the Census Bureau's estimated under/overcount for the same age and race/gender groups (Fay et al., 1988, Tables A.60.3, A.70.3, and A.80.3). The correction factor was created by dividing the sum of the estimated population for the age-appropriate race/gender group by the difference between the estimated population and the estimated undercount for that group. This correction factor was reduced to 75 percent of its value before it was applied to the experienced civilian labor force data because it was impossible to adjust against the unknown effect of the undercount numbers of the professions, an effect which would be *much less* than with the labor force as a whole, but impossible to estimate. This correction factor was then multiplied against the experienced civilian labor force numbers for each race/gender group for each census year. Given these changes, the numbers in the total experienced civilian labor force for 1960, 1970, and 1980 appear in Table A.6.

APPENDIX 2: DETAILED OCCUPATIONAL CENSUS CATEGORIES FOR PROFESSIONS AND TECHNICAL FIELDS

Detailed Occupational Census Categories Used in Different Levels of Occupational Domination Variable among *Professions and Technical Fields* Based on 1970 Detailed Census Categories, as Used to Analyze 1960 and 1980 Census Data Made Comparable to 1970 With Nam-Powers Occupational-Status Score

---

I. PROFESSIONS

MALE-DOMINATED PROFESSIONS (0 to 20 percent female)

Elite Male-Dominated Professions

lawyer	99
physician	99
dentist	99
optometrist	99
podiatrist	99
veterinarian	99
some college teachers*:	
agricultural science	96
atmospheric science	96
chemistry	97
physics	97
engineering	98
economics	98
law	99
psychology	96
geologist	97
physicist	99
life and physical scientist/nec	97
architect	97

some engineers:
    aeronautical/astronautical   96
    chemical   97
    metallurgical   96
    petroleum   96

Nonelite Male-Dominated Professions	
accountant	89
chiropractor	95
clergy	77
some college teachers:	
mathematics	95
sociology	94
trade/industry/technology	90
history	95
college and university, subject not specified	87
some engineers:	
civil	95
electrical and electronic	95
industrial	93
mechanical	95
mining	94
sales	94
not elsewhere classified (nec)	94
some scientists:	
agricultural	91
atmospheric/space	95
chemist	94
operations and systems research analyst	91
pharmacist	94
urban planner	95
farm management adviser	94
forester/conservationist	78
archivist and curator	80
actuary	94
designer	89
photographer	75
radio and TV announcer	71

**GENDER-NEUTRAL (Non-Sex-Segregated)
PROFESSIONS (20 to 60 percent female)**

math scientist/nec (mathematician)	96
statistician	88
computer systems analyst	93
computer programmer	89
biological scientist	91
some college teachers:	
biology	96
health specialties	96
business and commerce	95
social science/nec	96
art/drama/music	92
coaches and physical education	94
education	98
English	91
foreign languages	89
miscellaneous	94

psychologist	96	
social scientist/nec	91	
adult-education teacher	81	
secondary-school teacher	86	(public)
	77	(private)
vocational and educational counselor	92	
actor	71	
athlete	56	
author	90	
editor/reporter	86	
musician/composer	49	
painter/sculptor	77	
public relations and publicity writer	91	
writer/artist/entertainer/nec	80	
research worker, not specified	86	
personnel and labor relations specialist	89	
religious worker/nec	59	
recreation worker	58	
judge**	99	

FEMALE-DOMINATED PROFESSIONS (60 to 100 percent female)

elementary-school teacher	80	(public)
	66	(private)
nurse (registered)	66	
social worker	82	
librarian	75	
prekindergarten and kindergarten teacher	72	(public)
	47	(private)
noncollege teacher/nec	52	
home management adviser	77	
dietitian	56	
therapist	73	
dancer	40	
computer specialist/nec**	93	
theology college professor**	91	

II. TECHNICIANS

MALE-DOMINATED TECHNICIANS (0 to 20 percent female)

chemical technician	79
drafter	80
electrical and electronic engineering technician	82
industrial engineering technician	79
mechanical engineering technician	86
engineering and science technician/nec	77
surveyor	72
airplane pilot	94
air-traffic controller	85
embalmer	75
flight engineer	91
tool programmer (numerical control)	87
technician/nec	79
radio operator	60
therapy assistant**	54

GENDER-NEUTRAL TECHNICIANS (20 to 60 percent female)
agriculture and biological technician, except health   65
health technologist and technician/nec   63

FEMALE-DOMINATED TECHNICIANS (60 to 100 percent female)
clinical laboratory technologist and technician   70
dental hygienist   70
health-record technologist and technician   68
radiologic technologist and technician   64

*Only if the detailed census category was 0 to 20 percent female was it included in the male profes-
sions for college teachers. Others were classified according to their "percent female." Thus some
college professors fall into gender-neutral professions (and one into female-dominated professions). The principle used here was that every detailed occupational category provided by the 1970
census was used, not an aggregated category. However, the Census Bureau has indicated a certain
degree of unreliability in the specialties reported by college professors, since each census between
1960 and 1980 has an increasingly larger category of unspecified college-professor responses: in
1960 it was about one-third; in 1980 about two-thirds (John Priebe, personal communication,
1986).

**The categories of judge, computer specialist/nec, theology college professor, and therapy assistant
are classified according to the directions stated in Chapter 1. However, these four classifications
appear to be problematic since the classification on the basis of the "percent female" flies in the
face of what is typically expected. For example, judges are typically described as male, but here
are classified as a gender-neutral profession. For further discussion, see Chapter 1, "Methodological Note," p. 28.

In addition, six detailed occupations with *no* categories in 1960, but with categories listed in the
1970 census, had to be eliminated from this analysis: marine scientist, health practitioner/nec,
home-economics college professor, mathematical technician, political scientist, and sociologist.
All include very small numbers and should not affect the results.

NOTES

Preface

1. The 1990 census data are not yet available and promise to be long in coming to researchers given the more restricted access to government statistics begun under the Reagan administration.

Chapter I

1. My use of the term *racial/ethnic minorities* follows that of Evelyn Nakano Glenn: it designates "groups that are simultaneously racial and ethnic minorities. . . . blacks, Latinos, and Asian Americans, groups that share a legacy of labor exploitation and special forms of oppression. . . . It is offered as an alternative to more commonly used designations—minority groups, people of color, and Third World minorities—each of which is problematic in some way" (Glenn, 1987:73).

2. I use the term "black" instead of Afro-American, African-American, or some other term, because the overwhelming majority of blacks define themselves this way: visualize the "black power" movement of the late 1960s-1970s, and recent surveys where "Most [72 percent] Blacks Are Found to Favor Term 'Black'" (1991). In addition, Census Bureau data, on which my study is based, use the term black without distinguishing African-Americans from those born outside the United States.

3. The only other professions included in the list are kindergarten, elementary, and secondary school teaching; accounting and auditing; and computer systems analysis. One technical field, computer programming, is also listed in this grouping of the 20 occupations with the largest anticipated growth.

4. According to Bose (1985), registered nursing ranks 62 on the NORC/Siegal scores and 50 on the Ducan SEI score. It ranks 66 on the Nam-Powers (1983) occupational status score.

5. It is true that black enrollment in higher education overall peaked in the mid-late 1970s; but it declined throughout the 1980s (Carter and Wilson, 1989). And although black enrollment in professional schools actually increased during the 1980s, the latest figures reveal that in 1987 blacks received only 4.8 percent of all professional degrees (Carter and Wilson, 1989).

6. For a review of the theoretical literature on gender, class, and work, see Sokoloff (1980).

7. For a recent review of gender, race/ethnicity, and class as interconnected historical processes of domination and subordination that affect the economic and work lives of various groups of women quite differently, see Amott and Matthaei (1991).

8. The Latino/a (Hispanic) population, which is currently one of the fastest-growing minority groups along with Asians in the United States, has been variously classified as "white" and "nonwhite" by the Census Bureau during the period I cover, and before the 1970s Latinos/as were not even enumerated as a distinct category at all. (For problems associated with differential coding of Latino/a populations in 1960, 1970, and 1980, see USDC, Bureau of Census, 1983a.) Since the Latino/a population was not identified in 1960 and was classified only by race (black or white), I do likewise in my study by including white Latinos/as in the white population and black Latinos/as in the black population.

9. For that matter, neither do white men. However, the majority of white men do obtain what are considered to be very desirable jobs in our society: professional/managerial/skilled craftsmen.

10. I use the term *disadvantaged groups* to refer to black women and white women and black men who are generally disadvantaged in income, education, and employment in relation to the more privileged group of white men in this society. However, even among the disadvantaged groups, some members are better off than others—especially in terms of class advantage.

11. While Amott and Matthaei (1991) provide an excellent discussion of the overall changes in the labor force of different race/gender groups in the United States over the course of the 20th century, Reskin and Roos (1990, Chapters 1,2) discuss the employment experiences of women in male-dominated occupations in particular.

12. See Carr-Saunders and Wilson (1933) for a classic definition of professions. Also, see here Greenwood (1957).

13. Braverman (1974) includes professionals, but not technicians, along with managers and administrators in the professional managerial class.

14. This does not preclude the fact that different sectors of a profession might provide avenues of mobility for more economically disadvantaged men. For example, see Smigel's (1960, 1964) and Baron's (1983) discussions of the dual bar in the legal profession.

15. Of course the issue is simultaneously one of class as well as race and gender. However, since the current study focuses on the experiences of professional women, *some* of the class variables are already controlled for. For an analysis of the social mobility of different race/gender groups in the socioeconomic system into the professions, among other jobs, see Higginbotham and Cannon (1988).

16. More recently, even when race and gender are both included, the focus is often not on the equally important experiences of black women. For example, Farley (1984) has compared men and women by race, but has focused primary attention on men and has given more superficial treatment to women's experiences.

17. Although outside of the mainstream theory, both Marxist and socialist feminist theory can be said to provide a social structural analysis.

18. For a review of this perspective on race, gender, and work in general—that is, not specifically on women in the professions—see Amott and Matthaei (1991). For an earlier review of Marxist, Marxist feminist, and socialist feminist theory on women and work, see Sokoloff (1980).

19. The earliest of the classic studies on gender segregation are Gross (1968) and Oppenheimer (1970). Both look at the amount of gender segregation between 1900 and 1960. Further work includes Council of Economic Advisors (1973), Stevenson (1975), Blau and Hendricks (1979), Dub-

noff (1979), G. Williams (1979), Burris and Wharton (1982), and Jacobs (1989). Many of these studies are summarized in England (1981).

20. Other research supports the idea that despite the persistence of high levels of segregation in the 1980s, large and significant declines in gender segregation have occurred in the professions (and sometimes in management) since World War II, with the greatest changes having taken place during the 1970s. These include Beller (1984), Jacobs (1984, 1986), and Bianchi and Rytina (1986) as well as earlier works by Blitz (1974) and Fuchs (1975). For a review of this literature, see Sokoloff (1986).

21. See Freeman's (1976) analysis of educated black men. Also, for the conservative black male argument, see Sowell (1990). For a sympathetic review of Sowell emphasizing the belief that blacks are hindered by affirmative action, see Hacker (1990).

22. Note that Epstein's arguments are on the special treatment ensuing from the doubly disadvantaged status—*not* based on affirmative action, but on role theory.

23. For limited exceptions to this criticism during the 1970s, see Szymanski (1974), Almquist (1979). However, neither deals with the question of women's increase in male-dominated professions specifically between 1960 and 1980. This changes somewhat in the 1980s as racial/ethnic women in particular begin to explore the lives of many groups of racial/ethnic women in more detail, and somewhat of black women in the professions. For example, see Higginbotham (1987), Higginbotham and Cannon (1988), and Glenn (1987, 1992). See also Hill (1986), Landry (1987), Swinton (1990), Amott and Matthaei (1991).

24. It was not possible to include elite and nonelite distinctions for the female professions. As with the labor force in general, women were located in a much smaller range of occupations than were men in the professions. The men were in a large number of varied occupations in both elite and nonelite male professions; in contrast, large numbers of women were concentrated in a much smaller number of female professions. Moreover, because the numbers of black men and black women were so small, any attempt to utilize elite and nonelite classifications in the female and neutral professions and technical fields would have created too much statistical unreliability. Finally, although no such distinction is made for the 33 gender neutral professions, 7 of them qualify as elite according to the criteria used for the male professions. Their numbers are so small, however, that they would not constitute a large enough category for purposes of comparison.

25. No uniform procedure exists by which occupations are classified as male or female dominated (see Rytina and Bianchi, 1984). Instead, categories typically have been defined arbitrarily by using a 5, 10, or 20 percentage point spread around the female proportion of the total work force. Since the "percent female" differed for each of the three census years studied, I decided to use 40 percent, which is close to the average of 44.4 percent female in the professions for the three census years, as the point at which a particular occupation within the professional/technical labor force was gender segregated. Next, I selected a conservative 20 percentage point spread around the average of 40 percent to be used in defining male-, neutral-, and female-dominated professions/technical areas. This procedure is similar to the one used by Bianchi and Rytina (1984).

26. "That is, assignment of a score for the occupation depends on the relative position of the median for that occupation in the array of medians for all occupations. . . . a third ingredient for determining the status score is the number of persons in the occupations" (Nam and Powers, 1983:49).

27. Because of the extraordinarily high undercount of black men in the census (reaching almost one-fifth of all black men aged 40–49 years old in 1980) and therefore in the labor force (Fay et al., 1988), a correction factor was developed for the experienced civilian labor force in both indexes to minimize the distorting effect of this undercount. In fact, under/overcounts for the different race/gender groups required correction factors to be created for each group for each census year. See the end of Appendix 1, "Methodology," on "Correction Factor for Undercount of Race/Gender Groups in the Experienced Civilian Labor Force."

Chapter 2

1.   I have had to exclude race from this portion of the analysis for two reasons. First, the number of blacks in the professions is so small that it is impossible to set up race/gender occupational categories that are large enough to be meaningful. Second, although black women may be more heavily concentrated in some professional/technical fields than are white women, by and large both black and white women are concentrated in the same professions (e.g., elementary education, social work). Thus the differences between blacks and whites would not show up sufficiently at this level of occupational analysis.

2.   Individual status scores for selected professions and technical fields can be found in Table 1.1 Median incomes for each occupation are presented in Table 2.2, Column 1.

3.   Because of the small numbers and often very small percentages among all race/gender groups in the technical fields, as the analysis proceeds I focus on professional jobs but add technical fields where relevant.

4.   Reference to the 30 large detailed occupations can be found in Table 2.2. Otherwise, all 94 occupations included in the 7-category intermediate-level analysis (male, neutral, and female professions/technical fields) can be found in Appendix 2, "Detailed Occupational Census Categories . . ."

5.   Only 12 of the 94 professional/technical fields included in this study shrank between 1960 and 1980. More than half of these were in the specialized college-teaching professions. Another 15 college-teaching specialties showed a net increase between 1960 and 1980, but a serious decline during the 1970s. Secondary education is the only large profession that experienced a decline of 175,000 jobs during the 1970s but ended up with a net gain between 1960 and 1980 of almost 250,000 new jobs.

Chapter 3

1.   Note that while it is true that elite and nonelite male professions have very similar median occupational status scores, 97 and 94 respectively, the range of scores is quite different for the two groups: status scores for individual occupations in elite male professions range from 96 to 99; in nonelite male professions from 71 to 95.

2.   The reader should be aware that percentages and ratios are carried out six digits to the right of the decimal point. This is particularly important to remember when ratios are based on one very small percentage being divided by another very small percentage. Due to this fact, calculations made by hand for ratios from the percentages may come out somewhat differently from those given in the text.

3.   Findings for neutral and female-dominated technical fields are less reliable than for male-dominated fields because of the small number of detailed occupational categories included: two and four, respectively.

4.   The criterion for change is a move of at least 0.10 points on the index. Even though white men moved from a ratio of 1.50 to 1.42 in the nonelite male professions, they are considered to have remained at the same level of overrepresentation since the move did not reach the minimal criterion for change.

Chapter 4

1.   Note that nonspecific college teaching exhibited a trend in the same direction.

2.   For information on 1980 median income for each of the 30 large professions and technical fields, see Chapter 2, Table 2.2, Column 1.

3. In addition, white men were slightly underrepresented in both 1960 and 1980 (ratio = 0.79 both years) among secondary-school teachers. Although white men could not argue that they were losing out in relation to other groups since their rate of representation remained constant, they could stress the fact that they were not equitably treated here since they were not at parity.

Chapter 5

1. The largest growth rates are determined here by whether they are more than twice the average growth rate (1.18) in the professions/technical areas as a whole. (See Table 2.2.)

Chapter 6

1. While it is true that white women did not reach a 0.10 point change in the index among the elites, nevertheless they moved from very severe to severe levels of underrepresentation (0.09 to 0.17). For definition of these levels, see Chapter 1, "Methodological Note," p.31.

2. In addition, white women and white men reached or remained at parity with one another (as would be expected in neutral professions) only as personnel and labor relations specialists and as research workers. Only in one gender-neutral occupation did white women decrease their overrepresentation somewhat: secondary-school teaching.

3. Given this trend, one wonders if this tendency was happening among mechanical engineers (0.21 to 0.12) and physicians (0.72 to 0.63), who decreased only 0.09 points in the index.

4. In the female technical fields, white women's presence was 4 to 5 times greater than black men's or white men's.

Chapter 7

1. Black women increased in the gender-neutral technicians also, but this is a very small portion of the total.

2. I am here distinguishing between *technical-oriented* professions and the technical fields. They are not the same. *Technical-oriented* professions are those in comparison to *human or public service* professions. Technical fields are the Census Bureau's distinction between professionals and technicians.

3. See here Wilkie (1985), who also documents the decline in occupational segregation between black women and white women over the course of the 20th century, especially in expanding professional and clerical jobs after World War II.

4. This trend is supported in the detailed analysis for large professions (see Table 7.4, Columns 5,6). Black women became half as likely (or *less under*represented) as white women to be working as accountants, nonspecific college teachers, chemists, and engineers (electronic and electrical, mechanical, industrial, civil, and nec). This also applied to the elite male professions of medicine (which moved from a ratio of 0.24 to 0.53) and law (which moved from a ratio of 0.22 to 0.47).

5. Note that in computer programming, white women decreased and black women increased, but neither began nor ended as overrepresented.

6. In the gender-neutral professions, most of white men's decline in the Index of Representation hovered around parity except for counseling. This is the one neutral profession in which black women moved from moderately underrepresented in 1960 to severely overrepresented in 1980.

7. Black women, like white women, were better represented in 1980 than in 1960 in most of these same nonelite male and gender-neutral professions. However, black women were represented

at a far lower level than white women, who were either at or near parity. So one might conclude that black women experienced some gains if white men decreased their overrepresentation, but not to the extent that white women did.

8.   In addition, the intermediate-level analysis revealed that black women moved from moderate underrepresentation to slight overrepresentation in the smaller group of neutral professions. However, we cannot check these results with the detailed analysis because none of the neutral professions fit the criteria to be included among the "large" professions.

9.   It is worth repeating that the occupations did not necessarily become race/gender segregated; rather, black women as a group became resegregated into certain occupations.

Chapter 8

1.   Because the numbers of black men and black women in the professions are so small, it is impossible for a profession/technical field to become a "black" occupation—that is, over 50 percent black. However, black men or black women may be concentrated in a particular occupation, making it likely that, as a group, they will become locked into certain positions in the professions/technical areas. This is a form of segregation. For example, in New York City in 1990, the Human Resources Administration has become predominantly black in its managerial staff (Human Resources Administration report, 1991). This leads many whites to argue that this is proof of blacks getting all the advantages. I would argue, instead, that this is part of the process whereby blacks are resegregated into certain occupations and sectors of an organization (here a city bureaucracy), with the higher-level, still highly valued positions or sectors remaining predominantly white and male.

2.   Professions and technical fields as a group, as well as the 30 large ones, expand at a much faster rate than other jobs in the economy as a whole. Some of the smaller professions and technical fields (with less than 100,000 occupants in 1970) may operate differently.

3.   A young white man, sitting in the audience at a professional sociology meeting where I presented some of my findings, offered the following relevant observation: On the one hand, my findings suggest it is inappropriate to talk about the "displacement" of white men by women and minorities in the more advantaged professions; white men clearly are still in control. On the other hand, he continued, it may well be the case that the increasing number of white women, black women, and black men challenges white male "hegemony" in certain professions, creating a new sense of unease for this traditionally privileged group of white men.

4.   The fastest *growth rates* occurred in nonspecific college teaching, engineering (nec), counseling, personnel and labor relations, computer programming, social work, and clinical-laboratory technology. In addition, growth rates were above average for all professions and technical fields in law, accounting, research work, library work, elementary education, electronic technology, and engineering and science technology/nec.

5.   Despite the fact that the ministry traditionally has been an important occupation for black men, my data show that not only were white men severely overrepresented, but they became *more so* between 1960 and 1980.

6.   These were also occupations where men's incomes declined, but less than women's.

7.   The authors defined black women as overconcentrated in a profession if they were at least twice as likely to be represented in that profession as in the labor force as a whole.

8.   Here black men made up 3 percent, white women 23 percent, and white men 67 percent of managers.

9.   This finding is supported by a study of 1974 Harvard Law School graduates reinterviewed 10 years later. Of those Harvard Law women who entered private practice, only 23 percent were partners 10 years later, while 59 percent of the male attorneys who graduated Harvard Law School in 1974

were partners 10 years later (as reported in Hoffman, 1989). While this study refers to all women, and therefore primarily white women, the message is clear: graduating from a prestigious law school does not have the same impact for women (white or black) as for men.

10.   According to Gilkes, many of these women become "rebellious professionals" or "race women" in the black community. These terms refer to women who, despite being professionals—social workers, nurses, counselors, lawyers, or college professors—view their professional status on a moral, not an occupational, basis. In their work they reject professional ideologies that support traditional practices and values operating in white institutions, which they see as "part of, if not the root of, some of the problems they are trying to solve" in the black community (1982:307).

11.   Thus, for example, we know that not only white male elites, but historically many white working class men have fought hard against the inclusion of women into better off male jobs: crafts (Hartmann, 1976) and law enforcement (Price and Gavin, 1982) are but two examples. In addition, Glazer (1991) has documented the defensive reactions of many white women in nursing against policies imposed by (primarily white male) hospital owners, investors, some charities and the state, as well as offensive actions by (typically white) nursing associations trying to "professionalize" that exclude black women. These activities parallel actions taken by white male workers and professionals trying to protect their "turf" in the occupational arena.

Appendix I

1.   I am indebted to Suzanne Bianchi, who shared materials with me for 1970 and 1980 before the Census Bureau published them, thereby allowing me to develop the procedures used in this study to make the data comparable across census years and, ultimately, to do so for all four race/gender groups. John Priebe later made available the revised reports making 1970–1980 census data comparable as soon as they were published in 1986.

2.   In my study, I use the occupational-classification systems described in the following government documents. For 1960, see USDC, Bureau of Census, 1963; for 1970, USDC, Bureau of Census, 1975; and for 1980, see USDC, Bureau of Census, 1983a.

3.   Broad categories refer to occupations at the level of professional, administrative, clerical, service work, and so on.

4.   Certain minor changes are noted here: in my study, public and private classifications for school teacher were collapsed into one school category in 1960 and 1970, because no other public-private distinctions were made in the detailed occupational data. Also, most other census publications with detailed occupational categories did not include this distinction.

A different type of problem exists with college professors. Here, the number of college professors stating a specialty area declined from two-thirds of all responses to only one-third by 1980. This probably distorts some of the information in the professional categories—especially concerning the "percentage female" for college professors discussed below—since we do not know the type of college professors involved. See Appendix 2 for the breakdown of college-professor specialties among the occupational-status variable.

5.   It would have been more desirable to standardize the data according to the 1980 census as many more detailed changes were made in 1980. However, this was not possible at the time that this study was undertaken. It is true that Technical Report 59 came out in 1989 (Vines and Priebe, 1989) comparing 1970 and 1980 occupational and industrial detailed categories similar to that prepared by Priebe, Heinkel, and Greene (1972) comparing 1960 and 1970. However, the Census Bureau converted the 1970 data into the 1980 categories. I, on the other hand, needed the 1980 data converted into the 1970 categories so that I could likewise compare with 1960. Thus the way I have made the data comparable has not, to my knowledge, been done by anyone else.

6.   It would have been desirable for this information to be given by race/gender instead of gender alone. See below for discussion.

7.   The undercount of the black population continues at an even higher rate in the 1990 census. According to the Census Bureau's oversight committee, at least 2 million blacks were not counted (Barringer, 1991).

REFERENCES

Alexander, Keith. 1990. "Minority Women Feel Racism, Sexism Are Blocking the Path to Management." *Wall Street Journal*, July 25:B1.

Almquist, Elizabeth McTaggart. 1979. *Minorities, Gender and Work*. Lexington, Mass.: D. C. Heath.

Alston, Denise A. 1987. "Black Women in Management: Solving Problems; Asserting Authority." Paper presented at Fourth Annual Women and Work Conference, University of Texas at Arlington.

Altman, Lawrence K. 1988. "Few Women Attain Top Positions on Faculty." *New York Times*, December 15:B23.

————, with Elisabeth Rosenthal. 1990. "Changes in Medicine Bring Pain to Healing Profession." *New York Times*, February 18:A1, A34.

Amott, Teresa L., and Julie A. Matthaei. 1991. *Race, Gender & Work: A Multicultural Economic History of Women in the United States*. Boston: South End.

Angier, Natalie. 1991. "Women Swell Ranks of Science, but Remain Invisible at the Top." *New York Times*, May 21:C1,C12.

Babad, Elisha Y., Max Birnbaum, and Kenneth D. Benne. 1983. *The Social Self: Group Influences on Personal Identity*. Newbury Park, California: Sage.

Baron, Ava. 1983. "Feminization of the Legal Profession—Progress or Proletarianization?" *ALSA (American Legal Studies Association) Forum* 7:330–357.

Barringer, Felicity. 1991. "2 Million Blacks Not Counted in Census, Lawmaker Asserts." *New York Times*, March 12:A18.

Bartlett, Sarah. 1991. "New York Cost-Cutting Idea: City Jobs, Outside Workers." *New York Times*, July 7:1, 16.

Beale, Frances. 1970. "Double Jeopardy: To Be Black and Female." In Toni Cade (Bambara) (ed.), *The Black Woman*, 90–100. New York: New American Library.

Bell, Daniel. 1973. *The Coming of Post-Industrial Society*. New York: Basic Books.

Beller, Andrea. 1984. "Trends in Occupational Segregation by Sex and Race, 1960–1981." In Barbara Reskin (ed.), *Sex Segregation in the Workplace*, 11–26. Washington, D.C.: National Academy Press.

Bergmann, Barbara. 1974. "Occupational Segregation, Wages and Profits When Employers Discriminate by Race or Sex." *Eastern Economic Journal* 1 (April/July): 103–110.

————. 1985. "Is There a Conflict between Racial Justice and Women's Liberation?" *Rutgers Law Review* 37 (Summer): 805–824.

Bernard, Jessie. 1966. *Marriage and Family Among Negroes*. Englewood Cliffs, N.J.: Prentice Hall.

————. 1971. *Women and the Public Interest: An Essay on Policy and Protest*. Chicago: Aldine-Atherton.

Bianchi, Suzanne, and Nancy Rytina. 1984. "Occupational Change, 1970–1980." Paper presented at the Population Association of America, Minneapolis.

————. 1986. "The Decline in Occupational Sex Segregation during the 1970s: Census and CPS Comparisons." *Demography* 23(February):79–86.

Bielby, William T., and James N. Baron. 1986. "Men and Women at Work: Sex Segregation and Statistical Discrimination." *American Journal of Sociology* 91 (January): 759–799.

Birnbaum, Norman. 1971. *Toward A Critical Sociology*. New York: Oxford University Press.

Blackwell, James. 1981. *Mainstreaming Outsiders: The Production of Black Professionals*. Bayside, N.Y.: General Hall.

Blau, Francine. 1989. "Occupational Segregation by Gender: A Look at the 1980s." Revised paper presented at the 1988 American Economics Association meetings, New York.

————, and Wallace Hendricks. 1979. "Occupational Segregation by Sex: Trends and Prospects." *Journal of Human Resources* 14 (Spring): 197–210.

Blau, Peter, and Otis Dudley Duncan. 1967. *The American Occupational Structure*. New York: Free Press.

Blitz, Rudolph C. 1974. "Women in the Professions, 1870–1970." *Monthly Labor Review* 97 (May):34–39.

Bluestone, Barry, and Bennett Harrison. 1986. "The Great American Job Machine: The Proliferation of Low Wage Employment in the U.S. Economy." A Study Prepared for the Joint Economic Committee.

Bly, Robert. 1990. *Iron John: A Book about Men*. Reading, Mass.: Addison-Wesley.

Bock, E. Wilbur. 1969. "Farmer's Daughter Effect: The Case of the Negro Female Professionals." *Phylon* 30 (January): 17–26.

Bose, Christine E. 1985. *Jobs and Gender: A Study of Occupational Prestige*. New York: Praeger.

Bowman, Marjorie, and Marcy Lynn Gross. 1986. "Overview of Research on Women in Medicine—Issues for Public Policymakers." *Public Health Reports* 101(Sept.-Oct.):513–521.

Braverman, Harry. 1974. *Labor and Monopoly Capital: The Degradation of Work in the Twentieth Century*. New York: Monthly Review Press.

Brenner, Joel Glenn. 1990. "Minority Lawyers Missed Out on Hiring Boom." *Washington Post*, February 13:A8.

Broom, Leonard, and Norval D. Glenn. 1969. "The Occupations and Income of Black Americans." In Norval D. Glenn and Charles M. Bonjean (eds.), *Blacks in the United States*, 22–42. San Francisco: Chandler.

Brown, Carol A. 1974. "Women Workers in the Health Service Industry." Unpublished Ms., New York.

Burris, Val, and Amy Wharton. 1982. "Sex Segregation in the U.S. Labor Force." *Review of Radical Political Economics* 14(Spring-Winter):42–56.

Burstein, Paul. 1985. *Discrimination, Jobs, and Politics: The Struggle for Equal Employment Opportunity in the United States since the New Deal*. Chicago: University of Chicago Press.

Carey, Max L. 1981. "Occupational Employment Growth through 1990." *Monthly Labor Review* 104 (August): 42–55.

Carr-Saunders, Alexander M., and P. A. Wilson. 1933. *The Professions*. London: Oxford University Press.

Carter, Michael, and Susan Boslego Carter. 1981. "Women's Recent Progress in the Professions; or, Women Get a Ticket to Ride after the Gravy Train Has Left the Station." *Feminist Studies* 7 (Fall):477–504.

Carter, Deborah J. and Reginald Wilson. 1989 *Minorities in Higher Education, Eighth Annual Status Report*. Washington, D.C.: American Council on Education.

Castro, Janice. 1985. "More and More, She's the Boss." *Time,* December 2:64–66.

Catanzarite, Lisa M., and Myra H. Strober. 1988. "Occupational Attractiveness and Race-Gender Segregation." Paper presented at American Sociological Association meetings, Atlanta, August.

"Class of '86: Over 50 Percent Women Up from 25 Percent Twelve Years Ago." 1986. *NYU Law* (Spring):1–5,14.

Cohn, Samuel. 1985. *The Process of Occupational Sex-Typing: The Feminization of Clerical Labor in Great Britain*. Philadelphia: Temple University Press.

Collins, Patricia Hill. 1990. *Black Feminist Thought: Knowledge, Consciousness, and the Politics of Empowerment*. Boston: Unwin Hyman.

Collins, Sharon M. 1983. "The Making of the Black Middle Class." *Social Problems* 30 (April): 369–382.

———. 1989. "The Marginalization of Black Executives." *Social Problems* 36 (October): 317–331.

Corey, Mary. 1991. "Re-Inventing Man." *The Baltimore Sun,* May 16:1F,6F.

Cortese, Anthony J. 1987. "Affirmative Action: Are White Women Gaining at the Expense of Black Men?" Paper presented at American Sociological Association meetings, Chicago.

Cott, Nancy F. 1987. *The Grounding of Modern Feminism*. New Haven and London: Yale University Press.

Council of Economic Advisors. 1973. *Economic Report of the President 1973*. Washington, D.C.: U.S. Government Printing Office.

Cowan, Alison Leigh. 1992. "The New Letdown: Making Partner." *New York Times,* April 1: D1, D8.

Crustinger, Martin. 1990. "Study: Men in Most Top Jobs at Fed." *Washington Post,* September 4:B8.

Cummings, Judith. 1983. "Breakup of Black Family Imperils Gains of Decades," *New York Times,* November 20:1,56.

Daly, Kathleen. 1991. "Poverty, Prison, and Pregnancy: From Partners in Misery to Partners for Change." Paper presented at conference on Women and Crime, John Jay College of Criminal Justice, New York City.

Daniels, Lee A. 1989. "Experts Foresee a Social Gap between Sexes among Blacks." *New York Times,* February 5:1,30.

Davies, Margery. 1974. "Woman's Place Is at the Typewriter: The Feminization of the Clerical Labor Force." *Radical America* 8 (July–August):1–28.

Davis, Angela. 1971. "The Role of Black Women in the Community of Slaves." *Black Scholar* 3 (December):2–15.

Deutsch, Claudia H. 1987. "The Ax Falls on Equal Opportunity." *New York Times,* January 4:F1,F27.

———. 1991. "Don't Forget the White Males." *New York Times,* December 8:F29.

Dill, Bonnie Thornton. 1983. " 'On the Hem of Life': Race, Class and the Prospects for Sisterhood." In Amy Serdlow and Hannah Lessinger (eds.), *Class, Race and Sex: The Dynamics of Control,* 173–188. New York: G. K. Hall.

———, Lynn Weber Cannon, and Reeve Vanneman. 1987. "Race and Gender in Occupational

Segregation." In *Pay Equity: An Issue of Race, Ethnicity and Sex,* 10–69. Washington, D.C.: National Committee on Pay Equity.

DiTomaso, Nancy, and Donna E. Thompson. 1988. "Minority Success in Corporate Management." In Donna E. Thompson and Nancy DiTomaso (eds.), *Ensuring Minority Success in Corporate Management,* 3–24. New York: Plenum.

Dowd, Maureen. 1991. "Bush Appoints More Women, but It's All-Male Club at Top." *New York Times,* May 20:A1,B6.

Dressel, Paula. 1987. "Patriarchy and Social Welfare Work." *Social Problems* 34 (June):294–309.

Dubnoff, Steven. 1979. "Beyond Sex Typing: Capitalism, Patriarchy and the Growth of Female Employment, 1940–1970." Paper presented at the Eastern Sociological Society meetings, New York.

Dubois, W.E.B. 1967. *The Philadelphia Negro: A Social Study.* New York: Schocken Books. First published 1899.

Dullea, Georgia. 1984. "Women as Judges: The Ranks Grow." *New York Times,* April 26:C1,C12.

Ehrenhalt, Samuel. 1986. "Economic Scene: Work-Force Shifts in 80's." *New York Times,* August 15:D2.

Ehrenreich, Barbara, and John Ehrenreich. 1979. "The Professional-Managerial Class." In Pat Walker (ed.), *Between Labor and Capital,* 5–45. Boston: South End Press.

England, Paula. 1981. "Assessing Trends in Occupational Sex Segregation, 1900–1976." In Ivar Berg (ed.), *Sociological Perspectives on Labor Markets,* 273–295. New York: Academic Press.

———, and George Farkas. 1986. *Households, Employment, and Gender: A Social, Economic, and Demographic View.* New York: Aldine.

Epstein, Cynthia Fuchs. 1973. "Positive Effects of the Multiple Negative: Explaining the Success of Black Professional Women." *American Journal of Sociology* 78 (Summer):912–935.

———. 1983. *Women in Law.* Garden City, N.Y.: Doubleday.

Etzioni, Amitai (ed.). 1969. *The Semi-Professions and Their Organization: Teachers, Nurses, Social Workers.* New York: Free Press.

Farley, Reynolds. 1984. *Blacks and Whites: Narrowing the Gap?* Cambridge, Mass.: Harvard University Press.

Fay, Robert E., Jeffrey S. Passel, and J. Gregory Robinson with Charles D. Cowan. 1988. "Evaluation and Research Reports: The Coverage of Population in the 1980 Census." *1980 Census of Population and Housing* (PHC80-E4). Washington, D.C.: U.S. Government Printing Office.

Featherman, David L., and Robert M. Hauser. 1976. "Sexual Inequalities and Socioeconomic Achievements in the U.S., 1962–1973." *American Sociological Review* 41 (June): 462–483.

Fierman, Jaclyn. 1990. "Why Women Still Don't Hit the Top." *Fortune* 122 (July 30):40–42,46,50,62.

Fiske, Edward B. 1987. "Ethnic Separation Persists in Schools." *New York Times,* July 26:1,24.

Fox, Mary Frank, and Sharlene Hesse-Biber. 1984. *Women at Work.* Palo Alto, Calif.: Mayfield.

Frazier, E. Franklin. 1957. *The Negro in the United States,* rev. ed. New York: Macmillan.

Freeman, Richard B. 1976. *The Over-Educated American.* New York and London: Academic.

Freidson, Eliot. 1973. *Profession of Medicine: A Study of the Sociology of Applied Knowledge.* New York: Dodd, Mead.

Fuchs, Victor. 1975. "A Note on Sex Segregation in Professional Occupations." *Explorations in Economic Research* 2:105–111.

Fulbright, Karen. 1985–86. "The Myth of the Double-Advantage: Black Female Managers." *Review of Black Political Economy* 14 (Fall–Winter):33–45.

Gabriel, Trip. 1990. "Call of the Wildmen." *New York Times Magazine,* October 14:36–39,42,47.

Gartner, Alan, and Frank Reissman. 1973. "Notes on the Service Society." *Social Policy* 3 (March–April):62–69.

Gelman, David, et al. 1988. "Black and White in America." *Newsweek,* March 7:18–23.

Gilkes, Cheryl Townsend. 1980. " 'Holding Back the Ocean with a Broom': Black Women and

Community Work." In La Frances Rodgers-Rose (ed.), *The Black Woman,* 217–231. Newbury Park, California: Sage.

———. 1982. "Successful Rebellious Professionals: The Black Woman's Professional Identity and Community Commitment." *Psychology of Women Quarterly* 6 (Spring):289–311.

Glazer, Nona. 1991. " 'Between a Rock and a Hard Place': Women's Professional Organizations in Nursing and Class, Racial and Ethnic Inequalities." *Gender & Society* 5 (September):351–372.

Glenn, Evelyn Nakano. 1987. "Racial Ethnic Women's Labor: The Intersection of Race, Gender, and Class Oppression." In Christine Bose, Roslyn Feldberg, and Natalie Sokoloff (eds.), *Hidden Aspects of Women's Work,* 46–73. New York: Praeger.

———. 1992. "From Servitude to Service Work: Historical Continuities in the Racial Division of Reproductive Labor." *Signs* 18 (Autumn).

———, and Charles M. Tolbert II. 1987. "Technology and Emerging Patterns of Stratification for Women of Color: Race and Gender Segregation in Computer Occupations." In Barbara D. Wright et al. (eds.), *Women, Work, and Technology: Transformations,* 318–331. Ann Arbor: University of Michigan Press.

Goldman, Ari L. 1990. "Black Women's Bumpy Path to Church Leadership." *New York Times,* July 29:1,28.

Goldstein, Tom. 1988. "Women in the Law Aren't Yet Equal Partners." *New York Times,* February 12:B7.

Greenwood, Ernest. 1957. "Attributes of a Profession." *Social Work* 2 (July):45–55.

Greer, William. 1986. "Women Now the Majority in Professions." *New York Times,* March 19:C1,C10.

Gross, Edward. 1968. "Plus Ca Change . . . ? The Sexual Structure of Occupations Over Time." *Social Problems* 16 (Fall):198–208.

Hacker, Andrew. 1984. "Women vs. Men in the Work Force." *New York Times Magazine,* Section 6, December 9:124–129.

———. 1986. "Women at Work." *New York Review of Books,* August 14:26–32.

———. 1990. "Affirmative Action: A Negative Opinion." *New York Times Book Review,* July 1:7.

Hare, Nathan, and Julia Hare. 1970. "Black Women, 1970." *Trans-action* 8 (November–December):65–68,90.

Hartmann, Heidi I. 1976. "Capitalism, Patriarchy, and Job Segregation by Sex." *Signs* 1 (Spring, pt.2):137–169.

Hauser, Robert. 1992. "How Not to Measure Intergenerational Occupational Persistence." *American Journal of Sociology* 97 (May).

Heinz, John, and Edward Laumann. 1982. *Chicago Lawyers.* New York: Russell Sage.

Henriques, Diana B. 1991. "Piercing Wall Street's 'Lucite Ceiling.' " *New York Times* (section 3), August 11:1,6.

Herbers, John. 1983. "Census Shows Gains in Jobs by Women and Blacks in 70's." *New York Times,* April 24:1,38.

Hernandez, Aileen. 1981. "Dialogue: Almquist, Christian, Harley, Hernandez, Malveaux, and McAdoo." *Black Working Women. Proceedings of a Conference on Black Working Women in the U.S.,* 10–39. Berkeley: University of California.

Hesse-Biber, Sharlene. 1986. "The Black Woman Worker: A Minority Group Perspective on Women at Work." *Sage* 3 (Spring):26–34.

Higginbotham, Elizabeth. 1987. "Employment for Professional Black Women in the Twentieth Century." In Christine Bose and Glenna Spitze (eds.). *Ingredients for Women's Employment Policy,* 73–91. Albany: SUNY Press.

———. 1988. "We Have Not Yet Arrived: Racial Discrimination Limits Options for Professional Black Women." Paper presented at Southern Sociological Society Meetings, Atlanta.

———, and Lynn Weber Cannon. 1988. "Rethinking Mobility: Towards a Race and Gender Inclusive Theory." (Research Paper No. 8.) Center for Research on Women. Memphis State University.

Hill, Robert B. 1986. "The Black Middle Class: Past, Present, Future." In James D. Williams (ed.), *The State of Black America 1986*, 43–64. New York City: National Urban League.

Hilts, Philip J. 1991. "Women Still Behind in Medicine." *New York Times*, September 10:C7.

Hinds, Michael de Courcy. 1991. "Cash Crises Force Localities in U.S. to Slash Services." *New York Times*, June 3:A1,B6.

Hine, Darlene Clark. 1989. *Black Women in White: Racial Conflict and Cooperation in the Nursing Profession 1890–1950*. Bloomington and Indianapolis: Indiana University Press.

Hoffman, Doris S. 1989. "Statement on the Status of Women Lawyers." Statement delivered at the Hearing on Status of Women in the Professions, Committee on Women-New York City Council, February 23.

Hull, Gloria T., Patricia Bell Scott, and Barbara Smith (eds.). 1982. *All the Women Are White, All the Blacks Are Men, But Some of Us Are Brave: Black Women's Studies*. Old Westbury: Feminist Press.

Human Resources Administration. 1991. *EEO Quarterly Statistical Summary Report*. New York City. October–December.

Hyde, James C. 1989. "Defense Industry's Top Ranks Hold Few Women Execs." *Armed Forces Journal International* 127:55–57.

Jacobs, Jerry A. 1984. "Historical and Demographic Trends in Occupational Segregation by Sex." Unpublished manuscript, University of Pennsylvania.

———. 1986. "Trends in Workplace Contact between Men and Women, 1971–1981." *Sociology and Social Research* 70 (April):202–205.

———. 1989. *Revolving Doors: Sex Segregation and Women's Careers*. Stanford: Stanford University Press.

Jensen, Rita Henley. 1990. "Minorities Didn't Share in Firm Growth." *National Law Journal*, Volume 12, 4, February 19:1,28,29,31,35,36.

Johnston, William B., and Arnold E. Packer. 1987. *Work Force 2000: Work and Workers*. Indianapolis: Hudson Institute.

Jolly, D. Leeann, James W. Grimm, and Paul R. Wozniak. 1990. "Patterns of Sex Desegregation in Managerial and Professional Specialty Fields, 1950–1980." *Work and Occupations* 17 (February):30–54.

Jordan, June. 1985. "Report from the Bahamas." In June Jordan, *On Call*, 39–49. Boston: South End Press.

Kanter, Rosabeth Moss. 1977. *Men and Women of the Corporation*. New York: Basic Books.

Kaufman, Debra. 1984. "Professional Women: How Real Are the Recent Gains?" In Jo Freeman (ed.), *Women: A Feminist Perspective*, 3d ed., 353–369. Palo Alto, Calif.: Mayfield.

Kilborn, Peter T. 1991. "For Forlorn Millions, The Recession Goes On." *New York Times*, July 28:1,18.

Kilson, Marion. 1977. "Black Women in the Professions, 1890–1970." *Monthly Labor Review* 100 (May):38–41.

King, Sharon R. 1988. "Special Report: Black Women in Corporate America: At the Crossroads." *Black Enterprise* (August):45–61.

Kingson, Jennifer A. 1988. "Women in the Law Say Path Is Limited by 'Mommy Track.' " *New York Times*, August 8:A1,A15.

Ladner, Joyce. 1972. *Tomorrow's Tomorrow: The Black Woman*. Garden City, N.Y.: Anchor Books and Doubleday.

Landry, Bart. 1987. *The New Black Middle Class*. Berkeley and Los Angeles: University of California Press.

Laumann, Edward, and John Heinz. 1977. "Specialization and Prestige in the Legal Profession: The Structure of Deference." *American Bar Foundation Research Journal, no. 1* (Winter): 155–216.

Leon, Carol Boyd. 1982. "Occupation Winners and Losers: Who They Were During 1972–80." *Monthly Labor Review* 101 (June): 8–14.

Leslie, Connie. 1987. "Making Doctors Human." *Newsweek on Campus* (September):39–40.

Levin, Henry M., and Russell W. Rumberger. 1983. *The Educational Implications of High Technology.* (Project Report No. 83–A4, February.) Institute for Research on Educational Finance and Governance, School of Education, Stanford University.

Lohr, Steve. 1991. "Executives Expect Many '91 Layoffs to Be Permanent." *New York Times,* December 16:A1,D9.

Lorber, Judith. 1984. *Women Physicians: Careers, Status, and Power.* New York: Tavistock.

———. 1985. "More Women Physicians: Will It Mean More Humane Health Care?" *Social Policy* 16 (Summer):50–54.

———. 1987. "A Welcome to a Crowded Field: Where Will the New Women Physicians Fit In?" *Journal of American Medical Women's Association* 42 (September-October):149–152.

Loury, Glenn C. 1985. "The Moral Quandary of the Black Community." *Public Interest* 79 (Spring):9–22.

Luxenberg, Stan. 1985. *Roadside Empires.* New York: Viking.

Macdonald, Keith, and George Ritzer. 1988. "The Sociology of the Professions: Dead or Alive?" *Work and Occupations* 15 (August):251–272.

Malcolm, Shirley. 1989. "Increasing the Participation of Black Women in Science and Technology." *Sage: A Scholarly Journal on Black Women* 6 (Fall):15–17.

Malveaux, Julianne. 1981. "Shifts in the Occupational and Employment Status of Black Women: Current Trends and Future Implications." In *Black Working Women. Proceedings of a Conference on Black Working Women in the U.S.,* 133–168. Berkeley: University of California.

———. 1985. "The Economic Interests of Black and White Women: Are They Similar?" *Review of Black Political Economy* 14 (Summer): 5–27.

———. 1990. "Gender Difference and Beyond: An Economic Perspective on Diversity and Commonality among Women." In Deborah L. Rhode (ed.), *Theoretical Perspectives on Sexual Difference,* 226–238. New Haven and London: Yale University Press.

———, and Susan Englander. 1987. "Race and Class in Nursing Occupations." *Sage: A Scholarly Journal on Black Women* 3 (Spring):41–45.

Matthews, Nancy A. 1989. "Surmounting a Legacy: The Expansion of Racial Diversity in a Local Anti-Rape Movement." *Gender & Society* 3 (December):518–532.

McCrum, Hanna, and Hanna Rubin. 1987. "The Eighth Annual *Working Woman* Salary Survey." *Working Woman* 1 (January):53–64.

McElroy, Njoki. 1987. "The Vanishing Black Female Professional." Paper presented at the Fourth Annual Women at Work Conference, University of Texas at Arlington.

Menkel-Meadow, Carrie J. 1987–88. "The Comparative Sociology of Women Lawyers: The 'Feminization' of the Legal Profession." Institute for Social Science Research Working Papers in the Social Sciences, vol. 3, no.4, University of California, Los Angeles.

Mid-Atlantic Bureau of Labor Statistics. 1991. *New York-Northeastern New Jersey Mid-Year Report-1991.* New York City: Bureau of Labor Statistics.

Montagna, Paul. 1968. "Professionalization and Bureaucratization in Large Professional Organizations." *American Journal of Sociology* 74 (September):138–145.

———. 1977. *Occupations and Society: Toward a Sociology of the Labor Market.* New York: John Wiley.

Moynihan, Daniel P. 1967. "The Negro Family: The Case for National Action." In Lee Rainwater and William L. Yancey (eds.), *The Moynihan Report and the Politics of Controversy,* 39–124. Cambridge, Mass.: MIT Press.

Nam, Charles B., and Mary G. Powers. 1983. *The Socioeconomic Approach to Status Measurement.* Houston: Cap and Gown.

Nasar, Sylvia. 1992. "Employment in Service Industry, Impetus to Boom in 80's, Falters." *New York Times,* January 2:A1,D4.

Nelson, Charmeynne D. 1975. "Myths about Black Women Workers in Modern America." *Black Scholar* 6 (March):11–15.

Nesbitt, Paula D. 1986. "Implications of Gender Mobility on Organization Communication: An Occupational Analysis." Unpublished manuscript, Harvard University.

Nkomo, Stella. 1986. "Race and Sex: The Forgotten Case of the Black Female Manager." Paper presented at Sixth Annual International Conference on Women in Organizations. N.P.

Oppenheimer, Valerie Kincaide. 1970. *The Female Labor Force in the U.S.* Berkeley: University of California Press.

Parsons, Talcott. 1939. "The Professions and Social Structure." *Social Forces* 17 (May):457–467.

———. 1970. "Equality and Inequality in Modern Society, or Social Stratification Revisited." *Sociological Inquiry* 40 (Spring):13–72.

Phillips, Anne, and Barbara Taylor. 1980. "Sex and Skills." *Feminist Review* 6:79–88.

Phipps, Polly A. 1990a. "Industrial and Occupational Change in Pharmacy: Prescription for Feminization." In Barbara F. Reskin and Patricia A. Roos (eds.), *Job Queues, Gender Queues,* 111–128. Philadelphia: Temple University Press.

———. 1990b. "Occupational Resegregation among Insurance Adjusters and Examiners." In Barbara F. Reskin and Patricia A. Roos (eds.), *Job Queues, Gender Queues,* 225–240. Philadelphia: Temple University Press.

Pincus, Fred L. 1980. "The False Promises of Community Colleges: Class Conflict and Vocational Education." *Harvard Educational Review* 50(August):332–361.

Power, Marilyn. 1984. "Falling through the 'Safety Net': Women, Economic Crisis, and Reaganomics." *Feminist Studies* 10 (Spring): 31–58.

Prial, Frank J. 1982. "More Women Work at Traditional Male Jobs." *New York Times,* November 15:1.

Price, Barbara Raffel, and Susan Gavin. 1982. "A Century of Women in Policing." In Barbara Raffel Price and Natalie J. Sokoloff (eds.), *The Criminal Justice System and Women: Offenders, Victims, Workers,* 399–412. New York: Clark Boardman Ltd.

Priebe, John, Joan Heinkel, and Stanley Greene. 1972. *1970 Occupation and Industry Classification Systems in Terms of Their 1960 Occupation and Industry Elements.* (Technical Paper No. 26.) U.S. Department of Commerce, Bureau of Census.

Ramazanoglu, Caroline. 1989. *Feminism and the Contradictions of Oppression.* London and New York: Routledge.

Reskin, Barbara F. 1989. "Accounting." Unpublished manuscript, University of Illinois.

———. 1990. "Culture, Commerce, and Gender: The Feminization of Book Editing." In Barbara F. Reskin and Patricia A. Roos (eds.), *Job Queues, Gender Queues,* 93–110. Philadelphia: Temple University Press.

———, and Heidi Hartmann. 1986. *Women's Work, Men's Work: Sex Segregation on the Job.* Washington, D.C.: National Academy Press.

———, and Patricia A. Roos. 1990. *Job Queues, Gender Queues: Explaining Women's Inroads into Male Occupations.* Philadelphia: Temple University Press.

Roach, Sharon L. 1990. "Men and Women Lawyers in In-House Legal Departments: Recruitment and Career Patterns." *Gender & Society* 4 (June):207–219.

Robinson, J. Gregg, and Judith S. McIlwee. 1989. "Women in Engineering: A Promise Unfulfilled?" *Social Problems* 36 (December):455–472.

Roos, Patricia A., Barbara F. Reskin, Katharine M. Donato, and Elizabeth G. Hein. 1990. *1980 Occupational Characteristics File Codebook.* Unpublished Code Book. Department of Sociology, Rutgers University, New Brunswick, N.J.

Rosenthal, Jack. 1972. "For Women, A Decade of Widening Horizons." *New York Times,* April 10:1.

Rueschemeyer, Dietrich. 1964. "Doctors and Lawyers: A Comment on the Theory of the Professions." *Canadian Review of Sociology and Anthropology* 1(February):17–30.

———. 1973. *Lawyers and Their Society.* Cambridge, Mass.: Harvard University Press.

Rule, Sheila. 1982. "Blacks Believe White Women Lead in Job Gains." *New York Times,* March 25:B14.

Rumberger, Robert A. 1983. "The Job Market for College Graduates, 1960–1990." (Project Report No. 83-A3.) Institute for Research on Educational Finance and Governance, School of Education, Stanford University.

Rush, Marjorie E. 1989. "Women in School Administration: Two Views." *Women in Government* 12 (Fall):4. SUNY, Albany: Center for Women in Government.

Rytina, Nancy F. 1982. "Earnings of Men and Women: A Look at Specific Occupations." *Monthly Labor Review* 105 (April):25–31.

———, and Suzanne Bianchi. 1984. "Occupational Reclassification and Changes in Distribution by Gender." *Monthly Labor Review* 107 (March):11–17.

Rytina, Steve. 1992. "Scaling the Intergenerational Continuity of Occupation: Is Occupational Inheritance Ascriptive After All?" *American Journal of Sociology* 97(May).

Sacks, Karen Brodkin. 1984. "Computers, Ward Secretaries, and a Walkout in a Southern Hospital." In Karen Brodkin Sacks and Dorothy Remy (eds.), *My Troubles Are Going to Have Trouble with Me,* 173–190. New Jersey: Rutgers State University Press.

Schafran, Lynn Hecht. 1987. "Practicing Law in a Sexist Society." In Laura L. Crites and Winifred L. Hepperle (eds.), *Women, The Courts, and Equality,* 191–207. Newbury Park, California: Sage.

Scharf, Lois. 1980. *To Work and to Wed: Female Employment, Feminism, and the Great Depression.* Westport, Conn.: Greenwood Press.

Silver, Lori. 1990. "Few Women, Minorities at the Top." *Washington Post,* August 14:A1.

Silvestri, George T., John M. Lukasiewicz, and Marcus E. Einstein. 1983. "Occupational Employment Projections through 1995." *Monthly Labor Review* 106 (November):37–49.

Simpson, Gwyned. 1990. "Black Women in the Legal Profession." Unpublished manuscript, New York City.

Simpson, Richard L., and Ida Harper Simpson. 1969. "Women and Bureaucracy in the Semi-Professions." In Amitai Etzioni (ed.), *The Semi-Professions and Their Organization: Teachers, Nurses, Social Workers,* 196–265. New York: Free Press.

Skrzycki, Cindy. 1990. "Efforts Fail to Advance Women's Jobs: 'Glass Ceiling' Intact Despite New Benefits." *Washington Post,* February 20:A1.

Smigel, Erwin. 1960. "The Impact of Recruitment on the Organization of the Large Law Firm." *American Sociological Review* 25 (February):56–66.

———. 1964. *The Wall Street Lawyer.* New York: Free Press.

Snyder, David, Mark D. Hayward, and Paula M. Hudis. 1978. "The Location of Change in the Sexual Structure of Occupations, 1950–1970: Insights from Labor Market Segmentation Theory." *American Journal of Sociology* 84 (November):706–717.

Sokoloff, Natalie J. 1980. *Between Money and Love: The Dialectics of Women's Home and Market Work.* New York: Praeger.

———. 1986. "A Profile of the General Labor Force and the Professions: A Review of the Aggregate Gender and Race Segregation Literature." Revised version of paper presented at the American Sociological Association, New York.

———. 1987a. "The Increase of Black and White Women in the Professions: A Contradictory Process." In Christine Bose and Glenna Spitze (eds.), *Ingredients for Women's Employment Policy,* 53–72. Albany: SUNY Press.

———. 1987b. "What's Happening to Women's Employment: Issues for Women's Labor Struggles in the 1980s–1990s." In Christine Bose, Roslyn Feldberg, and Natalie Sokoloff (eds.), *Hidden Aspects of Women's Work,* 14–45. New York: Praeger.

———. 1988. "Evaluating Gains and Losses by Black and White Women and Men in the Professions, 1960–1980." *Social Problems* 35 (February):36–53.

Sowell, Thomas. 1983. *The Economics and Politics of Race.* New York, Basic Books.

————. 1990. *Preferential Policies: An International Perspective.* New York: William Morrow.

Spenner, Kenneth. 1985. "The Upgrading and Downgrading of Occupations: Issues, Evidence, and Implications for Education." *Review of Educational Research* 55:125–154.

Starr, Paul. 1982. *The Social Transformation of American Medicine.* New York: Basic Books.

Steele, Shelby. 1990. "A Negative Vote on Affirmative Action." *New York Times Magazine,* May 13:46–49,73,75.

Stevenson, Mary. 1975. "Women's Wages and Job Segregation." In Richard C. Edwards, Michael Reich, and David M. Gordon (eds.), *Labor Market Segmentation,* 243–255. Lexington, Mass.. D. C. Heath.

Stille, Alexander. 1985. "Outlook Better for Women, Asians: Little Room at the Top for Blacks, Hispanics." *National Law Journal,* December 23:1,6–10.

Strober, Myra. 1984. "Toward a General Theory of Occupational Sex Segregation: The Case of Public School Teaching." In Barbara Reskin (ed.), *Sex Segregation in the Workplace: Trends, Explanations, Remedies,* 144–156. Washington, D.C.: National Academy Press.

Swinton, David. 1990. "Economic Status of Black Americans during the 1980s: A Decade of Limited Progress." In Janet Dewart (ed.), *The State of Black America 1990,* 25–52. New York City: National Urban League.

Szymanski, Albert. 1974. "Race, Sex, and the U.S. Working Class." *Social Problems* 21 (June):706–725.

Theodore, Athena. 1971. "The Professional Woman: Trends and Prospects." In Athena Theodore (ed.), *The Professional Woman,* 1–35. Cambridge, Mass.: Schenkman.

Thurow, Lester. 1972. "Education and Economic Equality." *Public Interest* 28 (Summer):66–81.

Toner, Robin. 1991. "Racial Politics: Back with a Vengeance." *New York Times,* November 24 (Section 4):1,2.

Treiman, Donald and Kermitt Terrell. 1975. "Women, Work, and Wages." In Kenneth Land and S. Spillerman (eds.), *Social Indicator Models,* 157–199. New York: Russell Sage Foundation.

Tyack, David, and Myra Strober. 1981. "Jobs and Gender: A History of the Structuring of Educational Employment by Sex." In Patricia Schmuck and W. W. Charters (eds.), *Educational Policy and Management,* 131–152. New York: Academic Press.

U.S. Bureau of the Census. 1984. *Statistical Abstract of the United States: 1984, 104th ed.* Washington, D.C.:U.S. Department of Commerce.

U.S. Bureau of Census. 1988. *Statistical Abstract of the United States: 1988, 108th ed.* Table 729, Purchasing Power of the Dollar:1940–1986." Washington, D.C.:U.S. Department of Commerce.

(USDC) U.S. Department of Commerce, Bureau of the Census. 1963. *1960 Census of Population.* Table 3, "Race of the Experienced Civilian Labor Force and of the Employed, by Detailed Occupation and Sex, for the U.S., 1960." (PC(2)-7A.) Washington, D.C.: U.S. Government Printing Office.

————. 1975. *1970 Census of Population.* Table 2, "Race and Spanish Origin of the Experienced Civilian Labor Force by Detailed Occupation and Sex: 1970." (PC(2)-7A.) Washington, D.C.:U.S. Government Printing Office.

————. 1983a. *1980 Census of the Population.* Table 2, "Detailed Occupation of the Civilian Labor Force by Sex and Total Race: 1980." (Supplementary Report PC 80-S1–8.) Washington D.C.: U.S. Government Printing Office.

————. 1983b. *1980 Census of the Population.* Table 89, "Occupation of Employed Persons by Race and Sex: 1980 and 1970." (General Social and Economic Characteristics, U.S. Summary, PC80–1–C1.) Washington, D.C.: U.S. Government Printing Office.

————. 1984. "Detailed Occupation of the Experienced Civilian Labor Force by Sex for the U.S. and Regions: 1980 and 1970." (Supplementary Report PC80–S1–15.) Washington, D.C.: U.S. Government Printing Office.

―――. 1986a. "1970–1980 Census Comparability, Chart A, Detailed Occupation Sorted by 1970 Codes, Final Data." Unpublished manuscript Population Division.

―――. 1986b. "1970–1980 Census Comparability, Chart B, Detailed Occupation Sorted by 1980 Codes, Final Data." Unpublished manuscript Population Division.

(USDL) U.S. Department of Labor, Bureau of Labor Statistics. 1980. *Perspectives on Working Women: A Databook.* (Bulletin 2080.) Washington, D.C.

―――. 1983. "Employment in Perspective: Working Women." (First Quarter 1983, Report 683.) Washington, D.C.

Vanneman, Reeve, and Lynn Weber Cannon. 1987. *The American Perception of Class.* Philadelphia: Temple University Press.

Vines, Paula L., and John A. Priebe. 1989. *The Relationship between the 1970 and 1980 Industry and Occupation Classification Systems.* (Technical Paper No. 59). U.S. Bureau of the Census. Washington, D.C.: U.S. Government Printing Office.

Wallace, Phyllis. 1980. *Black Women in the Labor Force.* Cambridge, Mass.: MIT Press.

Weathers, Diane. 1981. "Winning Under the Double Whammy." *Savvy,* April:34–40.

Weisenhaus, Doreen. 1988. "Still a Long Way to Go for Women, Minorities." *National Law Journal,* February 8:1,48,50,53.

Westcott, Diane Nilsen. 1982. "Blacks in the 1970s: Did They Scale the Job Ladder?" *Monthly Labor Review* 105 (June):29–38.

Wilkie, Jane Riblett. 1985. "The Decline of Occupational Segregation between Black and White Women." *Research in Race and Ethnic Relations,* vol. 4:67–89.

Wilkinson, J. Harvie III. 1979. *From Brown to Bakke. The Supreme Court and School Integration: 1954–1978.* Oxford and New York: Oxford University Press.

Williams, Gregory. 1979. "The Changing U.S. Labor Force and Occupational Differentiation by Sex." *Demography* 16(February):73–88.

Williams, Lena. 1985. "For the Black Professional, the Obstacles Remain." *New York Times,* July 14:A16.

―――. 1991. "When Blacks Shop, Bias Often Accompanies Sale." *New York Times,* April 30:A1,A14.

Wilson, William Julius. 1987. *The Truly Disadvantaged: The Inner City, the Underclass, and Public Policy.* Chicago: University of Chicago Press.

"Women Doctors, by Specialty." 1990. *Washington Post,* January 16:5.

Woodson, Carter G. 1934. *The Negro Professional Man and the Community.* New York: Negro Universities Press.

Young, Anne McDougal. 1979. "Median Earnings in 1977 Reported for Year-Round Full-Time Workers." *Monthly Labor Review* 102 (June):35–39.

INDEX

Access, 29–30, 68, 114–22
Accounting, 59, 63, 81, 83, 89, 107, 120–21
Affirmative action
  black women and fallacy of double
    advantage, 20–21, 93
  debate over progress of black professionals,
    17, 65–66
  gains of white women from 1972 to 1977, 19
  job opportunities for blacks and political
    climate, 72, 122
American approach, 7
Arts, professions in, 86
Attrition, rate of, 12–13

Bakke, Allan, 56
Baron, James N., 23, 29, 123
Beller, 77
Benefits, employment, 130
Bernard, Jessie, 106
Bielby, William T., 23, 29, 123
Black men
  access to elite professions, 119
  black women compared to, 95–96, 102,
    106–108, 112
  deteriorating professions and lack of equal
    opportunity, 114
  growth in professions and technical fields
    from 1960 to 1980, 41

intermediate level of analysis of census data,
  65–74
movement into male technical fields, 51
occupational categories and conversion data,
  140–42, 144
patterns of race and gender segregation,
  117–18
study conclusions, 52
undercount of in census, 153n27
white women and job gains, 77
white women compared to, 87–92
Blacks (*See also* Black men; Black women)
  enrollment in higher education, 152n5
  as focus of study, 3–4
  history of in professions before 1960, 6–7
  race/gender composition of growth rate
    in professions between 1960 and 1980,
    39, 40
  social service jobs and politics, 122
  undercount of population in census, 158n7
  underrepresentation in professions in
    1980s, 3
  use of term, 151n2
Black women (*See also* Blacks; Women)
  access to elite professions, 119
  groups compared to, 55
  growth in professions/technical fields from
    1960 to 1980, 41

Black women *cont.*
  history of in professions before 1960, 6–7
  intermediate level of analysis of census data,
    93–112, 156n8
  occupational categories and conversion data,
    140–42, 144
  overstatement of progress in male-dominated
    professions, 22–23
  patterns of race and gender segregation,
    117–18
  segregation and stratification from 1980 to
    present, 127–30
  segregation in professions and parameters of
    study, 10–11
  structural transformations and nature of
    experience, 12
  study conclusions, 52
  white women compared to, 18–22, 155n4,
    155–56n7
Blau, Francine, 125
British approach, 7–8
Brown, George Hay, 15
Bush, George, 132

Carter, Michael and Susan Boslego, 29, 125
Census data, 9, 24–25, 135–46, 151n1, 157n5
Chemists, 89
Civil rights, 1–2, 65–66, 87, 113, 132
Class, 13, 152n15, 157n11 (*See also* Middle
  class)
Clergy, 73, 124, 156n5
Coalition-building, 131–34
Colleges, 65, 76, 121, 152n5
Collins, Sharon M., 74, 102
Computer programming, 5, 62, 86, 129,
  155n5
Conservatives, political, 66
Conversion data, 138, 139, 140–42
Core professions, 8
Correction factors, 144–46
Cortese, Anthony J., 77, 87
Counseling, 71, 86, 111, 155n6 (*See also*
  Vocational and educational counseling)
Cummings, Judith, 66

Design professions, 59, 63, 81, 83, 89, 107,
  120–21
Deskilling, 86, 120–21, 125
Dill, Bonnie Thornton, 134
Disadvantaged groups, 152n10

Economics, 1–2, 17, 65–66, 113, 131, 132–33
Editing, 86, 121, 125
Education, 15, 126, 128–29 (*See also* Colleges;
  Teaching)
Ehrenhalt, Samuel, 1–2, 39
Elite male professions
  access to, 119
  black women compared to black men,
    98, 106
  black women compared to white men, 100
  continued ghettoization of women, 125
  core professions, 8
  increased overrepresentation of white
    men, 51
  status scores, 154n1
  white women compared to black men, 88
  white women compared to white men, 80
Engineering, 67, 73, 89, 99, 124, 126
Epstein, Cynthia Fuchs, 21
Etzioni, Amitai, 8

Featherman, David L., 12
Female professions
  black women
    black men compared to, 107
    occupational growth and, 98, 99–100
    white men compared to, 102
    white women compared to, 109–110
  degree of race/gender segregation, 46–47
  elite and nonelite distinctions, 153n24
  findings using index representation, 49, 52
  semiprofessions, 8
  white women compared to black men, 88,
    89, 91
  white women compared to white men, 80,
    83, 91
Feminism, 133
Fox, Mary Frank, 20

Gender (*See also* Black men; Black women;
  Segregation; White men; White women)
  black women and race, 94–95
  censuses and occupational categories,
    138–40
  classification of professions,
    semiprofessions, and technical fields, 8,
    25, 27
  coalition building, 133–34
  composition of growth and change among
    professions, 37, 39–41

correction factors for undercounting in
  census, 145–46
occupational segregation
  aggregate data and underestimation of, 23
  from 1980 to present, 122–30
  increase in, 117–18
  persistence of, 2
  professions and parameters of study,
    10–11
  undercovering degree of, 44, 46–47
  structure of labor market, 13
  theoretical perspectives, 14–17
  underlying nature of job market, 34
Gender-neutral professions
  black women compared to black men, 107
  black women compared to white men, 102
  black women compared to white women,
    109–110
  degree of race/gender segregation, 46–47
  findings using index of representation, 49,
    51–52
  white women compared to black men, 88,
    89–90, 91–92
  white women compared to white men, 80,
    83, 86, 92
Ghettoization, 124–27
Glass ceiling, 18–19, 127, 129
Glenn, Evelyn Nakano, 129
Great Depression, 5
Grimm, James W., 36–37
Growth rates, 56–58, 66–67, 78–79, 156n4

Hacker, Andrew, 21, 43, 76, 96
Hare, Nathan and Julia, 106
Hauser, Robert M., 12
Hesse-Biber, Sharlene, 20
Higginbotham, Elizabeth, 123–24
Human capital/status attainment positions, 14–
  15, 16–17
Human services jobs, 71–72

Income
  black and white women compared, 20, 96
  black men and women compared, 96
  black men compared to white men, 73
  gap between male and female physicians, 76
  losses of women relative to men, 83
  paradox of partial change, 130
  white women compared to white men, 86,
    91

Index of Relative Advantage
  black men compared to white men, 69–71
  black women compared to black men, 87–
    88, 102, 106–108
  black women compared to white men, 100,
    102
  black women compared to white women,
    108–110
  methodology, 29, 30–31
  white women compared to white men, 79–81
  white women in detailed professions, 81, 83,
    86–87
Index of Representation
  findings using, 49, 51–52
  methodology, 29–30, 31, 48
  white women in large professions/technical
    fields, 58–59, 62
Interpretation, 14–19, 22–23, 47–49, 51–52

Jackson, Jesse, 134
Jacobs, Jerry A., 12
Jim Crow laws, 6
Johnson, Lyndon, 2
Jolly, D. Leeann, 36–37

Labor force, 66, 78
Landry, Bart, 20
Latinos/as, 152n8
Legal professions
  black women and interaction of race and
    gender, 95, 129–30
  gender segregation of specialties, 11
  ghettoization of women and deskilling of
    profession, 125
  growth of in 1970s and 1980s, 5
  women and partnerships in law firms, 76,
    126, 156–57n9
Legislation, 2, 6
Librarians, 73
Lucite ceiling, 19

Macdonald, Keith, 7
Male professions, 44, 46, 49, 99, 106–107
Malveaux, Julianne, 20, 21, 106, 128, 133
Managerial jobs, 128
Medical professions, 11, 76, 95, 125–26
Men's rights groups, 75
Methodology, 24–25, 27–31, 135–46
Middle class, 2, 8, 17, 74, 112
Mobility, individual, 11–13, 130–31

Nam-Powers scale, 27
Nonresponse cases, 144–45
Norton, Eleanor Holmes, 94
Nursing, 2, 8–9, 36, 151n4, 157n11

Occupational gender segregation position, 15–17 (*See also* Segregation)
Occupation summary data, 138–39
Oppression, 133–34

Personnel and labor relations, 71–72
Pharmacy, 81, 83, 89, 125
Phipps, Polly A., 89
Politics, 74, 112, 121–22, 131, 132–33
Professionalism, 119
Professional-managerial class, 8
Professions (*See also* specific topics)
    census codes, 136–42
    changes from 1960 to 1980, 9–11, 113–22
    definition in context of study, 7–9
    expansion of economy and civil rights in 1960s and 1970s, 1–2
    as focus of study, 4–5
    growth and change rates for race/gender groups, 37, 39–41
    growth of black men in, 66–67
    history of women and minority men before 1960, 5–7
    increased growth and benefits to groups, 34–36
    introduction to detailed, 36–37
    methodology and classification, 25
    profile of black women from 1960 to 1980, 97–100
    theoretical perspectives, 14–18
Public relations specialists, 124–25
Public service professions, 108, 110, 111–12
Publishing industry, 86

Queuing system, 116

Race (*See also* Black men; Blacks; Black women; White men; White women)
    black women and gender, 94–97
    censuses and occupational categories, 138–40
    coalition building, 133–34
    composition of growth and change rates among professions, 37, 39–41

correction factors for undercounting in census, 145–46
occupational segregation
    from 1980 to present, 122–30
    increases in, 117–19
    patterns of, 2–3
    professions and parameters of study, 10–11
    uncovering degree of, 44, 46–47
    structure of labor market, 13
    theoretical perspectives, 17–18
Racial/ethnic minorities, 151n1
Rainbow coalition, 134
Reagan, Ronald, 3, 132, 151n1
Resegregation, 13, 74, 83, 112, 124–27, 156n1
Reskin, Barbara, 12, 29, 30, 116, 118, 120, 124
Reverse discrimination, 3, 55–56
Ritzer, George, 7
Roos, Patricia A., 12, 29, 116, 118, 120, 124
Rule, Sheila, 21

Scientific professions, 124
Segregation, occupational (*See also* Gender; Race)
    black women and stratification from 1980 to present, 127–30
    gender and areas of specialization, 16
    gender and increase in disparity between black men and women, 112
    increase in from 1960 to 1980, 115–19
    race and gender from 1980 to present, 122–30
    racial and black women, 110
    status and white men in professions, 59, 62
    uncovering degree of race/gender, 44, 46–47
Semiprofessions, 8–9
Service industries, 132
Sexism, 90–91
Simpson, Richard L. and Ida Harper, 9, 129
Social service jobs, 74
Social work, 33, 71, 99–100, 121
Statistics, 22–23, 47–49, 51–52
Status, occupational
    black men compared to white men, 69–71, 73

black women compared to white women, 108–109
elite and nonelite male professions, 154n1
low and job deterioration, 120–21
nursing, 151n4
paradox of partial change, 130
segregation and white men in professions, 59, 62
socioeconomic classification of professions, 25, 27
white women compared to white men, 83, 91
Structural analysis, 11–14, 119–22
Structural-functionalism, 7
Success, measures of, 24
Suicide rates, 18

Teaching (*See also* Colleges; Education)
black women and low-status, low-income jobs, 106
college, 81, 83, 89, 120–21, 154n5, 157n4
elementary school, 62, 63
growth in professional jobs from 1960 to 1980, 36
public and private classifications, 157n4
secondary education, 154n5, 155n3
Technical fields
black women compared to black men, 107
black men compared to white men, 71–73
definition in context of study, 9
findings using index of representation, 49, 51, 52
growth of female-dominated occupations, 35–36
status of male versus neutral and female-dominated occupations, 27
study conclusions, 53
technical-oriented professions, 155n2
white women compared to black men, 88–89
white women compared to white men, 81
Tolbert, Charles M., II, 129

Vocational and educational counseling, 62, 63, 86, 98, 121

White men
access to elite professions, 119
black men compared to, 67–71
black women compared to, 96–97, 100, 102

degree of race/gender segregation, 44, 46
deteriorating professions and lack of equal opportunity, 114
growth in professions/technical fields from 1960 to 1980, 41
increase in overrepresentation in elite male professions, 51, 116
increase in traditional female professions, 46
intermediate level of analysis of census data, 55–59, 62–63
occupational categories and conversion data, 140–42, 144
patterns of race and gender segregation, 117–18
perception of threat from alleged gains of women and minorities, 75, 156n3, 157n11
structural change and occupational mobility and equity, 24
study conclusions, 52–53
underrepresentation among secondary-school teachers, 155n3
white women compared to, 79–81
White women (*See also* Women)
access to elite professions, 119, 127–28, 155n4, 155–56n7
black women compared to, 18–22, 94–95, 108–110, 127–28, 155n4, 155–56n7
growth in professions/technical fields from 1960 to 1980, 41
intermediate level of analysis of census data, 74–92
occupational categories and conversion data, 140–42, 144
patterns of race and gender segregation, 117–18
study conclusions, 52–53
Wilson, William Julius, 65–66
Women (*See also* Black women; Gender; White women)
deteriorating professions and lack of equal opportunity, 114
history of in professions before 1960, 5–7
race/gender composition of growth rates in professions between 1960 and 1980, 39
social service jobs and politics, 122
Women's movement, 87, 113
Wozniak, Paul R., 36–37

Zero-sum approach, 47, 48